THE CREATION OF LIFE

OF LIFE

PAST, FUTURE, ALIEN

THE CREATION OF LIFE

PAST, FUTURE, ALIEN

Andrew Scott

Basil Blackwell

First published 1986

Basil Blackwell Ltd
108 Cowley Road, Oxford OX4 1JF, UK

Basil Blackwell Inc.
432 Park Avenue South, Suite 1503,
New York, NY 10016, USA

British Library Cataloguing in Publication Data
    Scott, Andrew
        The creation of life: past, future,
        alien.
        1. Evolution
        I. Title
        575   QH366.2

        ISBN 0–631–14883–3

Library of Congress Cataloging in Publication Data
    Scott, Andrew.
        The creation of life.

        Bibliography: p.
        Includes index.
        1. Life–Origin.   I. Title.
        QH325.S39 1986   577   86–11749
        ISBN 0–631–14883–3

Typeset in 10/12 pt Palatino by Oxford Publishing Services, Oxford
Printed in the USA

For my parents

Contents

Nothing is so firmly believed as that which we least know.
Montaigne

Preface

This book about the 'creation' of life is largely concerned with the origins of life on earth, but it also considers the possible origins of life elsewhere in the universe and the new forms of life which mankind might create in the future.

The possibility that life might have originated spontaneously on the early earth, as a result of a long sequence of chemical reactions involving various carbon-containing 'organic' chemicals, has become an accepted part of the dogma of modern science. It has been repeated so often and with such conviction in our schools, textbooks and encyclopaedias that it has attained the status of virtual fact. Yet it remains only one rather insecure possible version of our origins.

This book is not an unquestioning regurgitation of the 'standard' account of the origin of life on earth, nor is it an attack aimed at demolishing that standard version. It attempts to cast a critical eye over the explanation of life's origins offered by modern science, identifying areas of both weakness and strength. It is not written from any deeply entrenched position, either scientific or religious.

I have tried to cover all of the essential aspects of this wide and controversial subject, but inevitably the coverage has been influenced to some extent by personal preferences and opinions. I apologize in advance to anyone I offend. It is impossible to write anything about the origins of life without offending someone.

The book will hopefully be of interest to a wide range of readers, from laymen to undergraduates and scientists themselves; but in writing it, I have tried to assume nothing about its readers other than an interest in science and the mystery of our ultimate origin. The ideal reader will already know some basic biology, chemistry and physics, to 'O' level, 'A' level or even undergraduate standard; but anyone with an interest in the subject should hopefully be able to read and understand most of the book with a little effort, even if school science is only a distant memory. Such readers might come up against difficult sections from time to time, which they will need to read through carefully and perhaps more than once; but such sections should not last long, and hopefully the effort of perseverance will be considered worthwhile.

Chapters 2 and 3 may be unnecessary for readers with a firm grounding in biology and chemistry, but are offered for the others, or as a quick reminder. Some might consider chapter 2 to be out of place in a book which is essentially about biology, but it describes the physics and chemistry without which there would be no biology at all.

Many thanks are due to Kim Pickin, and to Sue Banfield, Peter Whatley, Diyan Leake and Ann McCall for their help with the planning and production at Blackwell's. Graham Cairns-Smith and John Scott provided useful advice about the sections covering their own work, while Peter Atkins should be thanked for some helpful comments about part of chapter 2. I am also extremely grateful to Dick Wall, for reading the entire manuscript and making numerous wise comments and suggestions; and to my wife, Margaret, for her help in many ways. Finally, many thanks to my parents, David Scott and Margaret Scott, for playing so well their important part in my own creation.

1 Mysteries, challenges and fears

. . . all sentient things, born by the same stern law.
Voltaire

From birth until death we live out our lives in a world which is not of our making, and which we did not choose to enter. We experience consciousness and thought, making us certain of our own existence and confident that those fellow beings around us experience much the same thing. We know nothing when we arrive, and perhaps we still know nothing when we leave; but we soon discover that the world presents us with many mysteries, many challenges, and much to fear.

One of the deepest mysteries is the question of how we ever came to be here in the first place – the mystery of the origins of life. The challenge of searching for solutions to this mystery leads on to further mysteries and challenges: Is there life elsewhere in the universe? If we can work out how life can begin, could we re-create its origin in the laboratory? Could we create completely novel forms of life according to our own designs?

These mysteries and challenges can give rise to considerable fears. If life exists elsewhere, will it come here and what might it do to us? Has it been here already? If we learn to create life ourselves, could it be dangerous? Could it multiply out of control to threaten our own existence?

This book investigates the possible origins of life on earth and elsewhere, and considers some of the other mysteries challenges and fears thrown up by that investigation. In essence, it explores very simple questions which have troubled us all, such as 'Where have I come from? Why am I here? What am I?'

As children, the answers we receive to such questions range from tales of a God in heaven breathing life into his newly created world, to bewildering sagas of tadpoles wriggling enthusiastically in search of eggs, or of seeds planted mysteriously into stomachs. As we grow older, the story develops into the modern scientific version of Genesis; and this 'true' account of our ultimate creation goes something like this.

In the beginning there was something, and that something went bang. The bits of something went rushing out into the nothing which was all around. From that moment on, our eventual awakening (or at least the awakening of something) into consciousness may well have been inevitable. We have called the stuff released from the bang 'matter', and have discovered that it seems to come in all sorts of different lumps or 'particles'. The particles interact with one another through mysterious agencies which we call 'forces', and these forces can be resisted by an equally mysterious phenomenon known as 'energy'.

As the universe expanded following the big bang, the forces pulled the particles this way and that, and allowed the particles we call 'atoms' to form. At first, only very small and simple atoms were formed; but as the matter began to coalesce into hot seething masses called 'stars' (pulled by the force known as 'gravity'), so the simple atoms combined to form bigger ones.

From time to time, the stars would explode and spew out a harvest of atoms into 'space', where they could sometimes combine into groups of linked atoms known as 'molecules', and also be used as the raw material to form new stars. Eventually, a long time after everything had gone bang, firm solid bodies like the planet earth began to form around some stars. On the earth, perhaps in something we like to call the 'primordial soup', the forces made the atoms and molecules link up into ever more complex and varied clusters, forming all sorts of different chemical compounds.

At last, dramatically, some molecules were formed that were able to *make more of themselves,* simply by encouraging other chemicals to join up into similar structures as themselves. These 'self-reproducing' or 'self-*replicating*' molecules were of the type known as 'nucleic acids', and we find them still at the heart of the reproductive machinery which allows us all to breed. They form the celebrated 'genes', which teachers like to describe as the 'blueprints of life' – instructing our cells to form bodies that live and grow and reproduce.

In the early days though, the nucleic acids were on their own. These self-replicating nucleic acids went forth and multiplied, and eventually chanced upon a dramatic new chemical 'trick'. Some of them began to encourage the manufacture of other types of molecules

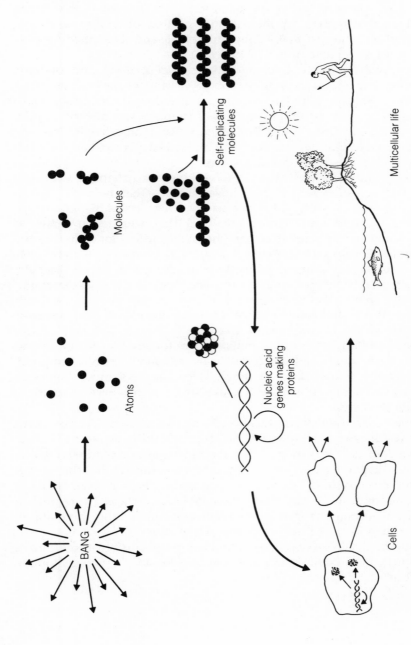

Figure 1.1   Modern science's version of the origin of life on earth.

known as 'proteins'; and these proteins had a remarkable ability to speed up particular chemical reactions out of the vast number of different reactions going on all around. Nucleic acids that made proteins that speeded up the reactions needed for their nucleic acids to multiply, did just that – they multiplied, and diversified further, and became capable of new chemical 'tricks'.

Eventually, simple combinations of nucleic acids and proteins became trapped in membrane-bound vesicles or 'cells'. And then different cells containing different nucleic acids and proteins began to compete for the dwindling supplies of chemical raw materials in the 'soup' around them. Cells that made proteins that helped them to survive and multiply, survived and multiplied. Those that could not help themselves died and disappeared.

Over billions of years the cells developed and changed thanks to the *'natural selection'* of only those changes that helped them to survive and multiply. In other words, they *'evolved'*. Single cells joined up into multicellular creatures that were even better at surviving and multiplying than the single cells alone. Eventually plant life flourished in the seas and on the land, fishes swam the seas and occasionally flopped about gasping between drying rock pools. Slowly they evolved into creatures able to walk across the land and directly breathe in the oxygen released by plants; and then some of the creatures that could walk and breathe developed into creatures that could 'think' and 'reason' and talk.

Four and a half thousand million years (or so) after the earth had formed, its atoms had given rise to us – spontaneously, using only mysterious 'matter' and all powered by the mysterious 'forces of nature' which some people (to take us back to where we started) attribute to God.

That, very briefly, is the tale now being recounted in the classrooms and lecture halls of the world. Although scientists vigorously debate the details amongst themselves, the message they send confidently out to the populace at large is that science essentially has the answer to the mystery of life's creation. That answer is truly astonishing: it was all the result of just a few basic types of particles being pushed and pulled and changed by 'fundamental forces'; and there are no more than four such forces, perhaps only one.

This book takes a close look at that happy conclusion, examining its validity, questioning its implications, and considering where it might lead us.

2   Sparse fabric

. . . the chaotic dispersal of energy as the purposeless motivation of change . . .
P.W. Atkins

The universe is made out of some sort of 'stuff' which can move and can change. Scientists refer to the stuff as 'matter', but don't be fooled by the scientific ring of that term – it is no more meaningful than 'stuff'. Nobody really knows what matter is, although many people are expert at describing its structure and predicting its behaviour, whatever it is. Certainly, it is the stuff that we are made of, so it is something we should take a closer look at.

It is obvious to everyone that the matter of the universe is assembled into many different individual things. Books and pens and tables and apples and cars and mice, and men, are just a few examples. One way of describing all such bits of matter would simply be to compile a list of them all. This would be of almost infinite length but of little real use. What has proved useful, however, is to examine matter in its many varied forms in search of underlying simplicities. This search has revealed that all of the objects which matter forms are made out of different arrangements of just a few fundamental 'little bits of matter' or 'particles'. This makes everything much simpler.

Over 23 centuries ago the Greek philosophers Democritus and Leucippus (and probably many other people as well) decided that the substances around them must be composed of little *indivisible* bits of substance too small to see. They reached this conclusion without the aid of any experiments, and their reasoning might have gone something like this: Suppose you took a piece of any substance, a piece of charcoal for example, and split it up into several smaller lumps. Then you took one of the smaller lumps, and split *it* into smaller lumps. Then you carried on splitting the smallest lumps you could find into ever smaller lumps. Obviously the lumps of charcoal would soon become far too small to handle or even to see, but we do not have to worry about such things in a 'thought' experiment. Instead, we can imagine splitting up the lumps for as long as there remain lumps that will split.

The big question is, would it be possible to go on splitting for ever, or would there come a point at which some smallest possible indivisible lump had been obtained? The idea of being able to repeatedly split something up for ever obviously did not appeal to Democritus. Instead, he decided that there must come a point at which further splitting would be impossible, and he called the indivisible lumps left at this point 'atoms' (which means 'indivisible' in Greek).

The concept of atoms has come a long way since the days of Democritus. Unfortunately (if you speak Greek) it no longer refers to indivisible lumps of matter, because the 'atoms' of today can be split into smaller 'sub-atomic particles'. Nevertheless, the term 'atom' does still represent an absolutely fundamental stage in the hierarchy of matter: *atoms are the smallest bits of matter that can possess the distinctive chemical characteristics of chemicals that we find up in the large-scale world all around us.*

So if you split up a piece of charcoal, it will remain charcoal until you get down to the level of individual atoms (pure charcoal is made up solely of carbon atoms). These individual carbon atoms will behave in chemical reactions just like the carbon of the original lump of charcoal. Chop the atoms up further, however, and the bits you get will no longer behave as carbon. Instead you will get some 'protons', 'neutrons' and 'electrons' – the familiar sub-atomic particles of school science classes (see figure 2.1).

What about all the other substances found in our everyday world – what happens if we split some other things up into ever smaller pieces? If we are lucky in our first choices, then we will discover that they behave just like charcoal. An iron bar, for example, could be split up into iron filings, iron powder, then all the way down to many individual iron atoms. At all these stages the bits would still behave chemically as iron; but split up the iron atoms, and the sub-atomic particles obtained will behave very differently. In fact, they will behave exactly like the protons, neutrons and electrons obtained by splitting up carbon atoms.

If we chance upon a lump of sulphur, then our splitting will yield the same results as before, telling us that sulphur is made up of lots of sulphur atoms, which are themselves composed of the same sub-atomic particles (protons, neutrons and electrons) used to make all other types of atom.

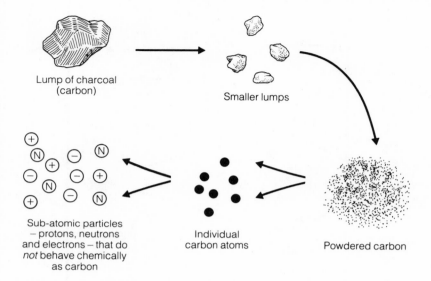

Figure 2.1   An atom is the smallest 'lump' of a piece of carbon that still behaves as carbon in chemical reactions.

But for the vast majority of substances, our results will be rather different. Suppose we took some water (frozen into an ice-cube to make our careful splitting a bit easier!), what would happen then? For a while we could split away, producing ever smaller bits of water which all behaved chemically just like the water we started with; but eventually something new would happen. Eventually we could break the water up into particles that would not be water, but equally, would not be the familiar sub-atomic particles obtained on splitting an atom. In fact, we would have particles of two quite different new substances – oxygen and hydrogen. If we then, perhaps in frustration at our neat pattern having been destroyed, smashed up these bits of oxygen and hydrogen, we would this time get back to the familiar sub-atomic particles (see figure 2.2).

So splitting up the smallest particle capable of behaving as water does not produce sub-atomic particles, instead it produces atoms of hydrogen and oxygen, which can then themselves be split up into sub-atomic particles. So water cannot be made up of single atoms. Instead, water is formed when two types of atoms (hydrogen and oxygen) become linked together in a certain way (actually two hydrogen atoms are needed for every one oxygen atom, hence water's famous formula, H_2O).

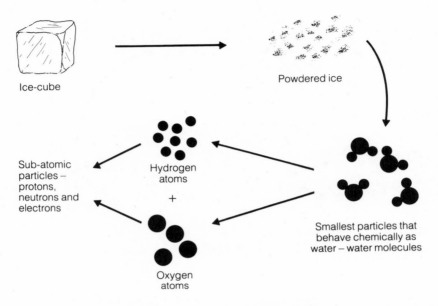

Figure 2.2   Splitting up an ice-cube would eventually yield water molecules, which could themselves be split up into atoms of hydrogen and oxygen.

Substances like water, whose properties depend on different types of atoms being linked or 'bonded' together in some way, are called 'compounds'.

So all of the chemicals we encounter are made up of either a single type of atom (e.g. carbon, iron, sulphur), or of larger particles composed of different types of atom joined together (e.g. water). The first type of substance is known as an 'element', while the second type are compounds.

There are actually 92 different types of element found naturally on the earth, all listed in the 'periodic table of the elements' (see figure 2.3), and they combine together to produce many millions of different compounds. Obviously then, there are 92 different types of atom found on earth – the chemical raw materials from which all living things on the planet are formed. These atoms are the fundamental building-blocks of chemistry, not because they are indivisible – they aren't – but because if you do split them up then their distinctive chemical properties are lost, leaving you with just a collection of protons, neutrons and electrons regardless of which atoms you began with.

So what about these protons, neutrons and electrons? Are *they* the

Legend:
- Atomic number (no. of protons)
- Symbol
- Mass (in atomic mass units)

1	2	3	4	5	6	7	8	9	10	11	12	13	14	15	16	17	18
1 H 1																	2 He 4
3 Li 7	4 Be 9											5 B 11	6 C 12	7 N 14	8 O 16	9 F 19	10 Ne 20
11 Na 23	12 Mg 24											13 Al 27	14 Si 28	15 P 31	16 S 32	17 Cl 35.5	18 Ar 40
19 K 39	20 Ca 40	21 Sc 45	22 Ti 48	23 V 51	24 Cr 52	25 Mn 55	26 Fe 56	27 Co 59	28 Ni 59	29 Cu 64	30 Zn 65	31 Ga 70	32 Ge 73	33 As 75	34 Se 79	35 Br 80	36 Kr 84
37 Rb 85	38 Sr 88	39 Y 89	40 Zr 91	41 Nb 93	42 Mo 96	43 Tc 98	44 Ru 101	45 Rh 103	46 Pd 106	47 Ag 108	48 Cd 112	49 In 115	50 Sn 119	51 Sb 122	52 Te 128	53 I 127	54 Xe 131
55 Cs 113	56 Ba 137	57 La 139	72 Hf 178.5	73 Ta 181	74 W 184	75 Re 186	76 Os 190	77 Ir 192	78 Pt 195	79 Au 197	80 Hg 201	81 Tl 204	82 Pb 207	83 Bi 209	84 Po 210	85 At 210	86 Rn 222
87 Fr 223	88 Ra 226	89 Ac 227															

58 Ce 140	59 Pr 141	60 Nd 144	61 Pm 147	62 Sm 150	63 Eu 152	64 Gd 157	65 Tb 159	66 Dy 162	67 Ho 165	68 Er 167	69 Tm 169	70 Yb 173	71 Lu 175
90 Th 232	91 Pa 231	92 U 238	93 Np 237	94 Pu 242	95 Am 243	96 Cm 247	97 Bk 247	98 Cf 251	99 Es 254	100 Fm 253	101 Md 256	102 No 254	103 Lw 257

Elements beyond atomic no. 92 do not occur naturally on earth

Figure 2.3   The periodic table of the elements.

ultimate indivisible 'atoms' of Democritus' dreams? Protons do not seem to be, because they apparently consist of still smaller bits of matter called 'quarks' (although nobody has ever split a proton into free quarks). And neutrons certainly aren't, because they can be split into protons and electrons and less familiar particles known as 'neutrinos' (and neutrons really do split up like this during certain forms of radioactive decay). Nobody has yet found any evidence of another layer of little bits of matter inside electrons, so maybe they really are indivisible; but the question of the ultimate indivisibility of bits of matter is not really uppermost in the minds of modern physicists and chemists. In fact many might try to persuade you that the question is meaningless, down in the bizarre world of the 'fundamental particles'.

Fortunately, there is no need for us to hack deeper into the jungle of particle physics to meet the modest aims of this book. Chemistry, including the chemistry that makes us live, can largely be described by settling on the familiar sub-atomic trinity of protons, neutrons and electrons as our most basic building-blocks. We can happily leave the physicists to worry about any 'even littler bits of stuff' which lie within them.

Particles and forces

The particles from which our living bodies are constructed do not sit apart from one another in lonely isolation. In the first place they are all constantly on the move – rushing about, spinning, tumbling, bumping into and bouncing off one another with the random chaotic motion we call 'heat'. The 'heat' of an object is simply a measure of how energetically its particles are in motion. Secondly, they *interact*, or they affect one-another, thanks to agencies known as 'forces'.

Consider a force everyone knows about – the force of attraction between positive and negative electrical charge, and of repulsion between like electrical charges. The concept of electrical 'charge' becomes so familiar to those of us interested in science as we struggle through our schooldays, that we can easily forget (or never realize) what a completely mysterious phenomenon it is. Our increasing ability to describe and use the effects of the phenomenon that has been labelled 'electrical charge' can easily seduce us into thinking that we really know what, or *why*, it is.

All we really know is that some things are attracted towards other things, and repelled from others, in a way which suggests that one consistent agency or 'force' is responsible. We have invented the term 'electrical charge' to denote the origin of this force, and have found that it makes sense to describe the workings of the force in terms of two types of opposite charges: positive and negative. Things that 'carry' opposite charges are attracted towards one another by this 'electric' force, while those carrying like charges are repelled away from one another.

We find electric charge and electric force to be what makes atoms form and interact. Protons in the nucleus, with their positive charge, are surrounded by negatively charged electrons which (in the naive description of the school chemistry class) 'whirl' about the nucleus like satellites in orbit. Neutrons, of course, are also found in the nucleus, but they do not carry a net charge. The idea of electric charge and electric force is a wonderful invention of the human mind, allowing us to describe and predict the workings of the universe with astounding success.

But the electric force is not the only one we have found necessary to describe and predict the behaviour of our universe. The force of 'gravity' for example, which appears to attract every object in the universe towards every other object, is another of the 'fundamental forces' which make things happen. For a long time the force of 'magnetism' which pulls together appropriate poles of a magnet, was thought to be another fundamental force; but in the 1870s the phenomenon of magnetism was shown to be produced simply by electric charges in motion, and so magnetism became merely another aspect of the electric or 'electromagnetic' force.

Up until very recently it has been believed that there were at least two other fundamental forces at work in the universe. One of these, called the 'strong nuclear force', is responsible for holding the positively charged protons together in an atomic nucleus – overcoming the repulsive effects of the electromagnetic force provided the distances involved are very short. The other one, the 'weak nuclear force' can be found at work within neutrons. According to the most recent theories, however, this weak force is really just another manifestation of the force responsible for electromagnetism; so we are left with only three fundamental forces to make everything happen: gravity, electromagnetism (or the 'electroweak' force, as it is increasingly becoming known) and the strong nuclear force.

The unification of the forces may well be taken further in the future. Some theories already combine electromagnetism with the strong nuclear force; and more ambitious ideas suggest that only the one basic 'superforce' may be behind gravity *and* the other one or two forces.

Whatever new discoveries the future holds, it certainly seems that everything which happens in our universe, including all of the chemical reactions that let us live, is the result of no more than four fundamental forces pushing and pulling and changing just a few different types of particles of matter. That is a remarkable conclusion to contemplate while out walking amid the complexity of today's living world – watching rabbits and hares and birds and flowers and trees; or rushing through the human whirlpool of a modern city; and all the time feeling the wind on your face and the steady heartbeat within your chest. How such complexity could possibly have been woven from the sparse fabric of a few particles and forces, is what this book is all about.

Energy

A few moments thought about a universe composed of particles which are pushed and pulled about by various forces will throw up a fundamental mystery: why are the forces not fully 'satisfied'? In other words, why do the forces not simply push and pull the particles into place, at which point all change would cease? Why do all the stars and planets not come crashing together, propelled by the force of gravity? Why don't all the electrons in our atoms dive into the positively charged nucleus which we know they are strongly attracted to?

The search for ultimate answers to such questions occupies endless hours of debate, but at least a part of the answer lies with that mysterious phenomenon known as 'energy'.

Energy is yet another scientific term which many people glibly use while rarely bothering to analyse what it really means. Most schoolbooks (and many university-level texts) offer us only some classic phrase such as 'energy is the ability to do work'. Now 'work' has been defined as 'movement against a force'. The word 'force' here, is the key to a better understanding of what the idea of energy is all about.· Although energy is an abstract, rather than a concrete concept, its definition as 'the ability to do work' can be made more concrete by realizing that energy must therefore be the ability to 'resist' (or 'push against') a fundamental force. It takes energy to pull a positive charge away from a negative one (against the electro-magnetic force). It takes energy to lift an object from the surface of the earth (against the gravitational force) and it would take energy to pull a proton out of an atomic nucleus (against the strong nuclear force).

This description of energy has centred on what is known as 'potential' energy, mainly because it has the potential to be converted into a more obvious form of energy called 'kinetic' energy, or *the energy of motion*. Potential energy, such as the energy held by water in a mountain lake, can be used to make things move, such as a water wheel powered by water falling from the lake. Equally, things that are moving (i.e. which have some kinetic energy) can generate potential energy when they are made to slow down or stop. Movement, and resistance against the fundamental forces, are *interchangeable* forms of the strange phenomenon we call energy.

Entropy

Having briefly explored the meaning of energy, I should now point out that the universe seems to have a certain amount of energy 'built in'. To create a very simple analogy, we might say that the universe is a bit like a compressed spring (see figure 2.4). The distribution of the compression can vary, with some regions being highly compressed (i.e. containing a lot of energy) while others are more relaxed, but

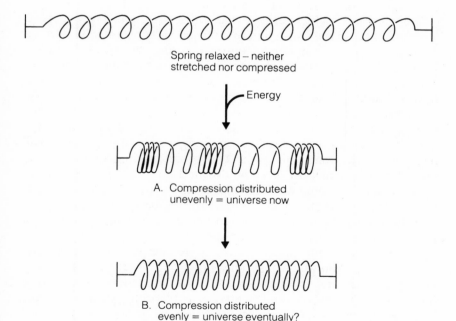

Spring relaxed – neither
stretched nor compressed

Energy

A. Compression distributed
unevenly = universe now

B. Compression distributed
evenly = universe eventually?

Figure 2.4   The universe as a compressed spring. As time goes by the compression (i.e. the energy) is becoming dispersed towards an even distribution.

overall the spring remains compressed to the same extent whatever happens.

The sun, or any other star, corresponds to a 'highly compressed' high-energy region, while our earth and the dust clouds of deep space are much more relaxed.

Now the most fundamental observation, or 'law' in all science is the second law of thermodynamics, and in general terms all this law says is that *'energy tends to disperse'*. To see this in action, consider the spring as it is shown in figure 2.4A. Obviously that state could not last for long, unless someone held the coils to keep the compression unevenly distributed. Instead, the compression – the energy – would soon disperse, until it became evenly distributed throughout the entire length of the spring.

This is what is happening in the universe all the time. Energy is unevenly distributed, concentrated in the stars, for example, and much rarer in planets and interstellar space; but the energy is constantly dispersing, and it is that dispersal of energy which we have to thank for our own existence. Energy dispersal is what makes chemical reactions work (as we shall explore a little later), and chemical reactions are what make us work.

The extent to which energy has dispersed, has been labelled 'entropy', and so the entropy of the universe is constantly increasing. Another popular definition of entropy is 'the degree of disorder', because 'disorder' (such as the increasing random motion of particles as a substance gets hotter) is what energy dispersal creates. No matter how it is defined and described, the driving force of all change is the dispersal of energy as the universe 'springs' from a state of uneven energy distribution towards a state of even energy distribution.

If that state is ever reached, nobody really knows what will happen. Maybe that will be the end of everything, or maybe the universe will somehow become 'wound up' or 'unevenly compressed' again in some way (perhaps as all its matter rushes inwards towards a 'big crunch' which reverses the big bang). The question of *how* the universe gained an uneven energy distribution in the first place, is also a source of great debate.

All such deep questions are yet more 'jungles' which we can happily skirt around. We should however, briefly consider *why* energy should tend to disperse, since that tendency is the driving force which created us all. The answer is blissfully simple – energy disperses because there are more *opportunities*, or more 'ways', for it to do so, than there are for it to become yet more unevenly distributed.

Think of an iron bar, hot at one end and cold at the other.

Remember that 'heat' is simply a measure of the random motion of the atoms in the bar, and clearly that random motion will spread along the bar as fast-moving 'hot' atoms jostle into slow-moving 'cold' ones and give up some of their energy to them as they do so. Fast-moving atoms obviously have more opportunity to jostle into and give up energy to slow-moving ones, than vice-versa. If, while standing in the street, you are hit by someone jogging, the jogger is hardly likely to bounce off moving faster than before, but you will!

Similar explanations could be given for all situations in which energy tends to disperse – it disperses because it has no other option. The quotation at the start of this chapter comes from P.W. Atkins' superb book *The Second Law* (published by W.H. Freeman). Consult its colourful pages if you want to learn more about 'the chaotic dispersal of energy as the purposeless motivation of change'.

All this discussion of particles and forces and energy and entropy might seem very abstract and of little direct relevance to the origins of life, which is presumably what you want to read about; but actually it is absolutely vital to the origins of life, because particles, forces, and energy and its irreversible tendency to disperse, are what allowed the universe to give rise to living things.

Back to atoms

All our descriptions of the universe, in terms of atoms, forces, energy and so on, are simply 'models' or 'representations' of reality. As science progresses, the models presumably draw ever closer to the real 'truth' about what actually happens and why it happens. Our model of the atom has undergone a series of drastic changes over the years, as you will find summarized in figure 2.5.

The idea of atoms as indivisible little spheres or 'billiard balls' was retained from the time of Democritus up to the days of John Dalton, who in the early nineteenth century devised a comprehensive atomic theory of chemistry, based on different types of atoms reacting with one another in fixed proportions. Over a short space of time, a series of discoveries then demolished this billiard ball model of the atom and replaced it with a sequence of refinements.

Firstly, as the twentieth century dawned, it became apparent that atoms were not indivisible, but contained equal numbers of positively charged protons, and negatively charged electrons. For a while, 'plum-pudding' models of the atom became the vogue, with the protons and electrons mixed together like the ingredients of a pudding.

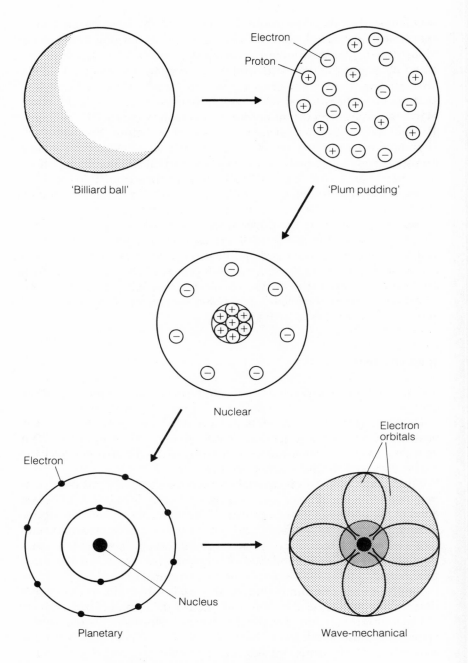

Figure 2.5   The development of our models of atomic structure.

This lasted only a few years, however, before Lord Rutherford's experiments revealed that all the protons of an atom must be concentrated into a tiny central 'nucleus', with the electrons distributed all around it. When James Chadwick discovered the neutron (in 1932) the nucleus became a mixture of protons and neutrons; but long before that (from about 1914 onwards) the Danish physicist Niels Bohr and others had wrought a major change in the model. They told us that the electrons surrounding the nucleus could not be just anywhere between the nucleus and the atom's extremities. Instead, they appeared to circulate in defined 'orbits'. In each orbit there was room for only a certain number of electrons, and electrons in 'low' orbits needed less energy to keep them there than those in the 'higher' orbits.

Many aspects of the resulting 'planetary' model of the atom fitted nicely with what we see happening up in the large-scale world all around us. It takes more energy to put a satellite into a high orbit than a low one; and after accepting that only a restricted number of possible orbits are allowed, the idea of planetary electrons matched pleasingly with the behaviour of the planets as they orbit around our sun.

Sadly for those who like to keep life simple, atoms do not really seem to be built like that. Around the 1920s to 1930s it became apparent that electrons were often better described as wave-like entities rather than as 'solid' particles. In other words, they behaved like periodic variations in the phenomenon of negative electrical charge.

This new description of electrons as waves was just one aspect of a new 'wave mechanics', which allowed physicists to treat all particles as waves, whenever it suited them, while leaving them free to return to the 'common-sense' world of solid particles when the need arose! We have hit the fringes of another jungle here – the jungle of 'wave–particle' duality – and once again there is no need for us to enter any deeper. The small-scale world of the atom seems to sometimes be best described in terms of waves, and sometimes in terms of solid particles. This does not mean that the small-scale world is nonsensical, or that it must be composed of things which are both waves and particles – it simply means that nothing happening up in our large-scale world can be used as a direct analogy for what goes on down there.

The important point, for our purposes, is that the emergence of wave mechanics led to yet another model of the atom. In this current model, electrons are represented by 'clouds of negative charge' (referred to as 'orbitals') distributed around the nucleus in various shapes. Electrons can be thought of as being 'smeared out' within their orbitals. Only certain defined orbitals are 'allowed', and to be in any particular orbital an electron must possess a set amount of energy.

If an electron shifts from one orbital into another of lower energy, then the energy it loses in this process is 'radiated' away as pure energy in the form of 'electromagnetic radiation' such as light. Equally, an electron can absorb electromagnetic radiation that provides it with just enough energy to jump up into a higher-energy orbital.

Chemistry

The universe would be dull indeed if it consisted merely of atoms which jostled around, occasionally bumping into one another and perhaps exchanging energy, but doing nothing else. To get a degree in chemistry you would simply need to memorize the periodic table of the elements. You could then turn to the study of more interesting topics, such as how atoms came into being and worked, or how on earth you were able to be alive in a world made solely of non-reacting atoms.

But of course atoms are not aloof and solitary travellers of a dull, uninteresting universe. Instead, they can become linked together in a great variety of different ways to form many millions of different chemical compounds.

Chemistry is really just the study of atoms interacting, or 'reacting' to the conditions and the company they find themselves in. Hydrogen and oxygen atoms react together to form water. Carbon and hydrogen atoms react together to form methane gas and petrol and rubber and oil. Carbon, hydrogen, nitrogen, oxygen and sulphur atoms react to form the seemingly miraculous protein molecules which make us all work; and carbon, hydrogen, nitrogen, oxygen and phosphorus atoms combine to produce the genes made of DNA which ensure we become men and women rather than buffaloes, or bacteria, or begonias.

The big question, of course, is how and why does all this happen? What makes the chemical reactions of the living and the non-living world take place? The answer is that the fundamental forces make them all happen, spontaneously shifting and shuffling the atoms into arrangements in which energy becomes more evenly dispersed throughout the universe than it was before the reactions took place. And in practice the answer is even simpler than that, because the reactions of chemistry are generally powered by only one of the fundamental forces – the force of electromagnetism, which attracts electrons to protons and repels electrons from electrons and protons from protons. Let's look at some very simple examples.

Hydrogen is by far the most common element in the universe, accounting for an astounding 92.7 per cent of its atoms (chapter 4 tells you why). Hydrogen atoms are also the simplest there are, consisting of a single proton surrounded by a solitary electron (see figure 2.6).

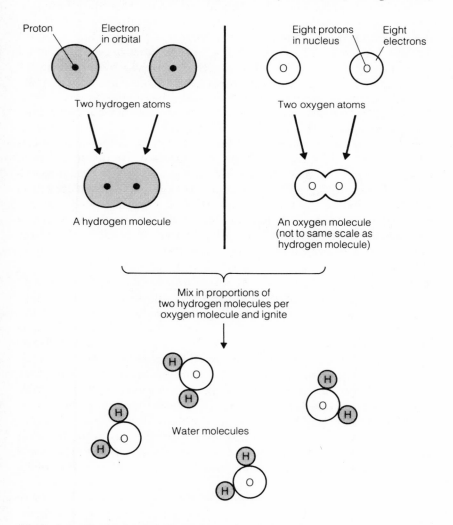

Figure 2.6   The formation of hydrogen, oxygen and water.

Whenever a number of hydrogen atoms are close to one another, the electron of any one atom is attracted, not only to its own proton, but also to the protons of neighbouring atoms. This can cause two hydrogen atoms to come together and 'share' their electrons.

In this sharing arrangement, the electromagnetic forces of both attraction and repulsion between the four particles involved are less resisted (more fully satisfied) than they were when the atoms were apart. That is the same thing as saying that the shared arrangement is a *lower-energy* one. So when the atoms come together they lose energy, which can be dispersed out to the surroundings (assuming the surroundings in general are in a fairly low energy state, which is usually the case). This dispersal of energy is what makes the shared arrangement stable. By coming together, the two hydrogen atoms have allowed the energy distribution of the universe to even out a bit.

In the shared arrangement the two atoms have joined up to form a 'molecule' (a particle composed of two or more atoms chemically bonded together). This molecular arrangement is the lowest energy, and therefore most stable, arrangement that hydrogen atoms can adopt. Push them closer together, and forces of repulsion between the two protons become stronger and the energy of the structure will rise. Pull them apart, and you have to fight against forces of attraction which act to keep the molecule together – so again, the energy will rise. Try to group three, or four or more hydrogen atoms together in a sharing arrangement, and you will find that all possible structures have a higher energy than the H_2 molecule.

Now similar arguments also apply to much more complex atoms and molecules. Oxygen atoms, for example, contain a nucleus of eight protons and usually eight neutrons, all surrounded by eight electrons. They, too, can come together to form a lower-energy molecule composed of two oxygen atoms sharing electrons. The energy lost as an oxygen molecule forms is dispersed out to the surroundings and so O_2 is the form in which oxygen is usually found.

So far we have looked at why two molecules can form, but they have not been very interesting molecules because both have contained only the one type of atom. The really interesting molecules, such as the ones that make us work, contain *different* types of atoms bonded together, in other words they are chemical 'compounds'. We can watch a simple compound being formed if we mix some hydrogen and oxygen molecules together in the same jar (figure 2.6 again).

Actually, if we simply mixed the two gases together at room temperature, nothing much would happen; but if we heated up a few of the molecules (i.e. made them move much faster) by dropping a burning match into the jar, then the results would be dramatic. The jar would explode, and if we then picked up a few fragments of the broken glass (assuming we were not more concerned about the wounds we had sustained during the explosion) we would find them covered in droplets of water. This water would have been produced by a chemical reaction between the oxygen and the hydrogen; but why?

Once again, the driving force behind the reaction was electro-magnetism. This force can be more fully satisfied by rearranging the nuclei and electrons of oxygen and hydrogen atoms into the form of water molecules. In this case, the effects of the dispersal of energy away from the reaction were dramatic. The energy caused such great heating and expansion of the reaction mixture that it exploded.

One problem about this reaction remains: why did it need the help of a burning match to get it started? One of the easiest ways to understand the answer is to leave the world of protons and electrons for a moment, and consider the more mundane situation of a rock lodged in some cleft on a mountainside (see figure 2.7). The fundamental force we call gravity is pulling the rock downwards, and yet it is not as far down the mountain as it could be. So the rock is in a state of higher energy than it would be if it fell to the bottom. Of course it will not fall to this lower energy state spontaneously, because it is lodged in the cleft; but if we give it a push just sufficient to lift it out of the cleft, then down it will go.

As it falls, the gravitational potential energy it had by virtue of

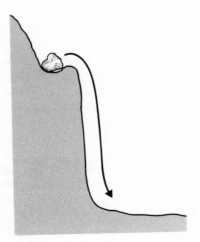

Figure 2.7   The rock needs a push to make it fall.

being half-way up the mountain rather than at the bottom, will be converted into the kinetic energy of motion. Then when it hits the bottom this kinetic energy will be dispersed away into the ground as heat energy (i.e. kinetic energy of motion on an atomic scale). So the net result is that, once the rock has fallen, the energy of the universe will be more evenly dispersed than it was before – some of it having been dispersed throughout the particles of the earth all around, rather than being locked up as the gravitational potential energy of one small rock. But remember, to get this to happen we first had to *increase* the potential energy of the rock by pushing it up and over the edge.

Chemical reactions are in much the same situation as our rock – they need a bit of a 'push' to get them to go. In the case of chemical reactions, the push is usually supplied as heat energy. This increases the rate at which the atoms and molecules rush about and jostle into one another, allowing them to disrupt their structures sufficiently to let all the electrons and nuclei become reorganized into new configurations.

In the reaction we are considering, the heat from our match was needed to make hydrogen and oxygen molecules bump together with a force that would disturb the fairly stable arrangement they were already in, and let them settle down into a new and even more stable arrangement. Once this had allowed a few water molecules to form, the energy given out as they formed would be available to jostle some more hydrogen and oxygen molecules into reacting. Very quickly the dramatic self-fuelling explosive conversion of hydrogen and oxygen into water would be under way.

The energy needed to jolt atoms and molecules into configurations in which reaction between them can occur is known as the 'activation energy' of a reaction. This activation energy can be represented by a diagram which looks very similar to our drawing of a rock on a mountainside (figure 2.8). In some cases, sufficient activation energy is supplied merely by the heat available when the chemicals involved are mixed at room temperature. But many reactions need more 'persuasion'; one of the main reasons for having bunsen burners in chemistry laboratories.

So where have we got to? We have seen that atoms and molecules can react together to reach more stable, lower energy configurations in which the electromagnetic force acting between protons and electrons is more fully satisfied. The energy difference between the start of the reaction and its end can be dispersed outwards into the environment all around. The irreversible dictum of the second law will have been complied with.

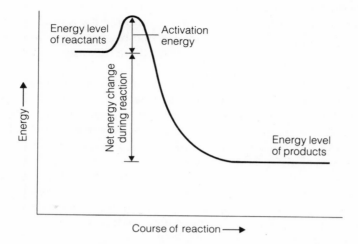

Figure 2.8   Chemical reactions also need an energy 'push' to make them go.

But once again, if that were all that happened, then chemistry would still be pretty boring. Whenever they met, atoms and molecules would rearrange themselves into the lowest possible energy configuration, and then sit about doing nothing much at all. That may be what will happen to the universe eventually, but for the moment, living as we do in a universe whose energy is still far from evenly dispersed, things are much more interesting.

Sometimes, the energy sloshing about the universe can actually push reactions all the way *up* the slope shown in figure 2.8, to leave the atoms and molecules in a higher energy configuration than they were before. How can we reconcile this with the irreversible tendency of energy to disperse? Quite easily actually – because whenever the surroundings around any chemical system contain *more energy* than the chemicals of the system, then the dispersal of energy will push it *into* the chemical system. Remember that the second law tells us energy tends to become dispersed evenly throughout the universe, moving from regions of high energy to regions of lower energy. In the examples looked at so far, the reacting chemicals were at a higher energy level than their surroundings, so reactions in which they gave out energy were favoured. The opposite situation can also occur, chemicals in low energy configurations can absorb energy from their surroundings and be pushed up into higher energy 'clefts'.

So the chemical form in which atoms and molecules find themselves is really determined by an interplay between two factors. The electromagnetic force is constantly pulling them towards lower energy states, in which that force is more fully satisfied; but the energy sloshing around the universe as it becomes ever more evenly dispersed, can be absorbed to push them up into higher energy states.

Chemicals react to reach an energy level that is in harmony with the energy level of their surroundings. In relatively low energy surroundings they will react to 'fall down' into relatively low energy states (provided the surroundings supply enough energy to surmount the activation barriers of the reactions). Heat them up, or supply energy in other forms such as light, and they can absorb energy and be 'pushed up' into higher energy states. And in all cases they react as they do because of the irreversible tendency of the energy of the universe to become more evenly dispersed as time goes by, a tendency which exists simply because a universe built of particles moving about in all directions provides *more opportunities* for energy to disperse than to spontaneously become concentrated in a few locations.

Protons, neutrons and electrons; between one and four fundamental forces; and a certain amount of 'force resistance' known as energy, gradually becoming evenly dispersed throughout the universe – that is indeed a sparse fabric from which to weave such a complex cloth as the living world around us. It is time to look at how that world manages to live.

3   Life on earth

. . . the DNA double helix and replication based on complementary
associations, genetic coding between nucleic acids and proteins: such are the
great secrets of life at the molecular level.
Jacques Ninio

Scientists interested in the origins of life on earth are embroiled in a complex detective story in which the mystery to be solved is us. How did we, and all other living things, ever come to be here? A first essential step towards solving that mystery is to find out everything we can about what we are and how we work. Answers to these questions will not only make it easier for us to speculate on the past origins of life on earth, they should also help us to consider how life elsewhere or new life in the future might originate. So in this chapter I want to consider how the living things of the modern earth manage to live, leaving the question of how they might have originated until later. If the material in this chapter is all new to you, then you may find it a bit of a challenge. Hopefully it will be a stimulating challenge, because it will reveal to you the chemical 'secrets' of life, secrets which are in general much simpler than you might suppose.

Humans have puzzled over the mysteries of their own existence ever since there were humans around to puzzle, but reliable answers have been very slow in coming. Only over the last few decades have we begun to understand the complexities of physics and chemistry that make us work. Many profound mysteries remain, especially concerning the minds that do the puzzling, but the barriers between puzzlement and perception do seem to be crashing down at last.

Our living bodies, and the bodies of all other living things, appear to be marvellously intricate chemical machines. We may not be *'mere'* machines, but machines we certainly are. Actually, creatures such as ourselves are confederates of many millions of individual chemical machines working in cooperation, because the basic machine which makes us work is the living cell.

The living cell

Even those unenlightened souls whose main memories of school science are that chemistry laboratories smell, and dissected dogfish smell even worse, usually also remember that the basic unit of life is the 'cell'. The differences between ourselves and all other creatures boil down to the types and numbers of cells we contain. An amoeba is made of a single cell which does little else but seek out food, take it in, and use it to grow and multiply. A human is made of around ten trillion cells, divided into many different types each specialized to do different things.

Although cells can differ enormously in what they do and what they look like, they all have a common core of essential features which let them work. Figure 3.1 outlines these features, using a cell

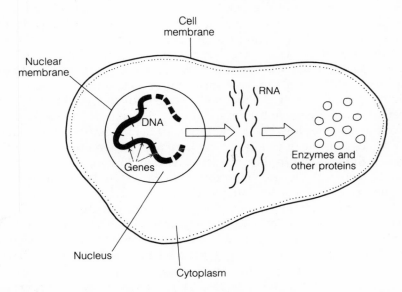

Figure 3.1   Living cells contain genes (made of DNA) which direct the manufacture of proteins. Proteins are the chemical catalysts ('enzymes') which speed up and direct the chemistry of life (although they have other roles to play as well – see text). RNA is a very similar chemical to DNA, which serves as a 'working copy' of a gene during the process of protein manufacture.

from a 'higher organism' such as ourselves as an example. The single cells of 'lower organisms' (such as bacteria) have a simpler structure – lacking a separate 'nucleus', for example – but the basic chemistry that makes them work is very similar.

Remember that all the structures labelled in the figure and described in the text are made up of atoms, or molecules (atoms chemically bonded together), or 'ions' (atoms or molecules that carry a net electrical charge by virtue of having lost or gained one or more outer electrons). And all the changes and interactions I will describe take place because they are essentially chemical reactions driven by the tendency of energy to become evenly dispersed throughout the universe.

The cells of higher organisms are split into two compartments – the 'nucleus' and the 'cytoplasm', thanks to the presence of the nuclear membrane, and it is inside the nucleus that we find our 'genes'. Many people who know nothing about the chemical nature or behaviour of genes are nonetheless well aware that they play a central role in determining the structure and activities of living things; and also that they make each generation of cells or organisms resemble their ancestors. Genes, in other words, are the agents of *heredity*, ensuring that all mice look like mice and all men look like men.

Genes are actually distinct regions of incredibly long thin molecules of the chemical 'DNA' (which stands for **D**eoxyribo**N**ucleic **A**cid). Some organisms, such as bacteria, contain only one main DNA molecule. Our own cells, and those of all other higher organisms, contain a number of separate bundles of DNA, each known as a 'chromosome'; and the DNA of each chromosome contains many genes.

So what do genes do that makes them so important? Very simply, *they carry the 'information' (in a chemically coded form) needed to make an organism, and they pass that information on to subsequent generations of cells.* The information carried by genes is called 'genetic information', and it can be thought of as the precise 'instructions' needed to construct another vitally important class of chemicals – the proteins. Broadly speaking, one gene is a section of a DNA molecule that contains the information needed to make one particular type of protein molecule. The full complement of genes contained within a cell's DNA is known as its 'genome', and the human genome probably contains about 100 000 distinct genes, all present within every one of our trillions of cells.

If the importance of genes is that they contain the information needed to make proteins, the next big question is what do proteins do? Proteins actually perform a wide range of essential tasks within cells and organisms, but by far their most important function is to act as the molecules that actually construct and maintain all cells. The proteins that do this job of cell construction and maintenance are known as 'enzymes', and they perform their seemingly miraculous task in a very simple way.

Enzymes are chemical 'catalysts' – with a catalyst being defined as something that *speeds up* a particular chemical reaction while itself remaining unchanged in the process. I have already emphasized that every living thing is a chemical machine, which implies that the overall activities of a living organism are the result of many interacting chemical reactions. Now countless different chemical reactions could take place between the chemicals found inside cells, most of which would not give rise to life; so for any meaningful form of life to be assembled from all the various possibilities there must be some way of encouraging desirable reactions, preventing (or at least not assisting) undesirable ones, and ensuring that all the detailed chemical reactions of life take place in the right places, at the right times, at suitable speeds and in the correct sequence. This is the job of the enzymes (see figure 3.2).

Each of the thousands of chemical reactions that combine to make you, me, a mouse or a bacterium, is catalysed by a particular enzyme. Without the help of catalysis by enzymes many of these reactions would never get going at any reasonable pace at all. It is the enzymes which make the integrated chemistry of life possible. They bring order, structure and balance to the chemical 'soup' within our cells.

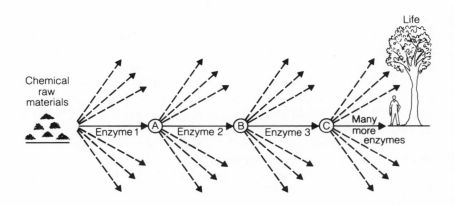

Figure 3.2   The importance of enzymes. Each enzyme speeds up a particular chemical reaction required for life (solid lines), while giving no help at all to undesirable reactions (dashed lines). See also plate 4.

So by containing the information needed to make enzymes (and other proteins), genes ultimately determine the structure and activities of all cells and organisms. But you should bear in mind that enzymes are not the only proteins that matter, for proteins do lots of important things other than speeding up chemical reactions. We will explore some of these other things a bit later.

The overall message so far has been that life on earth is based on genes that direct the manufacture of proteins, and the proteins act together to construct all living things. Before delving more deeply into the activities of genes and proteins, I should briefly mention the other class of chemical shown in figure 3.1 – RNA. RNA (which stands for RiboNucleic Acid) has a very similar structure to DNA, and in figure 3.1 it is shown performing one of its major roles in the cell – acting as a 'working copy' of the genetic information which travels out from the nucleus and into the cytoplasm, where protein assembly actually takes place. DNA is the 'master copy' of a cell's genetic information, and it stays secure within the nucleus. RNA copies of the genetic information stored in any gene are made and transported out into the cytoplasm when required, and it is these RNA copies of genes that actually direct the production of proteins. As their full names imply (see above) both RNA and DNA belong to a class of chemicals known as the 'nucleic acids'. We will be looking at their chemical structure more closely in chapter 4.

Genes and the double-helix

The obvious place to begin a journey through the workings of a cell is at its DNA, which stores the genetic information needed to make the cell. There are two main requirements for any chemical that is to serve as a carrier of genetic information. Firstly, it obviously must be able to *contain* information; and secondly, there must be some easy way for this information to be *copied*, so that when cells multiply by dividing there will be a copy available for each of the two new cells. Let's look at the structure of DNA, beginning with the entire molecule in all its complexity, and then simplifying it step by step to concentrate on only those features that make it a good carrier of genetic information.

Figure 3.3A (and plate 1) is as close as I can get to showing you what DNA actually 'looks' like. It shows a short section of DNA with spheres representing all the atoms. DNA is made out of hydrogen, carbon, nitrogen, oxygen and phosphorus atoms, and real DNA molecules are incredibly long compared with their breadth. A single gene, shown to the same scale as figure 3.3A, would be at least 6

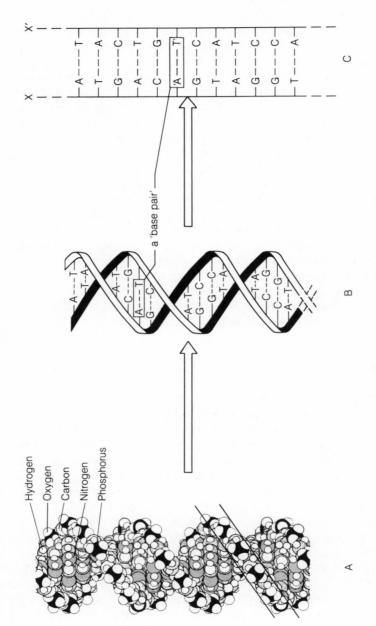

Hydrogen
Oxygen
Carbon
Nitrogen
Phosphorus

A

A----T
T----A
G----C
A----T
C----G
A----T
G----C
T----A
A----T
G----C
G----C
T----A

a 'base pair'

B

X   X'

A----T
T----A
G----C
A----T
C----G
A----T
G----C
T----A
A----T
G----C
G----C
T----A

C

Figure 3.3   The structure of the DNA double-helix.

metres long (often much longer); and a single DNA molecule usually contains many genes.

About one and a half million life-sized copies of the short section of DNA shown in figure 3.3A would need to join up to form a DNA molecule 1 centimetre long. That demonstrates how very small atoms are, compared to us; and that when we investigate how life works we must deal with things which are unbelievably tiny compared to the world of our everyday experience.

Looking at all its individual atoms makes DNA seem very complex, but it can readily be made to look much simpler. Even the complexity of figure 3.3A, however, can be used to point out the most celebrated feature of DNA's structure – its ability to form a 'double-helix'. Two helical ribbons of atoms, referred to as the helical 'backbones' of DNA, can be seen spiralling around the central core (part of one of them has been highlighted by drawing lines on either side of it). The double-helical structure can be seen much more clearly in figure 3.3B. This considerably simplifies the structure of DNA by distinguishing between its two main regions – the helical backbones and the central core – and by representing them in diagrammatic form.

The structure of the helical backbones never varies, so these parts of the molecule cannot contain any information. Actually, they serve simply to hold the crucial central core in place. So we can represent all the atoms of the helical backbones simply as two twisting ribbons. The structure of the central core has obviously also been simplified in figure 3.3B, with all the atoms being replaced by merely the first initials of the different types of chemical groups that make up the core. The core of a DNA double-helix is composed of only four different chemical groups, called 'bases'. These bases are 'adenine' (A), 'thymine' (T), 'guanine' (G) and 'cytosine' (C). The differences between different DNA molecules – the differences between the genes that make the proteins of mice or of men – simply involve the different sequences in which the four bases of DNA are arranged. So to understand how DNA works, we now only have to worry about the four bases – 'A', 'T', 'G' and 'C' – and the sequences in which they are arranged.

In figure 3.3C, the simplification process has been taken one final step. The helical backbones have been untwisted and are now represented by straight lines. This allows us to concentrate on the central bases which carry the genetic information. Having reached this stage, I should point out that a DNA double-helix is strictly speaking not a single molecule, but is composed of two separate DNA molecules wound around one another. In figure 3.3C the molecule or 'strand' labelled X carries one particular sequence of bases, while the other strand X′, carries another. The two strands are held together by weak forces of electromagnetic attraction (the attraction between positive and negative electrical charge, remember) represented by dashed lines between the bases on opposing strands. So the double-stranded DNA double-helix is held together by 'base-pairs', formed when the bases on opposing strands become linked by these weak bonds.

In only two steps the structure of DNA has been reduced from the real-life assembly of five types of atoms, to a simple array of letters (representing different chemical groups). Such arrays must somehow be deciphered to make living cells and organisms, but how?

The first clue to how DNA works is the hidden order present in its structure as shown in figure 3.3C. It isn't very well hidden, but it might escape a first glance. Take a look at the particular bases that make up individual base-pairs. Wherever an 'A' appears on one strand, it is paired with a 'T' on the opposite strand (and conversly, all 'T's are paired up with 'A's). The same applies to all the 'G's and 'C's – every 'G' is paired with a 'C' and every 'C' with a 'G'. These 'rules of base-pairing' result from the chemical structure of the individual bases, and they never vary. Throughout all the DNA of a cell there are only two types of base-pair – 'A's paired with 'T's, and 'G's paired with 'C's – although these two types of base-pair can appear either way round. Any two DNA strands whose base sequences 'match' according to the rules of base-pairing, are called 'complementary' strands. Obviously, two DNA strands able to bind together in the form of a double-helix must be complementary to one another.

Now remember the two things that the genetic material of a cell must be able to do. It must be able to be easily *copied*, so that copies can be made available for future generations; and it must be able to *contain information* – the information needed to make specific proteins. Clearly, the information must take the form of variations in the sequence of bases strung out along the length of a DNA molecule, but I will consider the copying problem first.

The answer to the copying problem stares you in the face as you examine figure 3.3C. The structure of DNA makes it easy to produce faithful copies of any particular double-helix, because *all the information needed to make an entire double-helix is contained in either of its two strands*. To appreciate this, imagine the two strands were pulled apart, and you were given only one of them (the strands can actually be pulled apart rather easily, because the bonds holding the base-pairs together are very weak). Given one strand and a supply of the four bases linked to the atoms that make up the helical backbone, you could quickly reconstruct the original double helix. You would simply need to pair up the appropriate bases according to the rules of base-pairing – pairing 'A's with 'T's, 'T's with 'A's, 'G's with 'C's and 'C's with 'G's (see figure 3.4)

The copying process outlined in figure 3.4 is very close to what actually happens when the DNA of living cells is 'replicated'. The DNA is unwound or 'unzipped' by enzymes, and then other enzymes link up the required bases into the newly forming strands of

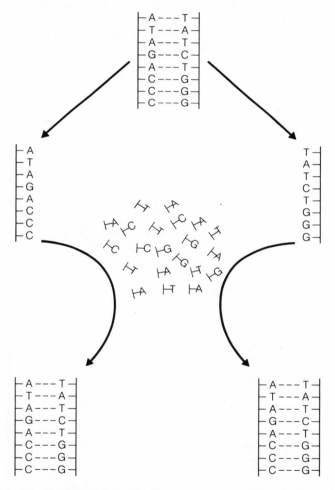

Figure 3.4 Anyone provided with only one strand of a DNA double-helix and a supply of nucleotides (bases linked to atoms that form the 'backbone' of DNA) could easily re-create the original double-helix by following the rules of base-pairing.

DNA, paired up in the only way the base-pairing rules allow (see figure 3.5). The bases actually come already joined to the atoms that will form the new helical backbone, as molecules known as 'nucleotides'.

It is important to realize that although enzymes catalyse all of the chemical reactions involved in DNA replication, the actual specificity of the process is due to the structure of the bases themselves. The 'correct' base-pairs are formed, simply because they are the only ones that *can* form in a way that allows the available enzymes to link the new bases into the growing helical backbone. If the 'wrong' bases should pair up, they will not be in the correct position for the linkage reaction to occur – that is why they are 'wrong'.

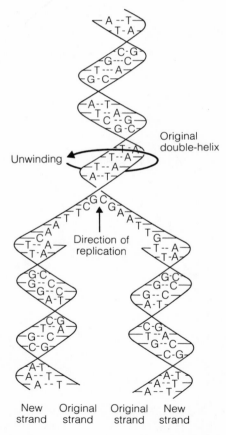

Figure 3.5 The replication of double-helical DNA.

Having seen the answer to the copying problem, we can now turn to the other one – the central question of how DNA manages to contain the information needed to make specific protein molecules.

I have already said that the information carried by DNA takes the form of variations in the sequence of bases strung out along the length of the DNA double-helix. The bases can be present in any sequence at all, provided the base-pairing rules are satisfied between the bases on opposing strands. Obviously, the information needed to make protein molecules must be *encoded* in the DNA base sequence in some way. The possibilities for using a base-sequence code to direct the production of proteins become more obvious when you take a look at the architecture of protein molecules.

Plate 3 shows you what a typical protein molecule actually 'looks like', and it suggests that once again we are dealing with incredibly complex structures which might be very difficult to understand. But just as we were able to simplify the structure of DNA, to make it comprehensible, so we can also simplify the structure of proteins to reveal the common architectural plan they all adhere to.

All proteins are long chain-like molecules, as shown in figure 3.6C (the rest of the figure is explained shortly). A protein chain is made by linking together many smaller molecules called 'amino acids', each composed of just 10 to 27 individual atoms. Each rectangle of figure 3.6C represents one particular amino acid molecule. A total of 20 different amino acids are used to make proteins, and most proteins contain several hundred of them linked into the protein chain.

Once a protein has been made by linking up the correct amino acids in the correct sequence (all catalysed by enzymes of course), then the long chain usually folds up into a highly specific shape (represented schematically by figure 3.6C, and more realistically by plate 3). Only once a protein has adopted its final precisely folded form can it actually carry out its chemical task, such as acting as an enzyme which speeds up some specific chemical reaction vital to the cell.

It is crucial to realize that the folding process is determined entirely by the type of amino acids in the protein chain, and by the sequence in which they are arranged. The protein is pushed and pulled into its folded structure by electromagnetic forces of attraction and repulsion acting between the amino acids and the watery surroundings inside the cell. So once the correct amino acids have been linked up in the correct sequence, the job of making a protein is essentially complete. The protein chain will fold up into the precise three-dimensional structure that the electromagnetic force pulls it into; and this will be the structure that allows it to carry out its highly specific biological task.

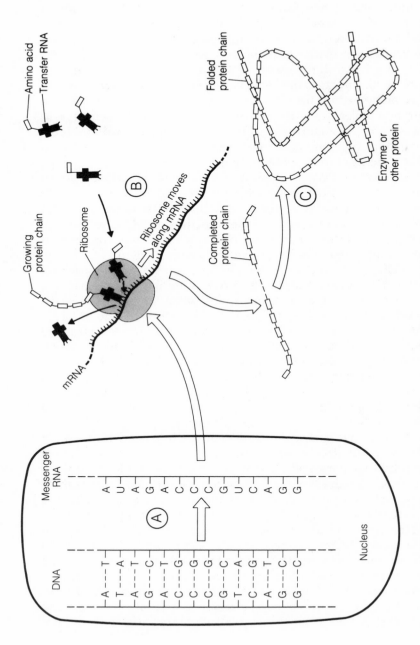

Figure 3.6 A summary of gene expression. The DNA of a gene is copied into single-stranded RNA. This messenger RNA (mRNA) moves out to the cytoplasm and binds to a ribosome. The ribosome moves along the mRNA, allowing appropriate transfer RNAs (tRNAs) to bind to the exposed mRNA codons by forming base-pairs between the codons and complementary anticodons on the tRNAs. Each tRNA brings with it the amino acid encoded by whichever codon the tRNA can bind to. The amino acids are linked up to form the protein encoded by the gene.

So things should be looking clearer and simpler now. The information needed to make a protein is stored in the form of a *linear* sequence of bases in DNA, and what that information must do is bring about the formation of a protein composed of a particular *linear* sequence of amino acids. To solve the problem of how the genetic information in DNA is decoded into proteins, we simply need to know the relationship between the base sequence of a gene and the amino acid sequence of the protein it codes for, and how the first gives rise to the second. The essence of the answer can be stated very simply: *each sequence of three bases in DNA can direct one particular amino acid to become linked up into a growing protein chain.*

That single sentence summarizes the results of a monumental amount of human effort and ingenuity. It tells us how to decode the 'genetic code' – the natural code which allows variations in the base sequence of DNA to direct the production of the protein molecules that go on to construct and maintain all living things. It will be explained to you in the next page or so, which may make tough reading if it is all new to you. If so, take things slowly, read each section over a few times and don't give up! You are learning nothing less than how life on earth manages to live! First of all, we will follow the whole decoding process through in outline (see figure 3.6 A–C).

It begins with DNA – the master copy of the cell's genetic information. A section of DNA encoding one particular protein is known as a 'gene', and the first thing to happen when a gene becomes active is that a working copy of the gene is made in the form of RNA. From the figure you can see two obvious differences between the DNA of a gene and its RNA working copy. Firstly, the RNA is single-stranded. It is actually a replica of just one of the strands of the double-helix (in the figure, the RNA is a replica of the left-hand strand of the unwound double-helix). Secondly, wherever the base 'T' appears in DNA, a different base known as 'U' appears in its RNA copy. 'U' stands for 'uracil', a very similar base to 'T' and one which forms a base-pair with 'A' just as 'T' does. So for our present purposes the bases 'U' and 'T' can be regarded as behaving identically.

The RNA replica of one strand of the double-helix is made in much the same way as new copies of the DNA itself. The two strands of the double-helix become temporarily separated, allowing enzymes to use one strand (the right-hand one in figure 3.6) as a template on which nucleotides (i.e. bases linked to the backbone atoms, remember) can be linked together into a complementary strand of RNA. The production of this RNA is known as 'transcription', since the genetic message is being transcribed from a DNA version into an RNA version, and obviously it too depends on the rules of base-pairing to make it work. As the RNA copy of a gene is made, the double-helix snaps together once more, releasing the RNA.

The RNA copy is known as 'messenger RNA' (mRNA), since it then moves out from the nucleus and into the cytoplasm, carrying its genetic message from the cell's central 'data bank' out to the site of protein synthesis in the cytoplasm. Proteins are actually constructed on large conglomerates of protein and RNA known as 'ribosomes' (figure 3.6B). A ribosome attaches to an mRNA molecule, and then works its way along the message from one end to the other. Each time it passes a sequence of three bases, the appropriate amino acid (the one 'encoded' by the three bases) can be linked up by enzymes into the growing protein chain.

The amino acids are actually brought to the ribosome attached to another class of RNA molecules called 'transfer RNAs' (tRNAs). Each tRNA has a set of three bases which can form base-pairs with the three bases on mRNA that code for the amino acid the tRNA carries. The bases 'UAC' on mRNA, for example, can form base-pairs with the bases 'AUG' on the tRNA that carries the amino acid 'tyrosine'. This means that the sequence 'UAC' in mRNA always causes tyrosine to be linked into a growing protein.

Figure 3.7 shows which amino acids are encoded by each of the sets of three bases (known as 'codons') that can be found in mRNA.

Second base/nucleotide

		U	C	A	G	
First base/nucleotide	U	UUU ⎫ Phe UUC ⎭ UUA ⎫ Leu UUG ⎭	UCU UCC Ser UCA UCG	UAU ⎫ Tyr UAC ⎭ UAA STOP UAG STOP	UGU ⎫ Cys UGC ⎭ UGA STOP UGG Tryp	U C A G
	C	CUU CUC Leu CUA CUG	CCU CCC Pro CCA CCG	CAU ⎫ His CAC ⎭ CAA ⎫ GluN CAG ⎭	CGU CGC Arg CGA CGG	U C A G
	A	AUU ⎫ AUC ⎪ Ileu AUA ⎭ AUG Met	ACU ACC Thr ACA ACG	AAU ⎫ AspN AAC ⎭ AAA ⎫ Lys AAG ⎭	AGU ⎫ Ser AGC ⎭ AGA ⎫ Arg AGG ⎭	U C A G
	G	GUU GUC Val GUA GUG	GCU GCC Ala GCA GCG	GAU ⎫ Asp GAC ⎭ GAA ⎫ Glu GAG ⎭	GGU GGC Gly GGA GGG	U C A G

(Third base/nucleotide shown at right)

Figure 3.7   The genetic code table. The amino acids specified by each codon are represented by their common abbreviations.

Notice that three codons ('UAA', 'UAG' and 'UGA') do not code for amino acids, but instead indicate the points on mRNA at which protein synthesis should stop. Also, there is more than one codon available for most amino acids. The sets of three bases on tRNA that can form base-pairs with the mRNA codons are known as 'anticodons', and obviously an anticodon is complementary to its codon.

So as ribosomes travel the length of an mRNA molecule, tRNA molecules bind to the codons as they become exposed at a special site on the ribosomes. The tRNAs bring along the amino acids encoded by the codons they can bind to, and as each amino acid arrives, it is linked up into the growing protein chain. Each tRNA is released from the ribosome when the growing protein chain is passed on to the next tRNA and the ribosome moves on. Eventually, the ribosome will reach one of the 'stop' signals, causing both the mRNA and the now completed protein to be released. The protein will fold up in the precise way determined by its amino acid sequence, and will then be able to begin to perform whatever chemical task its structure allows it to perform.

This process of protein synthesis is known as 'translation', since the genetic message is now being translated from the language of DNA and RNA (i.e. from the language of nucleic acids) into the language of proteins. The entire process of decoding a gene into a protein, involving both transcription (the production of the mRNA) and translation (use of the mRNA to make protein) is known as gene 'expression'. And remember that all of the enzymes needed to catalyse gene expression are themselves produced by the expression of *their* genes; and all the other types of RNA, such as tRNAs and the RNAs found in ribosomes, are produced by the transcription of genes that encode them.

So DNA and RNA are needed to make proteins, while proteins are needed to make DNA and RNA, and also to assemble proteins. This presents us with a 'chicken and egg' type of dilemma: how could DNA and RNA (or any similar nucleic acid) have first formed and been replicated without proteins; or how could proteins have first formed without the DNA genes and mRNAs needed to encode them, and without the other proteins needed to catalyse their manufacture? That is really the central issue facing scientists trying to explain the origin of life on earth – how did self-replicating systems of genes encoding proteins that make new genes and proteins . . . first arise? (See figure 3.8.)

If you have found the last few pages confusing, don't despair! They contain all the essential secrets of the chemistry of life. If you have

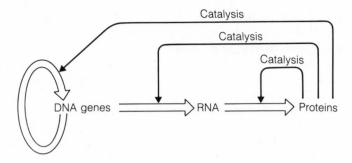

Figure 3.8   The central molecules of life on earth are as dependent on one another as chickens and eggs. Proteins are needed to catalyse the chemical reactions which make proteins, RNA, and which replicate DNA. DNA genes and RNA are needed to make proteins. How this interdependent system first arose, is the major mystery facing scientists trying to explain the origin of life on earth.

understood them, then you know how life on earth lives and multiplies – simply by containing genes which replicate (to pass their 'information' on to succeeding generations), and which direct the manufacture of proteins (which make all living things by catalysing the necessary chemical reactions). Humans have been searching for these secrets for millennia, so if you found them hard to understand on a first reading of only a few pages, you should at least be prepared to have another go! But first of all, run through the quick summary given in the paragraph below.

Genes are long sections of DNA in which the four different bases are arranged in differing sequences. This sequence of bases is converted into a sequence of amino acids in a protein molecule according to a code; and in this 'genetic code' each group of three bases directs the incorporation of one particular amino acid into a protein molecule. Once formed, the protein automatically folds up and, if it is an enzyme, begins to catalyse a specific type of chemical reaction involved in the construction or maintenance of cells (and therefore of organisms). The differences between all organisms result from the different chemical reactions taking place within them. Which reactions occur is dependent on which proteins are encoded in an organism's DNA. The 'secret of life' is that replicating genes direct the manufacture of the proteins (and some RNAs) that make life live. All life on earth is essentially based on genes that encode proteins.

The powers of proteins

Since proteins are the molecular 'workers' that build cells and organisms, we should at least briefly consider how they manage to do that work; and we should also look at some of the other things they do in addition to acting as enzymes.

The first problem is how do enzymes manage to catalyse so many different chemical reactions with such speed and efficiency, often increasing their rate many thousandfold, while giving no help at all to unwanted reactions? In essence, the answer is very simple. In its final folded form an enzyme has grooves and clefts on its surface into which only the chemicals involved in the reaction it catalyses can fit (see figure 3.9 and plate 3). When bound to the enzyme surface, the reacting chemicals are held in an orientation that makes the desired reaction much more likely. Chemical groups on the enzyme itself, belonging to the various amino acids, can also participate in the reaction – pushing or pulling the electrons of the reacting chemicals in ways that encourage the reaction to proceed (by lowering the *activation energy* of the reaction). There are amino acids that can act as acids, and others that can act as alkalis; some that carry a positive charge and some whose charge is negative; some that bind tightly to water molecules and others that can hold on to 'oily' hydrocarbons. Together, they comprise a formidable chemical repertoire which makes the chemistry of life work.

Some enzymes are assisted in their catalytic wizardry by 'co-enzymes' – simple small molecules, or even single metal ions, that can bind to such enzymes to provide chemical assistance. The ability to grab hold of and utilize such co-enzymes is of course a result of the amino acid sequences of the enzymes involved.

So enzymic catalysis depends on the folding of protein chains to produce a final folded structure in which appropriate amino acids come together in appropriate conformations to allow the reacting chemicals (and perhaps some co-enzyme) to bind to the surface of the enzyme and react. The chances that any protein with a randomly chosen amino acid sequence will act as an efficient catalyst for any particular reaction, are very small. But throughout the course of evolution countless numbers of amino acid sequences must have been 'tried out', with only the most useful being 'selected' and modified further. The superbly efficient enzymes found in modern organisms are presumed to be the end products of millennia of gradual improvement – a process which no doubt often began with very coarse 'enzymes' whose catalytic effects were only very slight.

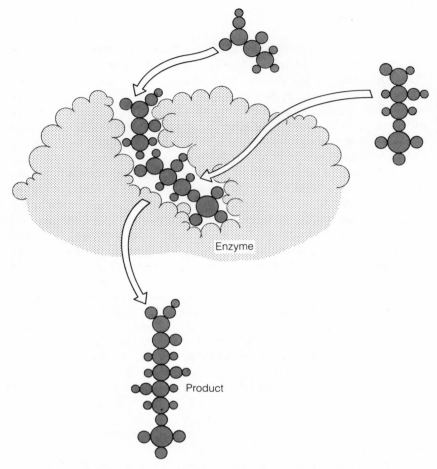

Figure 3.9   Enzymes have grooves and clefts on their surface into which only the chemicals involved in the reactions they catalyse can fit. This allows the chemicals to bind to the appropriate enzymes in orientations and environments that greatly encourage the reactions to proceed.

The way in which different protein sequences could have been 'tried out' and 'selected' is a major part of our story.

Enzymes are so spectacular and so efficient that it is easy to forget that proteins do lots of other very important things in addition to acting as enzymes. You will find some of them listed in figure 3.10. Apart from enzymes, the next most fundamental type of proteins are probably the 'structural proteins' which, as their name suggests, form

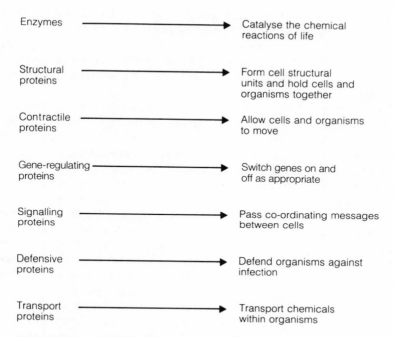

Enzymes ⟶ Catalyse the chemical reactions of life

Structural proteins ⟶ Form cell structural units and hold cells and organisms together

Contractile proteins ⟶ Allow cells and organisms to move

Gene-regulating proteins ⟶ Switch genes on and off as appropriate

Signalling proteins ⟶ Pass co-ordinating messages between cells

Defensive proteins ⟶ Defend organisms against infection

Transport proteins ⟶ Transport chemicals within organisms

Figure 3.10   Some of the things that proteins do.

much of the structural framework or 'scaffolding' holding cells and organisms together. The exterior surfaces of many organisms, including us, are made largely of protein. Other structural proteins form much of the 'connective tissue' found in bones, ligaments, tendons and which generally holds the cells of our bodies together. And many cells contain a complex intracellular 'scaffolding' of tube-like proteins known as the 'cytoskeleton'. This is not a static skeleton, but one that can contract and disassemble and then assemble again where and when required. It pulls the components of the cell around and gives cells the ability to move.

This brings us on to the 'contractile proteins' – a class of structural proteins that clump together into bundles or fibres which can contract and relax in response to various stimuli. The contractile proteins of your muscles are straining and stretching as you sit reading this book. Complex cycles of their contraction and relaxation are needed to prevent you from slumping to the desk or to the floor, and to perform the intricate process of flipping from one page to the next.

Some proteins are able to bind to specific regions of a cell's DNA and switch various genes 'on' or 'off' as appropriate. These 'gene-regulating' proteins must play a vital role in allowing cells to grow and develop properly, and to respond in appropriate ways to changes in their environment. Thanks to them, various cells of an organism can become specialized to perform many different tasks (as muscle cells, liver cells, brain cells etc.) despite containing identical genomes.

Many other small proteins act as signalling or 'messenger' molecules within our bodies. These are made and released by one type of cell to influence the activity of other types of cells in appropriate ways. The most famous protein messengers are some 'hormones', such as 'insulin' or 'growth hormone', which circulate through the bloodstream until they meet up with the cells whose activities they control. Other less well known messengers called 'tissue factors' are constantly being passed around the various tissues of your body. These act a bit like 'local hormones' restricted to just one type of tissue rather than being circulated widely throughout the bloodstream. Some protein messengers can be passed from one organism to another, such as some of the sex pheromones used by various creatures to attract and prepare a suitable mate.

The celebrated 'defensive proteins', such as 'antibodies' which allow us to fight off infection, form another vital and almost infinitely variable class of protein molecules. Other defensive proteins such as 'inteferon', 'interleukin', and many others with complex unfamiliar names, all cooperate to save us many times from the threat of viruses, bacteria, fungi and so on.

The final class of proteins I want to mention are the 'transport proteins', responsible for transporting various essential substances around large creatures such as ourselves. The best-known example is probably haemoglobin, which sits in our red blood cells and carries oxygen molecules from our lungs to all the parts of the body that need them.

So the proteins are a remarkable class of chemicals which make cells and organisms into the marvellously intricate chemical machines they are. Genes are important simply because they contain the information needed to make the life-creating proteins. The major task of the proteins is to catalyse all of the chemical reactions of life, although they perform other important functions as well. Before winding up this chapter, I should introduce you to two very important types of chemical which are assembled or manipulated by enzymes, and which have vital roles to play in the structure of life – carbohydrates and lipids.

The most familiar carbohydrates are various simple 'sugars'

(sucrose, glucose, fructose etc.), and the more complex types known as starch and cellulose. They play a major structural role in many cells and organisms, as well as acting as versatile sources of chemical energy (see chapter 8). All carbohydrates are essentially composed of carbon, hydrogen and oxygen atoms. The simple carbohydrates known as sugars can form more complex ones by becoming linked up into chains, as you can see in figure 3.11. The 'amylopectin' shown in the figure, and formed by the linkage of many glucose molecules, is a major constituent of starch. Carbohydrates are often found attached

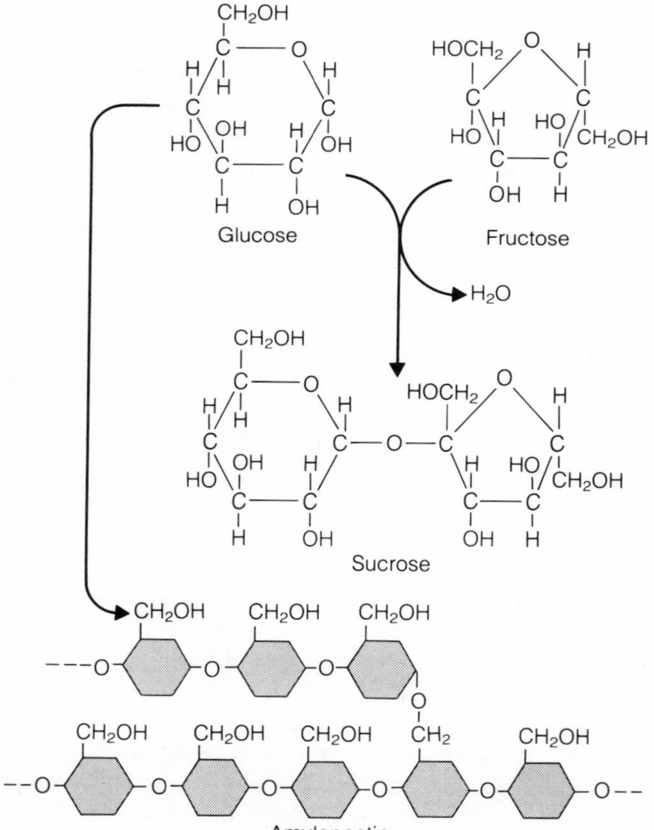

Figure 3.11 The structure of some carbohydrates. Simple sugars such as glucose and fructose can become linked into slighly larger sugar molecules such as sucrose (common 'sugar'). They can also become linked into complex carbohydrates such as amylopectin (a major constituent of starch, made of linked glucose molecules).

to the surface of various protein molecules, forming protein–carbohydrate complexes called 'glycoproteins'.

The substances that biochemists call lipids are a diverse group of chemicals with one major property in common – they are not soluble in water. The term includes everything that a layman would call 'fat'. Lipids act as energy storage molecules, and also play many other important roles within cells; but their major function is to form the thin membranes found at the boundary of all cells and also the various intracellular bodies such as the nucleus (see chapter 5).

In addition to carbohydrates and lipids, living things contain a wide variety of different types of chemicals all reacting and interacting in ways that give rise to life. But all of the many thousands of chemical reactions are catalysed by the proteins we call enzymes, which are encoded by genes (see plate 4). So the mystery of how living things ever got going in the first place really boils down to a question of how genes first arose and began to direct the manufacture of proteins. And the mystery of how the first living things evolved into such complex organisms as ourselves, boils down to the question of how the first protein-making gene systems were amplified and diversified to make the thousands of different proteins that make us work.

The common foundation of genes that encode proteins has given rise to a myriad of very different living things, all based on different types of cells. Genes and proteins manage to make bacterial cells, plant cells and animal cells; cells specialized to form leaf and stem, muscle, bone, liver and kidney; cells adapted to transport oxygen around our bodies and to fight off disease; and many many more, including the cells of the brain which presumably contain the still secret chemistry of consciousness which lets us think and study and worry about it all.

Many such different cells are different because they contain different genes, but many others are different because a common set of genes is used in different ways. Consider all of the different cells within your own body. They all came from just a single fertilized egg cell which began to divide until it had given rise to you. Each of your cells is believed to contain the same complement of genes as was present in the original cell, and yet the cells of your skin are obviously very different from those of your bones, or muscles or brain and so on. These differences must be due to differences in the *activity* of the genes, with the genes that make blood cells being active only in blood cells, the genes that make nerve cells being active only in nerve cells, and so on. Each human cell probably contains the genetic information needed to make any type of human cell, and therefore an entire human, but in each cell only a selected portion of that information is used.

How this control (or 'regulation') of gene activity within different cells is achieved is one of the major mysteries facing biology today. Scientists do know of lots of ways in which genes can be switched on or off when appropriate (largely by starting or stopping their copying into messenger RNA), but they still have little idea about how all the various gene control systems mesh together to let a single fertilized egg cell create a superbly efficient thinking being rather than a chaotic proteinaceous mess.

So the diversity of living cells is literally bewildering. Nobody should let statements that attribute it all to differerent genes and different proteins seduce them into thinking that we know precisely *how* the different genes and proteins actually integrate to create such complex variety – we don't. And the baffling diversity of cells is at least equalled by the more familiar diversity of creatures all around us. Think of tigers and spiders, elephants and flies, geese and gooseberries, mushrooms and whales, yeasts, lobsters, bacteria, geraniums, mussels, mice and men. All work because they contain genes that encode proteins. All are powered by the fundamental forces pushing and pulling atoms and sub-atomic particles into place, as energy gradually disperses; and all are supposedly derived from a common origin that dates from a time when mere clusters of atoms spontaneously took on characteristics that changed them from what we call 'dead' to what we call 'alive'. It is at last time to look more closely at modern ideas about how atoms might have 'come alive'.

4 Stardust in a pond

It is generally believed that a variety of processes led to the formation of simple organic compounds on the primitive earth. These compounds combined together to give more and more complex structures until one was formed that could be called living.
Stanley Miller, Leslie Orgel

In December 1983 the American physicist William Fowler delivered his Nobel Prize acceptance speech to the Swedish Academy of Sciences in Stockholm. He had been given the physics prize, along with Subrahmanyan Chandrasekhar, for many years of research into the origin of the elements – the raw materials of all chemistry and all life. After a long and complex talk he closed with a final point which summed up everything with clarity and drama:

> My major theme has been that all of the heavy elements from carbon to uranium have been synthesized in stars. Our bodies consist for the most part of these heavy elements. Apart from hydrogen, we are 65 percent oxygen, and 18 percent carbon, with smaller percentages of nitrogen, sodium, magnesium-phosphorus, sulphur, chlorine, potassium and traces of still heavier elements. Thus it is possible to say that each one of us and all of us are truly and literally a little bit of stardust.

So most of the atoms that have been used to make ourselves and all earlier forms of life were created inside stars. The few other lighter atoms, such as hydrogen, were produced in the direct aftermath of the cataclysm we call the 'big bang'; or else were cleaved from larger atoms out in interstellar space. Our own sun and the earth formed from interstellar dust containing a rich mixture of atoms, including many created within the fires of earlier generations of stars. It is on the newborn earth that the atoms are believed to have reacted together to form life, but how?

Charles Darwin has little to say about the origin of life itself in his immortal *Origin of Species*, but musing on the topic in a letter he wrote of the life-creating possibilities of '. . . some warm little pond, with all sorts of ammonia and phosphoric salts, light, heat, electricity etc.'. This is one of the earliest versions of what has become the modern scientific story of the origin of life. In essence, it says that given enough time and energy the simple chemicals found in the waters of the early earth could have themselves, spontaneously, given rise to life. This genesis need not necessarily have occurred in Darwin's pond – it might have happened in some primeval ocean or muddy riverbank; but regardless of where it happened, this modern version of Genesis tells us that the origin of life required no outside intervention, from God, from spacemen, or from whatever.

Science has replaced the first chapter of the Bible with a single simple recipe – 'take some matter, heat while stirring, and wait'. The fundamental forces are presumed to have done the rest. What makes scientists so confident of this simple recipe for such a seemingly complex and almost infinitely variable phenomenon?

One historic experiment, performed by Stanley Miller in 1951, has probably done more than anything else to convince people that life on earth really could have arisen spontaneously from some suitable chemical 'soup'; and yet what he did was incredibly simple, and what it produced was certainly not alive.

Miller was studying for his Ph.D. degree at Chicago University, under the supervision of Professor Harold Urey, a physical chemist who believed that a logical scientific explanation could be found for the origin of life. Together, Miller and Urey decided to construct a simple piece of apparatus that would simulate the 'likely' conditions in the atmosphere and oceans of the early earth (see figure 4.1). A mixture of methane (CH_4), hydrogen (H_2), ammonia (NH_3) and water vapour (H_2O) (three simple gases then expected to have been abundant in the primordial skies), was exposed to a powerful electric spark which leapt repeatedly between two electrodes in the vapour. The water was continually condensed and revaporized to simulate the cycle of rainfall and evaporation which linked the primeval oceans to the sky; and the electric sparking was meant to inject the violent energy of the first lightning storms.

After about a week (many accounts insist on the biblical seven days!), the contents of the flask had turned a deep dramatic blood red. Miller stopped the experiment to investigate, and the results of his analysis could scarcely have been more satisfactory. The flask

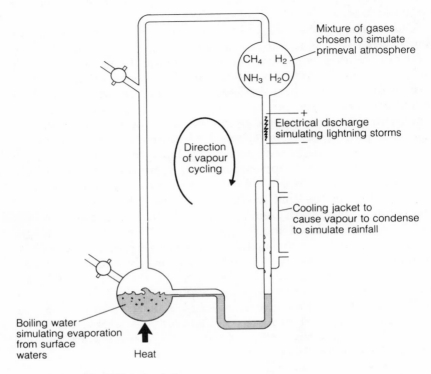

Mixture of gases
chosen to simulate
primeval atmosphere

CH_4 H_2
NH_3 H_2O

Electrical discharge
simulating lightning storms

Direction
of vapour
cycling

Cooling jacket to
cause vapour to condense
to simulate rainfall

Boiling water
simulating evaporation
from surface
waters

Heat

Figure 4.1   The Miller simulation.

turned out to contain significant amounts of amino acids – some of
the most fundamental 'stuff of life' itself!

Further simulations by Miller and by many other scientists have
since yielded many of the other simple 'building-blocks' of life. This
has led scientists to believe that the most essential chemical
components of life must have been available, and perhaps abundant,
on the early earth. This view has been further strengthened by the
discovery of a wide range of amino acids, nucleic acid bases and other
organic compounds in the meteorites which reach us from outer
space.

Difficulties arise if we try to take the simulation process much
further, by leaving the products of the first simulations lying around
in the conditions expected to have prevailed on the early earth.
Genes, enzymes, ribosomes, transfer RNAs and so on, certainly do
not arise with as much ease as their basic components. New life will
not come conveniently crawling at us out of a test tube – at least not

yet. But encouraged by the success of the more basic simulation experiments, and egged on by a multitude of 'thought experiments' which *speculate* on how things might have developed further, most scientists have become fully convinced that life on earth really did originate spontaneously within some primordial chemical soup or slurry or slime. In the rest of this chapter I want to take you through the key steps of the resulting modern 'standard' story of how we might all have originated from 'stardust in a pond', leaving any doubts and criticisms for chapter 5. I want to start back at the very beginning, with a bang.

Elements, stars and planets from a bang

Physicists tell us that the universe was born in the most violent explosion there ever could be – when all the matter and energy in existence, somehow constrained or newly created within an incredibly tiny space, went bang. For the first minute or so the exploding universal fireball contained only naked sub-atomic particles, unable to come together due to the phenomenal amount of energy available to rip any such attempts apart; but during the next couple of minutes the rapid expansion of the fireball reduced the energy density enough to let protons (i.e. the nuclei of hydrogen atoms) begin to fuse together into more complex clusters including helium nuclei. Some time later, further fusions began to create nuclei of the third element – lithium; but the temperature quickly fell too low to allow any further 'nucleosynthesis' to occur. It was at least a 100 000 years before things calmed down sufficiently for electrons to be captured by the nuclei to form hydrogen, helium and a few lithium atoms; and that was as far as the universe got in creating the periodic table (figure 2.3) until the first stars were formed a few thousand million years later.

The first stars began as dark and tenuous clouds of gas which slowly condensed together under the pull of gravity. At last the increasing energy generated by forcing all the atoms of the gas together became sufficient to ignite the fires of a new phase of nuclear fusion. Stars are massive 'fusion reactors' in which the nuclei of light atoms, such as hydrogen and helium, become fused together to form larger nuclei, accompanied by the release of the energy that shines out as starlight. This stellar fusion is believed to have generated most of the heavier atoms, such as carbon, oxygen, nitrogen and so on, that are so essential to life on earth.

Even the stars are not immortal – eventually they can explode and scatter a harvest of newly made atoms into space. These explosions, known as 'supernovae' may also provide the energy to manufacture some of the larger atoms. Other less spectacular mechanisms can also scatter the atoms generated within stars, such as smaller outbursts called 'novae', or the continual release of particle 'winds'. Regardless of how they are released, the atoms formed within one generation of stars serve as the seeds for future generations.

Within later stellar generations, still more complex types of atoms can be formed and then scattered in their turn. Thus from the raw material of hydrogen, helium and a little lithium, all the elements of the familiar periodic table were constructed by the stepwise combination of the nuclei of simpler atoms. There are only three exceptions: beryllium and boron (elements four and five), and also most lithium, are now believed to have been made out in interstellar space when atoms of heavier elements were split by cosmic radiation.

The big bang is currently dated at somewhere between 10 and 20 thousand million years ago, yet that has still been insufficient time for much of the raw material to be used up. Even today, hydrogen is estimated to account for about 92.7 per cent of all the atoms in the universe. Helium takes up a further 7.2 per cent, leaving a tiny 0.1 per cent or so for all other atoms, including most of the ones inside us! The furnaces of the universe would seem to have a long time yet to burn. Many more larger atoms may need to be added to the cosmic periodic table after a further 10 to 20 thousand million years. The heavier atoms of the present periodic table will become much more abundant, and may turn up within a wide variety of living things more complex than ourselves.

This is not a book about cosmology, and still less a critical analysis of that difficult field; but we should allow ourselves a short pause to consider the possibility that the story told above is wrong. The big bang theory of the universe's creation has become popular within only the last 30 years, particularly because it so neatly explains why the universe appears to be expanding, with all the galaxies rushing away from one another in all directions. It is not unknown to find respected physicists questioning its validity – even as I write a few are raising doubts about the reasoning that tells us the universe is expanding at all. If the history of science tells us anything, it is that our ideas can very quickly undergo radical change as the cherished 'facts' of one generation become the quaint old-fashioned fantasies of the next. Nevertheless, physics has presented us with a seemingly reasonable account of how the atoms that make life possible were themselves created, given the existence of mysterious 'matter', 'force' and 'energy' (and 'space') in the first place. We can ask for little more. But how were planets such as our earth formed, and what happened then?

When I was a child (in the sixties) I remember reading a dramatic tale about the origin of the solar system. It told me of great gobbets of glowing gases being pulled from our spinning sun by the gravity of a passing star. One of the gas clouds was then supposed to have coalesced and cooled to form a liquid earth whose surface then slowly turned to solid. This stirring tale was accompanied by a vivid double-page artist's impression of the very moment of earth-birth itself – filled with swirling reds and yellows as the two stars shot past one another in a riot of colour and energy. The legend told me that scientists had provided this answer to the mystery of the earth's formation, making me reflect on what clever people scientists must be and how nice it might be to become one. Alas, this tale which may have shaped my life now lies discredited, but I often think of its fate as I read and write about the modern ideas of science.

Modern science tells us that the earth and its sister planets were formed by the gradual accretion of dust and debris left behind from the dust cloud that gave rise to the sun (see figure 4.2). Little bits of dust came together to form bigger bits. The little stones and rocks that formed were then pulled together by gravity into boulders; boulders crunched together into bigger boulders and so on until the barren stony earth was born, perhaps looking a bit like the moon of today. The early earth must have shone brightly as the light of its sun was reflected back from a dry surface, unprotected by any water or atmosphere of gas. But the engines that would provide our skies and oceans would already be at work deep inside.

The dust that gave rise to the earth contained a fair proportion of large and heavy atoms (all the way up to uranium – element 92) produced by previous generations of stars. Some of these larger atoms (particularly some forms of uranium, thorium and potassium) were unstable and therefore 'radioactive' – spontaneously splitting up into simpler atoms and releasing considerable amounts of energy as they did so. This energy was trapped within the earth's rocky insides as heat, causing the interior of the planet to grow increasingly hotter over millions of years. Eventually, the hot centre of the planet began to melt, and this allowed the denser materials (such as iron and nickel) to slip downwards to the centre of gravity while less dense substances (such as silicates composed of silicon and oxygen) floated towards the surface.

Great convection currents of molten rock began to sort out the components of the earth according to their density, no doubt causing great upheaval on the surface in the form of volcanic eruptions and earthquakes. And molten rock was not the only thing on the move – the heating would also have released gases whose atoms had previously been trapped by chemical bonding within involatile

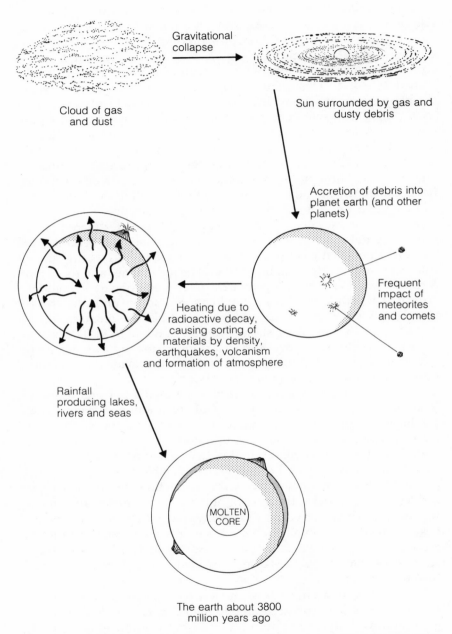

Cloud of gas
and dust

Gravitational
collapse

Sun surrounded by gas and
dusty debris

Accretion of debris into
planet earth (and other
planets)

Frequent
impact of
meteorites
and comets

Heating due to
radioactive decay,
causing sorting of
materials by density,
earthquakes, volcanism
and formation of atmosphere

Rainfall
producing lakes,
rivers and seas

MOLTEN
CORE

The earth about 3800
million years ago

Figure 4.2 Likely events in the formation of the earth (most details are still the subject of debate).

materials. Hydrogen, nitrogen, carbon dioxide, sulphuric and hydrochloric acid vapours and oxygen (which would quickly react with the other gases to form water) are some of the most likely gases to have hissed and gurgled up into the earth's first atmosphere.

A fierce debate still rages about exactly what was present in that first atmosphere, something which has great bearing on our simulations of the prebiotic ('before life') chemistry taking place in the early skies and oceans – the chemistry that is supposed to have created us. But to begin with there were no oceans; not even a trickle of water. The first water would have been formed by reaction between some of the released gases, and would have initially remained in the atmosphere as water vapour; but eventually the atmosphere would have become saturated with that vapour and the first rain would have begun to fall. It would not have been the pure life-giving water of the poets, but would have been a corrosive acidic solution which would have eaten into the alkaline rocks on the earth's surface to create the salt solutions that would form the earliest lakes and seas. From time to time great reservoirs of such solutions may have evaporated to leave behind vast flat salt plains.

This account of the earliest days of our earth may not be the whole truth. Some scientists believe that the entire earth might have become sufficiently hot to have gone through a molten phase, others believe that much of the heat might have come from the impact of comets and meteors, rather than from radioactive decay; and these are just a few of the points of contention. But volcanoes, earthquakes, acid rain, harsh ultra-violet radiation from the sun, widely varying temperatures and an atmosphere of gases which would certainly kill us, are all likely characteristics of the young earth as it waited for life to be born.

The birth of the earth itself is usually dated at around 4.6 thousand million years ago. From the time of birth to the formation of oceans and atmosphere probably took about 800 million years. By then, the first stirrings of the chemistry of life may well have begun.

First life

Creating life from lifeless atoms is a form of cosmic cookery whose outcome, like that of all cookery, depends on the initial ingredients and the conditions of their mixing, boiling, baking and so on. One of the first problems facing us as we try to re-create the recipe for life is that we can never be sure of what ingredients were available in what conditions. I have already mentioned the great debate about the composition of the early atmosphere, and many other things are also uncertain. We can never know the precise composition of the earliest lakes, oceans and seas, the concentrations of the various dissolved substances, or even which substances were there. We cannot be sure of the exact temperatures of the primeval waters, land and atmosphere; or of precisely how much light and ultra-violet radiation struck the early earth; or how many comets and meteors crashed into the surface or burnt up in the atmosphere, and what contribution such objects from space made to the chemistry that created life. So providing plausible answers to the mysteries of our origin is certainly not easy – there should be no doubts about that.

Stanley Miller's now classic simulation experiment provided the first real encouragement to suggest that the creation of life from the ingredients on the newborn earth might not have been *too* difficult. The mixture of gases he chose to represent the primeval atmosphere is no longer believed to represent the likely mix on earth, but a wide range of different possible atmospheres have all been used to create many of life's basic building-blocks in simulations subsequent to Miller's historic attempts (see figure 4.3). These later simulations did not restrict themselves to electrical sparking as the energy source needed to drive the various reactions forward. Instead they often used heat (to simulate the heat due to volcanism or the primordial sun), light and other electromagnetic radiations (to simulate the flood of radiant energy from the sun), or even the passage of shock waves through the reaction mix (to simulate the shock waves associated with the impact of a comet or meteorite on the earth's surface).

All such energy sources (either individually or combined in various proportions) are able to power the production of some of the building-blocks of life (amino acids, bases etc.), from a wide range of possible prebiotic environments. In every case the chaotic dispersal of the energy, in accordance with the second law of thermodynamics, pushes the raw materials into slightly higher energy and possibly life-making configurations.

The precursor chemicals used to prime the simulation reactions were all rather simple substances such as hydrogen cyanide (HCN), ammonia (NH_3), formaldehyde (CH_2O) and water (H_2O). From 1969 onwards astronomers have used their radiotelescopes to detect an abundance of these very molecules (and many others used in earlier simulations) in the deeps of interstellar space. Similar precursors, and even fully formed amino acids and bases, have been found inside the meteorites which reach us from space. So the very chemicals needed to make our sort of life may well be widely distributed throughout the entire universe. All this accumulated evidence has led even most critics of the standard version of life's origin to accept that the

Some important chemical precursors expected to have been present on the early earth, and which have been found in space or within meteorites		Biochemical 'building-blocks' that have been formed from the precursors during simulations of possible prebiotic conditions	Main components of living cells that are formed from the biochemicals (formation not yet satisfactorily simulated)
Hydrogen	H_2	Amino acids (all except histidine and arginine)	Enzymes and other functional proteins
Water	H_2O	Peptides and small proteins	
Ammonia	NH_3		
Carbon monoxide	CO	Bases – Adenine, guanine, cytosine, uracil and thymine	Nucleic acids – DNA and RNA
Formaldehyde	CH_2O		
Acetaldehyde	CH_3CHO		
Thioformaldehyde	CH_2S	Simple sugars, e.g. ribose and deoxyribose	Complex carbohydrates
Methylmercaptan	CH_3SH		
Hydrogen cyanide	HCN		
Cyanoacetylene	HC_2CN	Fatty acids	Membranes
Cyanamide	H_2NCN	Hydrocarbons	
Phosphine	PH_3		
Phosphates	PO_4		

Figure 4.3 Some of the precursors and products of prebiotic simulation experiments, and the main components of living cells that they are presumed to have given rise to.

simplest building-blocks of life such as amino acids, bases and various sugars, must certainly have been around on the early earth.

So suppose we take for granted the presence of reasonable amounts of amino acids, bases, sugars and many other types of simple organic (i.e. carbon-containing) and inorganic substances (phosphates, nitrates, sulphates etc.), perhaps all present in some sort of primordial 'soup', 'slurry' or 'slime'. How could this still lifeless mixture have developed further?

All living things on earth today are built on a foundation of nucleic acids – DNA and RNA. These are the chemicals that contain the information needed to construct an organism; and they are also the chemicals that allow us to reproduce, thanks to their own molecular reproduction or 'replication'. Of course the importance of nucleic acids to present-day life is that they can direct the manufacture of protein molecules. Both nucleic acids and proteins are long 'chain-like' molecules made when many smaller molecules become linked up end to end. All such chain-like molecules are known as 'polymers', formed by the linkage of many separate 'monomers' (poly = many, mono = one). The monomers of proteins are the amino acids. The monomers of nucleic acids are nucleotides (which are themselves composed of a base, a sugar, and a phosphate group all joined together – see below).

The standard version of our origins assumes that amino acids and nucleotides were able to form and to link up spontaneously into their appropriate polymers, or at least short-chain 'oligomers' (oligo = a few), on the early earth. Since it is the nucleic acids which lie at the very heart of present-day life (by carrying the genetic information needed to make living things and passing it down through the generations) the first significant step towards the creation of life is usually assumed to have been the spontaneous formation of chains of nucleic acids (or something very similar) somewhere on the primordial earth.

All nucleic acids are composed of 'bases' strung out along a molecular 'backbone', which itself consists of many sugar and phosphate groups linked in alternating sequence (see figure 4.4). Modern nucleic acids don't form by the attachment of bases to a preformed backbone, or by the linking up of phosphates with already linked bases and sugars. Instead, they are assembled by linking up molecules that already contain all three components – bases, sugars, and phosphates – bonded together. These molecules, the ones that are the raw materials of nucleic acid replication and transcription, are known as 'nucleoside triphosphates' because they consist of a 'nucleoside' (a base joined to a sugar group), linked to three

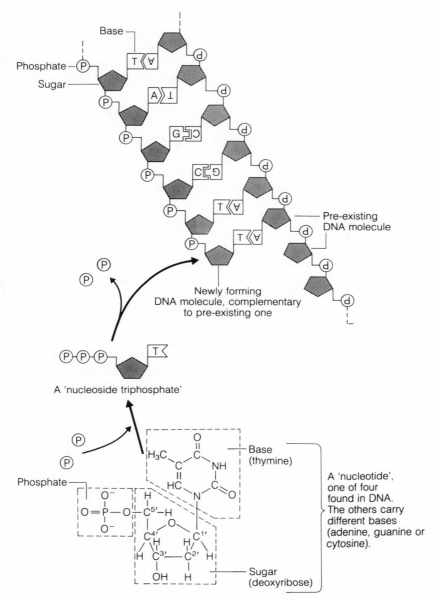

Figure 4.4   The structure of DNA, illustrated by showing one step in the formation of a new strand of DNA complementary to a pre-existing one (follow arrows showing incorporation of a nucleotide carrying the base 'T'). Any DNA molecule is composed of a string of linked nucleotides. Each nucleotide itself consists of a base, a sugar and a phosphate group (see text for details).

phosphate groups. During the enzyme-catalysed reaction that links nucleoside triphosphates into new DNA (or RNA) strands, they lose two of their phosphate groups. Now a nucleoside linked to just one phosphate group is a nucleotide, so, as you can see from figure 4.4, DNA is made out of many nucleotides all linked together in the same way.

The only difference between DNA and RNA is that DNA lacks an oxygen atom found in RNA, on the carbon atom of the sugar group labelled 2', and RNA uses the base 'U' in place of the 'T' found in DNA.

So having introduced you to the characters of nucleic acid chemistry, I can continue the story of how they are supposed to have created life. As you were told earlier, under the conditions of the primeval earth, bases, sugars and phosphate groups are supposed to have been formed, from simpler raw materials, and then been able to link up into short chains of nucleic acid. Nobody insists that these first nucleic acids must have been identical to modern DNA or RNA, but they are generally believed to have been quite similar. And remember that all of the chemical reactions involved in their formation had to proceed spontaneously, powered only by the chaotic dispersal of the energy provided by sunlight, volcanism, lightning storms or whatever.

Once these first nucleic acids (presumably of random or at least unspecific base sequence) began to form, then the chemistry of the earth was supposedly primed for the vital spark that really set it on the road towards living things. That spark would simply have been the spontaneous emergence of nucleic acids that were able to *make more of themselves*; able, in other words, to replicate themselves, or 'reproduce'.

To appreciate why the origin of replication is so important, consider for a moment what living things actually do. At its most basic, the phenomenon we call 'life' is associated with two simple properties – the ability to *replicate* (i.e. to reproduce) and the tendency to *change* from time to time during the act of replication, giving rise to new forms. Replication must not continue to forever produce *identical* replicas of the original form, but must occasionally give rise to offspring that are slightly different from their progenitors. These changes may arise out of 'mistakes' during the replication process, or be driven by some inbuilt mechanism promoting change.

Any population of entities that can replicate themselves, and occasionally change from one generation to the next, has the ability to 'evolve' by 'natural selection' – an evolution that can lead to the development of new and ever more efficient replicators and perhaps eventually to creatures such as us. We should consider these two crucial concepts of 'evolution' and 'natural selection' in more detail, before returning to our fledgling nucleic acid replicators to see how they might have got on.

The process of evolution by natural selection is believed to be the fundamental driving force that turned atoms into animals. When reduced to its bare essentials this process is so simple and obvious that some are tempted to dismiss it as a self-evident truth, based on circular logic, and therefore of no great significance.

Imagine a collection of 'things' that can make more copies of themselves, but in a way that is prone to occasional random errors – producing new things slightly different from their progenitors. Obviously we find it easiest to think of some sort of animals or cells as the chosen 'things', but they really could be anything at all. Now suppose that these things inhabit a world in which the raw materials needed to make more things are limited in supply and perhaps quite scarce; and also accept that in a world in which nothing is permanent each individual thing will eventually 'die'. What will happen to our thing population?

The things will replicate themselves, from time to time giving rise to slightly different things due to errors in the replicative process (I am not supposing a replicative process that involves any union or 'mating' between the things, but rather the direct self-replication of a thing, similar to the replication of a molecule of DNA, or the splitting in two of a cell). An original small population of identical things would soon give rise to a much larger population of things all different from one another in various small ways. Many of the differences might have no effect at all on the way the things worked, but at least a few of them would be likely to affect the *longevity* of the things, and also the efficiency with which they replicated (i.e. their *fecundity*). At least some of the random changes, in other words, would make the new things either better or worse at surviving and making more of themselves than the old things.

Obviously variants that are poorer survivors and replicators than the original things will neither live as long nor multiply as quickly as those more similar or identical to the original form. So the proportion of these 'poorer' things in the population will decrease from generation to generation, especially if a multitude of things are all 'competing' for a restricted supply of the raw materials needed to make new things. Conversely, those variants that are better at surviving and replicating than their progenitors will obviously multiply more quickly than all poorer forms. So the proportion of *these* things in the population will increase from generation to generation. All the time new and occasionally even better variants will be produced thanks to the continuing process of random change, and whenever a better variant does arise it will inevitably multiply faster than poorer variants, and account for an ever-increasing proportion of the thing population.

Overall then, what will happen? A population of self-replicating things will be continually giving rise to new variant things due simply to random errors in the copying process. The vast majority of these variants may well be much poorer at surviving and multiplying than their progenitors, so they will never multiply into a significant proportion of the thing population, and indeed will probably soon die out. But from time to time a few of the variants will be better at surviving and multiplying than existing forms. The future will inevitably belong to these few, because they will multiply faster than all other forms until they come to dominate the population. Of course that dominance may be short-lived, lasting only until some even better survivors and replicators arise from within their own ranks.

Anyone watching and puzzling over the changes in our thing population through many generations would make two main observations. Firstly, they would observe that the population is 'evolving', or in other words it is progressively changing towards increasingly more efficient forms (with efficiency measured simply in terms of replicative, or 'reproductive' success). Secondly, they would observe that overall a process of 'selection' seems to be driving this evolution, with those variant things that are the best survivors and replicators constantly being selected from all the other poorer variants, which are rejected. *But of course nobody is actually doing the 'selection'.* There is no technician or 'God' continually reaching down into the 'thingy soup' to pick out the improved variants and use them as breeding stock for the future, while throwing away the poorer versions. There is no need for such a God. By virtue of their own ability to survive and multiply better than other variants, the best variants (in terms of survival and multiplication) will always be *naturally selected* from all the others. Natural selection is simply the preferred survival and multiplication of things that are best at surviving and multiplying. It allows a continuous process of undirected change to power an overall directed evolution towards more efficient things.

Charles Darwin is remembered as the man who popularized the idea of natural selection, and who pointed out that it might explain the gradual evolution of living things. Darwin did not invent the ideas of natural selection or of evolution – many people had thought and written about them long before his time. His name is justly immortalized in our modern theories of 'Darwinian' evolution, however, because it was Darwin who made the power of evolution by natural selection clear for all to see. His book *Origin of Species* remains gripping and relevant reading even today.

Graham Cairns-Smith (a chemist from Glasgow University whose ideas we will be meeting in chapter 6) has suggested that a more appropriate term for Darwinian evolution might be 'natural rejection', since that may be what happens most: undirected change may usually produce variant organisms which are less fit than their progenitors, and which are therefore naturally rejected, because by being less 'fit' we mean less able to survive and multiply. Natural rejection and natural selection certainly both occur; they are the two inseparable facets of an inevitable process of evolution driven by undirected change.

Let's now return to the short chains of nucleic acids that we left floating around in the primordial soup. They will show us how evolution by natural selection might have got life on its way. Remember that the key requirement of any population that is to evolve by natural selection is the ability of its individuals to replicate in a manner that at least occasionally gives rise to altered versions of themselves. The simplest way for this requirement to be met is for the process of replication to be 'error-prone'.

On paper it is extremely easy to see how short-chain nucleic acids might undergo error-prone replication. Look back to figures 3.4, 3.5 and 4.4, illustrating how modern nucleic acids become replicated. This occurs thanks to the rules of base-pairing, which lets the base sequence of an existing nucleic acid strand direct the formation of a new matching 'complementary' strand. So maybe the first short single-stranded nucleic acids could have replicated in a similar way, simply by acting as templates or 'molecular moulds' on which free nucleotides could line up in sequences dictated by the rules of base-pairing, and then be linked up into new complementary strands. These new strands could then have themselves acted as the templates for the manufacture of strands complementary to themselves, and therefore identical to the original strands.

In modern cells the replication of nucleic acids as directed by the rules of base-pairing is catalysed by a host of complex enzymes which make sure everything runs smoothly, efficiently, and with as few errors as possible. Nonetheless, errors do still occur. In the earliest days of life's origin the replication of short nucleic acids is often supposed to have taken place *without* the help of any enzymes – they would not have been 'discovered' by evolution yet. Obviously, if such non-enzymic replication did occur, then it must have been much slower, much less efficient and much more prone to errors than the replication of modern nucleic acids within a cell.

Nobody suggests that early nucleic acid replication could have been anywhere near as efficient as it is now. Maybe it originally allowed only short runs of identical base sequence to be replicated, such as AAAAAAA or TTTTTTT. Perhaps in the first place it was barely specific at all, serving simply to encourage the further formation of nucleic acids of almost any sequence, regardless of whether or not they were complementary to those already present. But whatever the details, the modern standard view on the origin of life firmly holds that it involved the non-enzymic and probably very inefficient self-replication of short-chain nucleic acids. You will find this proposition in every textbook of biology, sometimes stated boldly as virtual fact, sometimes accompanied by many caveats and cautions. Although slow, error-prone and inefficient, the replication is presumed to have been sufficiently faithful to allow any 'good' variants to spread throughout the population; and sufficiently error-prone to continue creating new and sometimes 'better' variants often enough to keep evolution moving relentlessly forwards towards ever better replicators.

Imagine a population of short-chain and at least inefficiently self-replicating nucleic acids forming, and then gradually evolving within some primordial soup, slurry or slime. At first, there might be a plentiful supply of all the precursors needed to allow the nucleic acids to form spontaneously. Eventually, however, this supply would become insufficient to allow all the different nucleic acids to replicate as quickly as they could. At this point 'competition' between the nucleic acids would become very evident. Any nucleic acids that happened to be able to replicate faster, or more faithfully, than the others, would obviously become a larger part of the population as time went by. The other, poorer, replicators, would diminish in number (see figure 4.5). Evolution, like the evolution of 'things' already considered, would be on its way.

What sort of things could nucleic acid chains actually *do* to make themselves better survivors and replicators? Two very obvious variables are those of length and base sequence. Longer nucleic acids, for example, might be at a disadvantage simply because shorter ones could replicate more quickly (since there is less to be done). Nucleic acids containing a high proportion of the bases 'G' or 'C', might do better than those with lots of 'A's and 'T's, because the 'GC' base-pair happens to be stronger than the 'AT' one, so it might form more readily. Conversely, strong base-pairs might be a disadvantage in some circumstances, because they discourage the separation of newly

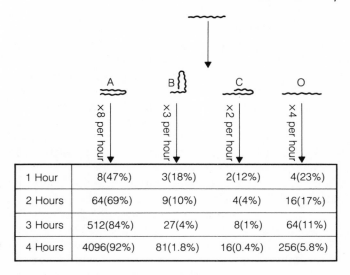

	A	B	C	O
	×8 per hour	×3 per hour	×2 per hour	×4 per hour
1 Hour	8(47%)	3(18%)	2(12%)	4(23%)
2 Hours	64(69%)	9(10%)	4(4%)	16(17%)
3 Hours	512(84%)	27(4%)	8(1%)	64(11%)
4 Hours	4096(92%)	81(1.8%)	16(0.4%)	256(5.8%)

Figure 4.5   Suppose that one original 'species' of self-replicating nucleic acid gave rise to three new variants – A, B and C, each able to replicate at a different rate from the original (O). The fastest replicator would soon come to dominate the population. If the environment could only sustain some maximum number of the replicators, the fastest replicator might drive all or some of the others to extinction. Generation times of hours, months, years or millennia would all yield the same inevitable result.

formed strands from their templates – an essential part of the replication cycle.

Some nucleic acids might have arisen whose base sequence allowed them to encourage some of the chemical reactions involved in their own replication. Others might have been able to encourage the reactions that generated nucleic acid precursors. Such more sophisticated possibilities might be strongly dependent on the ability of nucleic acid chains to fold-back on theselves and form complex three-dimensional structures held together by base-pairing. Single strands of nucleic acid can fold up into specific three-dimensional structures just as proteins can (although probably to a more limited extent), and the precise pattern of such folding will be determined by the base sequences of the nucleic acids – particularly the opportunities they offer for base-pairs to form between different parts of a nucleic acid strand.

Some long chains might have been able to fold up into tightly packed structures that were able to survive longer in an environment containing many reactive and potentially damaging chemicals.

Others might have been able to act as quite efficient 'RNA enzymes' catalysing many reactions that helped them to survive and multiply (see chapter 5). There are many possibilities and we have no way at the moment of knowing how they might have all sorted themselves out, what the best compromise might have been between long and short chains, chains with lots of 'A's or lots of 'C's, chains of uniform or of more variable base sequence, chains that folded and others that did not, and so on. The point is that *in principle*, while musing about it with pencil and paper, fairly short and simple nucleic acid chains seem to have considerable scope for variation and evolution – provided they can replicate themselves.

Given a primitive form of self-replication, and the ability to vary in ways that altered their chances of surviving and replicating further, nucleic acids might on their own have taken the first tentative steps up the 'ladder of life'. All biologists agree that a 'soup' composed of lots of different chemicals slopping about and reacting with one another in a more or less haphazard manner, would not be 'alive'. Many would argue that a population of self-replicating nucleic acids slowly evolving by the natural selection of the best survivors and replicators, would be 'alive'. If we are to grant the outwardly grand title of 'living organisms' to mere chains of nucleic acid composed of a few hundred atoms bonded together, then we should consider in some detail what we really mean by that mysterious word 'life'.

What is life?

Many laymen feel that there must be some clear-cut distinction between the living and the non-living world, because the difference between the things they normally consider as living and non-living is often so obvious. Few people would try to convince anyone that a rock or a stone was alive, while everyone can agree that they themselves, their pet cat and even a flea upon the cat most certainly are all alive. This clarity stems from examining nature at its *extremes*. Just as a beach is obviously 'low ground' and a mountain-top is obviously 'high ground', so a stone is obviously not alive and we obviously are. But as you climb from a beach towards a mountain-top, where does the low ground end and the high ground begin? Most people would recognize this to be a rather pointless question, because 'low ground' and 'high ground' are imprecise relative terms with no clear dividing line between them. 'Life' appears to be a similarly imprecise term. The fact that many people have difficulty accepting this suggests that they are reluctant to recognize their 'brotherhood' with rocks and stones as fellow aggregates of the matter which makes up the universe.

Since this is a book about the origins of life I should make a better attempt to define what I mean by 'life', than simply dismissing it as a vague, imprecise term. Fortunately, we can make a slightly better job of distinguishing between the living and the dead than we can between high ground and low ground, although it will force us to accept as 'alive' many things which most people would dismiss as 'mere chemicals'.

All the creatures that everyone accepts to be alive without question, such as ourselves, and cats and fleas and so on, are believed to have developed from simpler creatures by *evolution*. The ability to evolve by natural selection is what has allowed simple things to give rise to more complex things like ourselves. So if we can identify the point in life's history at which evolution began, and if we can divide everything around us into those that can evolve and those that cannot, then I think we will have marked the dividing line between the dead and the alive as best we can (although still somewhat ambiguously, since there can be arguments about what counts as true evolution).

What are the requirements for any thing to be able to 'evolve'? The first point to make is that individual things never evolve, in the biological sense of the word – it is *populations* which evolve. Each individual human, or ape or cat or other living thing, stays the same creature throughout its life, but they are all part of evolving populations, since the structure of the individuals of the populations changes over many generations.

Some people use the term 'evolution' simply to describe any changes over a period of time, but that is not the sense in which it is being used here. I am using it in the strict biological sense of 'change in a population through the generations, powered by the continuous selection of favourable characteristics'. I purposely avoided using the term 'natural' selection in that definition, because we ourselves make some species evolve by 'artificial' selection. When we select hounds with particularly floppy ears, or horses that run faster than others, or flowers with the heaviest scents, and use them for further breeding, we are artificially selecting characteristics that would not necessarily be selected in nature. This artificial selection can still make hounds and horses and flowers evolve – in fact they evolve much more quickly than they would normally, because we, God-like, reach down and do the selecting; and they evolve in directions often different to the ones that natural selection would have taken.

So to define 'life' we are looking for the requirements for evolution, and in fact we have already met them. The members of any population that is to evolve by natural or artificial selection must be *replicated* from time to time; during the course of that replication *changes* must sometimes occur that make the replicas slightly different from the originals; and these changes must be able to affect the speed and efficiency with which the individuals become replicated. Anything that has these properties will be able to give rise to a population of things that evolves by selection. How *far* that evolution will take the population towards things we would clearly accept as alive, depends on how much scope there is for variant things to alter and organize their environment in ways that favour their own replication. But populations of things that can evolve clearly have the potential to give rise to things we would all accept as 'alive'. That is why, if we are to decide on a dividing line between the dead and the living, then the threshold of evolution seems to be the place to draw it.

Many people find that a very unsatisfactory decision, because it does grant the status of 'life-forms' or 'organisms' to such things as self-replicating chains of nucleic acid that seem barely more complex than the molecules of sugar we stir into our tea. In a way it is still unsatisfactory, because it tries to give a firm well-defined meaning to what is probably a vague and indefinable term.

The ability to evolve, in the biological sense, is certainly not the only definition of life which has been offered through the years. Some books will recite lists of the 'characteristics of life', such as reproduction, locomotion, nutrition, growth, respiration, excretion and sensitivity. The problem with such lists is firstly, that they neither encompass all of the things we accept as alive, nor eliminate all of the things we do not; and secondly, they merely give rise to endless disputes about what the terms used in them really mean. They replace the debate about the meaning of 'life', with debates about the precise meanings of 'reproduction', 'locomotion', 'nutrition' and so on. They seem to me (and to many other people as well) to be totally unsatisfactory attempts to define a clear division of the natural world which probably does not exist. Much the same could be said of the definition of life as 'things capable of evolution', but to a lesser extent.

Some people think that living things have the magical property of defying the second law of thermodynamics. This is the law, remember, which tells us that energy always tends to disperse, or in other words that natural systems move irreversibly in the direction of increasing disorder (increasing 'entropy'). They point to the assembly of a living thing as a blatant violation of that law, since a highly organized and ordered object is arising from the more chaotic environment all around it. It is certainly true that living things impose organization and order on the chemicals they are composed of. It is true, in other words, that life is associated with *localized* decreases in entropy (i.e. localized increases in order) rather than the inevitable increase in entropy imposed by the second law. But the second law is never broken by living things, because it states simply that in any natural change the entropy of *the universe* must increase. Small localized decreases in entropy are a perfectly natural, in fact inevitable, consequence of the second law, *provided they are linked to and counterbalanced by a greater increase in entropy elsewhere.*

Small regions of the universe are decreasing in entropy all around us, not only in living things but also in many simple chemical reactions; but they are always accompanied by greater increases in entropy elsewhere. Thus living things decrease the entropy of a small part of their environment, the part that becomes incorporated into themselves, but only thanks to chemical reactions which are always accompanied by an increase in entropy overall (due to the release of heat away from the products of the reaction, for example). The overall effect of the chemistry of life is to increase the entropy of the universe, just as the second law demands. Any apparent 'violations' of the second law by living things are ultimately powered by the flood of energy arriving on the earth from the sun. That energy arrives in complete accordance with the second law, as part of the gradual dispersal of energy towards an even distribution.

In any case, if 'entropy decrease', or the more correct 'localized entropy decrease' is to be accepted as the definition of life, then fridges are alive, because they cool their interiors in apparent violation of the second law, moving heat from a cool place to a warmer one. They can do this simply because they are supplied with sufficient electrical energy through a flex to power their 'defiance'. In cooling their interiors, fridges increase the dispersal of energy throughout the universe overall, as do all forms of natural change. 'Localized entropy decrease within self-replicating systems' might be a more acceptable definition of life, but then what counts as 'self-replication'? Does crystallization count? Does our own complex 'replication' count, as dependent as it is on the energy and nutrients provided by plants and other forms of life?

We should be careful not to become completely bogged down in a fretful debate on definitions. In many ways the best response to the question of 'what is life', is simply to say 'what does it matter?' Is it not best to recognize that 'life' is an imprecise term bequeathed to us by people who wrongly presumed it represented a real division between some of the different things found in the universe? If it turns out that there is *no* clear fundamental difference between us and plants and rocks and stars – what does it matter? Stars, rocks, plants and humans all exist and interact. It is the interactions and the changes they cause that really matter, not definitions.

Let me settle the matter, for the purposes of this book, by declaring that when I speak of life, and discuss the search for the origins of life, I mean the ability to evolve in the biological sense of the word – particularly the ability of a population of replicators to gradually change in structure thanks to natural selection. We can move forwards with an investigation into the origins of evolution, even if disagreement remains about whether that is the same thing as the origins of life.

This definition clearly makes a population of self-replicating and evolving nucleic acids alive. If we are to accept pieces of self-replicating nucleic acid composed of a few hundred or so atoms as 'living organisms', then we must obviously also accept that they are rather poor and pathetic organisms compared to such magnificently complex creatures as ourselves. Judged by the standards of modern life, naked nucleic acids certainly do not have the capacity to *do* that much. The 'doers' of modern life are the proteins. Nucleic acids are important because they direct the production of protein molecules, and because they carry the necessary directions forwards into future generations; but it is our proteins that really make us, and make us work. So if modern science's version of Genesis is correct, at some point on the way up from molecules to man nucleic acids had to begin to direct the manufacture of specific proteins.

Enter proteins

How and why did nucleic acids begin to direct the manufacture of proteins? It is easy enough to see *why* they should have done so. Proteins can catalyse a virtually infinite range of chemical reactions, as well as being able to do many other useful things which could have helped fledgling organisms to survive and multiply.

Suppose that a population of evolving nucleic acids suddenly gave rise to a few variants able to encourage the formation of particular proteins, or merely very short chains of linked amino acids (known as 'peptides'). This ability would be due to some quirk of structure brought about by the specific base sequence of the nucleic acids. The first of these peptide- or protein-making variants might not have had a great advantage over their less 'clever' relatives, because it is unlikely that the proteins they made would by happy chance have been able to catalyse specific reactions that helped the nucleic acids to survive and multiply. But the proteins might have had some slight non-specific beneficial effects – forming a protective coat around the nucleic acid, for example.

As long as the proteins conferred some benefit on the nucleic acids that made them, then the protein-making trait could be expected to spread throughout the population over a number of generations. Fairly soon, nearly all of the nucleic acids might have been making some sort of simple protein, having driven their less sophisticated progenitors to extinction.

Thanks to chance variations in the nucleic acids' structures through the generations, variants would have arisen making peptides or proteins that helped their makers to survive and replicate in new and more specific ways. The first 'enzymes' would have been born. These would undoubtedly have been very poor enzymes compared to the massive and superbly efficient ones around today. They might have consisted of only a few amino acids linked in sequences that happened to catalyse the formation of the nucleotide derivatives needed as raw material for nucleic acid replication. They might have directly catalysed the replication reactions themselves – who knows? Obviously we can never find out exactly what the first simple enzymes did, but the potential benefits they might have bestowed on their nucleic acid makers are clear to see.

Once replicating nucleic acids making specific proteins (or peptides) had originated, then the fires of evolution and life would have been well alight. The differences between them and us appear to simply be ones of great elaboration, amplification and slow perfection. Whenever blind chance created nucleic acids making better proteins than those around already, these nucleic acids could be expected to thrive and multiply and displace their more primitive relatives. Individual nucleic acids making several different proteins might have arisen, perhaps formed by the chance linking together of two previously separate 'individuals'. Other nucleic acids might have been able to work together for their mutual benefit, in which case anything they did to encourage their joint containment within an enclosing membrane would be selected for – the first 'cells' would be born. Nucleic acids to whom we would only rather reluctantly grant the status of 'life-forms', would have given rise to replicating cells much closer to the sorts of things we freely accept as being 'alive'.

So it is easy to see *why* self-replicating nucleic acids should have begun to make proteins; but it is much harder to see *how*. Nobody knows how it happened, but there is no shortage of ideas. Looking through the multitude of research papers published on this topic, one gets the impression that every scientist interested in the origin of life has personally created at least one theory to explain this crucial step! I do not want to delve into their ideas in any detail at this point, but I will outline one suggested chain of events which many scientists feel may be close to the truth. Unlike many alternative ideas, it is at least supported by a little experimental evidence.

Recall, first of all, the way in which proteins are made within the cytoplasm of the modern cell (figure 3.6). An RNA 'working copy' of the genetic information stored in DNA is made first, known as messenger RNA (mRNA). The mRNA then moves out from the nucleus and into the cytoplasm, where it binds to large complexes of protein and RNA known as 'ribosomes'. A ribosome moves along its attached mRNA from start to finish, exposing the 'codons' (sequences of three bases each coding for one amino acid) of the mRNA at a special site on the ribosome, one by one. Appropriate transfer RNA (tRNA) molecules bind to exposed codons thanks to base-pairing between the mRNA codons and complementary 'anticodons' on the tRNAs. Each tRNA also carries, elsewhere on the molecule, the particular amino acid encoded by the codon it can bind to. In this way the various tRNA molecules bring the correct amino acids to the ribosome in the correct sequence, where enzymes link them up into the protein encoded by the mRNA.

Nucleic acids are able to direct the manufacture of specific proteins because of the correspondence between the sets of three bases we call codons, and the amino acids they code for. Our main problem in searching for the origins of protein synthesis is to explain how this correspondence first arose. There is one rather weak but suggestive piece of experimental evidence to help us: the individual amino acids found in modern proteins may be able to bind weakly to the anticodons that mediate their incorporation into protein, in preference to the anticodons of other amino acids.

The chemical evidence backing up this claim is rather complex and indirect. Overall, it suggests that the amino acid lysine, for example, will form a stronger and more stable association with the anticodon of the lysine tRNA than with that of say the phenylalanine tRNA. Look at figure 4.6 to get a clearer idea of what I mean. Such preferential binding may play no part in the manufacture of modern proteins, since nowadays the amino acids are held on their tRNAs at a special site far away from the anticodon, *and they are put there by enzymes*. It may, however, have been important when the link between genes and proteins was first being forged – when the enzymes which nowadays maintain that link would not have been available.

The results of the experiments which suggest the preferential

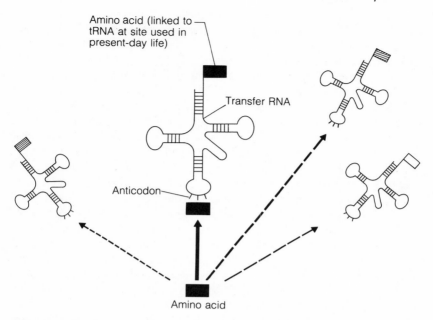

Amino acid (linked to tRNA at site used in present-day life)

Transfer RNA

Anticodon

Amino acid

Figure 4.6 Amino acids may have stronger affinities for the anticodons of their own transfer RNAs (and to a lesser extent of the tRNAs of chemically similar amino acids) than for the anticodons of the tRNAs of chemically very different amino acids. Thus the amino acid in the figure binds more strongly to its own anticodon (bold arrow) than to the anticodons of other amino acids (light dashed arrows). This selective binding might have been crucial during the early days of evolution, although in present-day life the amino acids are attached to their tRNAs at a site well away from the anticodon.

binding are far from clear cut, and any preferences must be very slight and overlapping. No amino acids are expected to associate strongly and specifically with only their own anticodons; but any other anticodons they associate with are probably more likely to be ones encoding amino acids very similar to themselves, than ones for completely dissimilar amino acids. So in general, amino acids may be able to bind by very weak forces of attraction to their own anticodons, and the anticodons of structurally similar amino acids, more strongly than they do to the anticodons of very different amino acids.

Although this effect must be slight and indistinct, if it exists at all, many scientists feel that it may be telling us something crucial about the way in which nucleic acids first began to make proteins. The obvious suggestion is that originally proteins (or more likely very short peptides) were assembled when certain amino acids became bound preferentially and directly to particular sequences of bases on nucleic acids. These base sequences then evolved into the anticodons of modern tRNAs, through a series of steps which might have been similar to the ones outlined in figure 4.7.

To begin with, a population of small self-replicating RNAs would have been set up, as we have considered already (figure 4.7A). The chemical reactions needed to make and replicate these RNAs might have been catalysed to some extent by mineral ions, crystal surfaces or small organic compounds; and by folding up in various ways some of the RNAs might themselves have been able to act as primitive catalysts helping the chemistry of their 'life' to proceed (see next chapter); but the precise and highly efficient catalytic effects of proteins would still be waiting for evolution to 'discover' them.

This discovery would begin when variant RNAs arose that could bind with some specificity to particular amino acids (figure 4.7B). These RNAs would have been the ancestors of the modern tRNAs. They might have allowed simple peptides or proteins to form, simply by aggregating side by side on some suitable surface such as a rock or a crystal. This might have encouraged the amino acids to link up into peptides or proteins of undirected amino acid sequence (figure 4.7C).

Other nucleic acids (probably also RNAs) might then have become able to act as primitive genes by binding to a series of the primitive tRNAs by base-pairing; or alternatively, some of the tRNAs might themselves have grown longer until able to perform both functions (figure 4.7D). At this point nucleic acids would have begun to direct the production of *specific* proteins for the first time – an evolutionary breakthrough second in importance only to the origin of self-replication.

The workings of this earliest form of protein synthesis would have been very imprecise, each 'gene' perhaps giving rise to a range of different short proteins of broadly similar sequence. But once nucleic acids had begun to direct the manufacture of proteins with any degree of specificity at all, then the way would have been open for natural selection to direct the evolution of ever more specific and more efficient systems able to make ever better proteins. By 'better', of course, I mean increasingly able to promote the survival and replication of the nucleic acids involved in their manufacture – by catalysing the reactions of nucleic acid replication, nucleotide formation, protein manufacture itself, and so on.

The smooth running of these earliest protein-making systems would have required the cooperation of several different nucleic acids (at the very least one 'gene' and a few 'tRNAs'), so the most successful systems might have had their various components held together within some restricted space or 'cell' (see later).

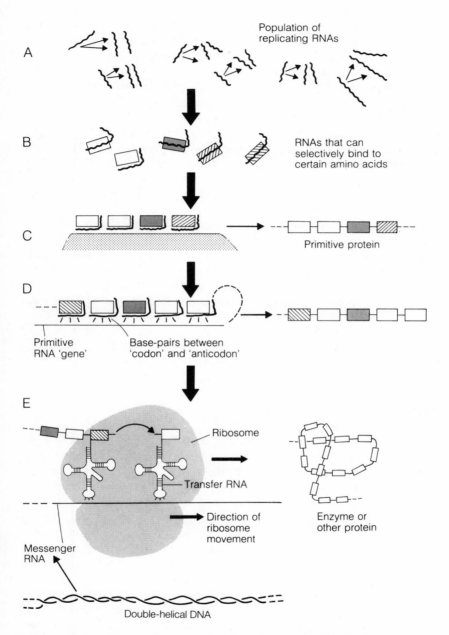

A — Population of replicating RNAs

B — RNAs that can selectively bind to certain amino acids

C — Primitive protein

D — Primitive RNA 'gene' — Base-pairs between 'codon' and 'anticodon'

E — Ribosome — Transfer RNA — Direction of ribosome movement — Enzyme or other protein — Messenger RNA — Double-helical DNA

Figure 4.7   A general outline of some of the stages that might have been involved in the evolution of nucleic acids that encode proteins (see text for details).

All of the RNAs, and therefore all the proteins, would be continually evolving into ever more efficient and versatile forms. The direct association of amino acids with their own anticodons would have gradually become less important, as the emerging enzymes took over the job of specifically linking the right amino acids to the right tRNAs; and so with time the amino acids could come to be held at a new site on the evolving tRNAs, away from the anticodon, just as they are in the tRNAs of the modern cell (figure 4.7E).

Also, at some point the original 'genes' might have begun to be copied into separate 'hard copies' of double-helical DNA, to form what we now call genes. The original genes of figure 4.7D would have slipped into the intermediary role of messenger RNA. Over billions of years the relentless power of natural selection would have generated the sophisticated protein-making machinery of the modern cell.

Don't take the scheme shown in figure 4.7 too literally, in fact don't take it literally at all! It is presented as merely a much simplified summary of some of the essential steps of only one possible path from the first self-replicating nucleic acids up to the central chemistry of modern life. There are countless variations on the same general theme, and many variations on different themes. None have ever been re-created in the laboratory, and the evidence supporting them all is extremely thin. I offer figure 4.7 simply to give you a general impression of the sort of ideas being dreamt up by scientists to explain how nucleic acids first began to make proteins.

Making cells

Suppose we accept for the moment, as most biologists do, that the story related so far bears at least some rough resemblance to what actually happened on the earth three or four or more thousand million years ago. With self-replicating nucleic acids that have evolved the ability to make some sort of proteins, we have arrived very quickly (some would say far too quickly) at the central core of modern life. But of course present-day life is based upon living cells, each containing its own complement of genes that encode proteins. So how and why did the first cells originate, and why were they selected as the sole basis for further evolution?

I have already given you some answers to the whys. We have seen that the manufacture of even the most rudimentary of proteins would probably have required the interaction or 'cooperation' of quite a few different nucleic acids. At the very least it would have needed some sort of primitive gene and a few of the primitive ancestors of transfer RNAs. And if these nucleic acids were to benefit (in the evolutionary terms of long life and bountiful multiplication) from the effects of whatever proteins they made, then they would probably need to interact with one or all of the proteins in some way.

If all of these required interactions were taking place between molecules floating free in a 'soup' containing many other molecules all undergoing interactions of their own, then the working of each particular protein-making 'cooperative' would be extremely inefficient. Lots of different genes would be competing for transfer RNAs and amino acids, nucleotides and other raw materials. Also the beneficial effects of any protein encoded by a gene would not be enjoyed by that gene alone. Instead, the protein molecules could be expected to drift throughout the 'soup', perhaps also assisting other 'rival' nucleic acids as well as the ones that encoded them. So 'clever' nucleic acids (i.e. those encoding some useful protein) would not enjoy the maximum evolutionary advantage over their more 'stupid' relatives. Protein-making cleverness would be being shared rather than greedily kept for the benefit of the clever nucleic acids alone.

Another, perhaps even more significant, problem with a large unified soup (or slurry, or slime) of evolving nucleic acids, is that the opportunities for various clever nucleic acids to cooperate for their mutual benefit would be very limited. Imagine two nucleic acids each making a different protein from the other, which could be of benefit to both. Both would multiply more quickly if their proteins were somehow kept near to the two nucleic acids for their mutual benefit, rather than being lost and shared out amongst all the other less versatile nucleic acids of the soup.

Any nucleic acids capable of such cooperation that somehow became entrapped within the confined space of a 'cell' might be at a considerable advantage; as might be any that could encourage cells to form around them, either directly or by encoding cell-forming proteins. All the nucleic acid members of the cooperative would be kept together and so be able to interact much more efficiently. All the proteins they made would be kept for the benefit of the nucleic acids of the cooperative alone. Provided the cells could enlarge and divide from time to time, as the nucleic acids multiplied, this cellular way of life might have rapidly become much more efficient and successful than the life that had to rely on the uncontrolled vagaries of an acellular 'soup'. But what would the first cells have been made of, and how might they have formed?

Modern cells are enclosed within a thin cell membrane composed of a 'lipid bilayer'. As has been said already, lipids are a diverse group of 'fatty' chemicals with one major property in common – they are not soluble in water. If appropriate lipid molecules are mixed together in some watery solution, they can spontaneously form 'lipid bilayers' by lining up 'back to back' as shown in figure 4.8. To form such bilayers the lipid molecules need to consist of a long 'tail' region composed of atoms such as carbon and hydrogen that have no chemical affinity for water molecules, and a compact 'head' region containing atoms that have a strong affinity for water molecules (see figure 4.8). Many naturally occurring lipids do have this sort of composition. When mixed with water they spontaneously form structures which allow the chemical 'preferences' of both parts of the molecules to be satisfied at the same time. The lipid-bilayer membrane is one such structure, because all of the tail groups are clustered together in the middle of the membrane, away from the water, while all the head

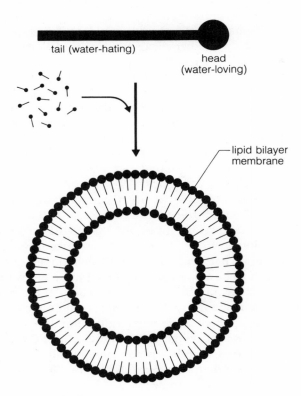

Figure 4.8 Generalized lipid structure and cross-section through a spherical vesicle bounded by a lipid-bilayer membrane.

groups are clustered together in direct contact with the water on either side of the membrane.

Suitable lipids are forced into the lipid bilayer structure by electromagnetic attractions and repulsions between the atoms of the lipids and those of water molecules. Scientists often say that the heads 'like' water and the tails 'hate' it, but what they really mean is that the head atoms are electromagnetically attracted to water molecules, while the tail atoms are not.

With their usual sense of urgency and economy of thought (and effort?), most biologists seem happy to assume that the first cells must have been bounded by roughly spherical lipid bilayer membranes similar to the ones found around all modern cells. They suggest that suitable lipids formed spontaneously in the chemical reactor that was the early earth (and some lipids certainly have been formed in various simulations of primordial chemistry), so maybe small membranous sacs or 'vesicles' were forming all the time, entrapping a selection of self-replicating nucleic acids as they did so. Every now and then a vesicle might have by chance entrapped nucleic acids that were able to cooperate together more than they competed. In other words, the nucleic acids within such a vesicle would all live longer and multiply faster inside the vesicle than outside.

Thus the first cells containing cooperating genes that encoded proteins would have been born and naturally selected for further evolution. That evolution could be expected to have gradually perfected the cellular way of life: selecting genes encoding proteins that helped the cells to form and grow (by the steady incorporation of more lipids into the membrane) and divide (perhaps spontaneously when the cells reached a certain critical size). Genes would also be selected that encoded proteins able to transport vital raw materials into the cell from the outside, or remove harmful by-products of the emergent cellular metabolism. We will be looking at how the first cells might have evolved all the way up to us in chapter 8. In the meantime, we must leave our neat little story in which the spontaneous origin of self-replicating nucleic acids set light to the fires of life, and briefly consider some alternatives.

The protein alternative

All modern life rests on the two great supporting layers of nucleic acids and proteins. Popular accounts of biology (including this one, so far) emphasize the fundamental role of nucleic acids as the most basic layer of this twin foundation. Proteins are presented as the versatile 'slaves' of their nucleic acid 'masters'. Nucleic acids contain the information needed to direct protein manufacture, and they alone are capable of *replicating* that information to pass it on to future generations of life. They alone can accumulate favourable changes (i.e. 'mutations') in their structure, and faithfully pass them on. Surely then, nucleic acids must either have preceded proteins in the history of life, or at the very least have evolved alongside them. That is the essence of the version of life's origin presented to you so far, but one major alternative is given credence by some of the biologists who muse over our distant past. What if the proteins came first?

At first sight the idea that proteins rather than nucleic acids took the first steps towards life seems to make a lot of sense. Amino acids, the building-blocks of proteins, form much more readily in prebiotic simulations than the sugars and bases needed to make nucleic acids. And peptides and simple proteins themselves can also be created in simulations much more readily than nucleic acids, let alone self-replicating nucleic acids. So amino acids, peptides and simple proteins could well have arrived on the prebiotic stage long before nucleic acids appeared, and in much greater abundance than their more reluctant partners; and proteins, of course, can do lots of 'clever' chemistry which might have helped them to form and survive.

Some scientists, most notably Sydney Fox who now works at Miami University, suggest that these early proteins may have lain at the heart of the first simple 'organisms'. He has managed to get simulated prebiotic proteins to spontaneously aggregate into spherical 'cell-like' structures which he calls 'proteinoids'. He suggests that within these proteinoids primitive proteins may have catalysed the chemistry that allowed them to grow and divide and therefore multiply; and he has even recreated some forms of proteinoid growth and division in his laboratory. So why should such proteinoids, which might grow, multiply and compete, not be credited with the status of life-forms? The answer, according to many scientists, is because they lack the ability to evolve by natural selection, simply because there is no way for them to replicate themselves in a manner that encourages the progressive selection of new and more efficient variants.

The abilities of the proteinoids would surely be restricted to the chance abilities of proteins that could form spontaneously. Certainly, there might have been a lengthy period of proteinoid competition and change, until the population became dominated by the most efficient possible proteinoids, all composed of the most useful and versatile of the spontaneously formed proteins, but then how could things develop further? Unless a protein spontaneously emerged that could catalyse its own self-replication, it is hard to see how evolution could have ever got on its way.

Suppose that by chance a new 'mutant' protein were formed in a proteinoid, able to catalyse a new reaction that let the proteinoid grow much more rapidly. For example, the 'clever' mutant might greatly increase the speed at which amino acids were linked up into new proteins within the proteinoid. This mutant would be able to perform its dazzlingly clever feats for a while, but eventually, like all individual molecules, it would become damaged or degraded down to peptides and amino acids again. Its cleverness would eventually be lost to the proteinoid. All individual molecules are mortal, surviving for only a certain time until falling victim to the vagaries of undirected chemical change. The only way for a clever mutant protein to spread its cleverness throughout the proteinoid population, would be for the protein to somehow encourage the formation of proteins with an amino acid sequence similar or identical to its own. In other words, it would have to be specifically *replicated*.

Nucleic acids are such favourites of scientists interested in the origins of life because (at least on paper) it is easy to see how they might have been replicated. Nobody has yet constructed any really plausible schemes for the replication of proteins, other than via nucleic acid intermediaries that encode them.

Evolution by natural selection relies on the occasional spontaneously formed 'clever' molecules (or the genes that encode them) being replicated, so that their cleverness can survive despite the mortality of each clever molecule itself. Proteins and proteinoids may well have formed in abundance on the early earth, and they may even have played a crucial role in creating the first nucleic acids, but unless they were capable of some form of specific replication they surely could never have evolved into forms of 'life'.

But maybe some of the proteins that formed spontaneously *were* capable of self-replication, something that would certainly have let evolution get on its way without waiting for the arrival of nucleic acid genes. Some scientists still consider this a possibility, and various schemes have been proposed for ways in which protein replication might have occurred. Most of these schemes involve a similar sort of 'template-dependent' replication to that employed by nucleic acids, with a protein of a given amino acid sequence acting as a 'template' on which an identical or somehow 'complementary' protein could form; but nobody has ever been able to get such schemes to work, and nothing like them has ever been found within modern cells. That is why most scientists disappointedly turn their backs on the proteins as they seek out the origins of replication, evolution and life; favouring instead the nucleic acids which certainly mediate the replication of modern life.

But the plausible suggestion that the first nucleic acids may have arisen only with the help of some spontaneously formed protein or proteins, may intriguingly reverse the 'master' and 'slave' relationship described earlier. Suppose that some spontaneously formed protein or peptide was able to attract nucleotides to its surface and cause them to be linked up into a nucleic acid chain. The attractions between the nucleotides and the amino acids of the protein could be governed by the selective bindings considered earlier – each amino acid preferentially attracting three nucleotides with a base-sequence similar to that of the tRNA anticodon associated with it today. When the nucleic acid was released from the protein the same selective attractions might have allowed it to bind to free amino acids and link them up into a replica of the original protein. In this situation proteins would be replicated *via a nucleic acid intermediary*, and the nucleic acid would be replicated via a protein intermediary. Protein replication would be dependent on nucleic acids, and nucleic acid replication would be dependent on proteins, just as these two great classes of polymer are totally interdependent today, but if anyone were to be described as the 'masters', it would be the proteins. The nucleic acids would be most entitled to the label of 'slaves'. The direct replication of nucleic acids by complementary base-pairing, might only have arisen later, once the process outlined above had allowed the enzymes needed to catalyse nucleic acid replication to evolve.

Many scientists feel that arguments about 'which came first – proteins or nucleic acids?' are a misguided irrelevance. They argue that both arose and evolved *together*, mutually dependent from the start. As with most proposals concerning the origins of life, a great variety of different possible scenarios along these lines have been put forward, but (again, as with most proposals concerning the origins of life), none have ever been convincingly re-created in the laboratory.

Scientists interested in the origins of life argue endlessly with one another about the details of how it all took place. They spend many happy hours in feverish speculation with pencil and paper, sometimes coming up with complex mathematical 'laws' which supposedly tell us how the contents of the primeval waters and skies must *inevitably* have given rise to life. They fly off to conferences and earnestly debate the complex mechanisms of events presumed to have occurred thousands of millions of years ago. They get excited, frustrated, insulted and elated about possible solutions to a problem which is, of course, completely insoluble. No matter how plausible they feel their theories to be, no matter how convincing the simulations of possible primordial events become, nobody can ever go back to check that they have got it right.

The very fact that the real answer is forever hidden by the irreversibility of time may be what encourages many scientists in this field to make much more forceful and flamboyant claims than those engaged in other areas of research. As Montaigne has said, 'Nothing is so firmly believed as that which we least know.' If you make a dogmatic assertion about the chemistry of the modern cell, you run the risk of being irrefutably proven to be wrong. No theory about life's origin, no matter how crazy, can ever be completely dismissed.

Despite the great debates that rage *within* the relatively small circle of scientists researching into the origins of life, their fundamental belief that organic life did originate spontaneously and rather directly on the newly formed earth is virtually unshakeable. I choose to describe it as a 'belief', because many scientists seem to have a faith in this outline of our origins as firm as the beliefs of any religious devotees. In their more public pronouncements some of them behave rather like the creationist opponents they so despise – pretending to have firm answers which they have not got at all, and glossing over the many great mysteries that remain.

In this chapter I have given my own 'edited highlights' of the story which most scientists, and certainly most teachers of science, present to the public at large as virtual fact. The public has undoubtedly come to regard it as virtual fact, apart from the religious fundamentalists. Even when it is accompanied by commendable caveats and cautions, these tend to be ignored or soon forgotten, such is the inspiring appeal of the idea of organic life crawling directly from some earthly chemical broth. In their book *The Origins of Life on the Earth*, Stanley Miller and Leslie Orgel followed the quote that heads this chapter with the caution that 'No one should be satisfied with an explanation as general as this.' but quotes such as the first one are remembered and publicized, while the cautions tend to slip from view. Most scientists will freely admit their lack of knowledge about the details of the origins of life, but remain insistent that 'something along these lines' must have happened, that *somehow* organic chemicals can spontaneously give rise to life.

The next chapter casts a sceptical eye over such confidence. It neither attempts to demolish the standard scientific version of our origins, nor presents it gloriously victorious over the assaults of the disbelievers. It is simply intended to illustrate that the 'standard tale' is far less secure and certain than is popularly supposed, raising the possibility that things may well have been very different.

5 A gulf unbridged

There is no waste in molecular biology and all shaky concepts are recycled
towards the origins of life . . .
Jacques Ninio

It is easy to understand and sympathize with the excitement
originally generated by Stanley Miller's historic simulation experiment. At virtually the first attempt to re-create the chemistry of the
ancient earth, the vital amino acid building-blocks of life obligingly
formed in significant amounts. Further experiments soon yielded
other essential building-blocks, such as sugars and bases. The
conclusion that life itself might have easily arisen from these
primordial ingredients was eagerly drawn and publicized by an
increasingly secular scientific community in an increasingly secular
world. But science must be careful not to replace the mythology of
religion with a substitute mythology of its own. What does the Miller
experiment, and the multitude of subsequent simulation experiments, really tell us?

These simulations certainly suggest that the simplest chemical
building-blocks of life could have formed spontaneously on the early
earth; although whether they would have accumulated to any great
extent is another matter, which we will return to later. They certainly
do not tell us that life could have originated easily from these
building-blocks, although they are often presented as doing just that.
All they really show us is that the creatures of the earth are
constructed out of chemicals that might well have been around, and
perhaps abundant, on the earth shortly after it was formed. Now that
is hardly surprising. If we assume for the moment that the creatures
of the earth really did originate on the earth, then we would hardly
expect them to be made of chemicals that could never have formed on

the earth. But any temptation even to hail the simulation results as proof that life did originate on earth, should be held in check by the discovery of many of the same 'building-block' chemicals in the meteorites that reach us from space.

Simulation experiments, and the analysis of meteorites, the composition of interstellar dust clouds and so on, have so far told us only that life on earth is constructed out of chemicals that probably form fairly readily in many places throughout the universe. The conclusion that our first living ancestors must have originated somewhere in the universe is hardly a great breakthrough!

In its day, the Miller experiment was significant and important, because it was the first to tell us that the basic chemicals of life may form with unexpected ease. But now that we suspect these same chemicals may be common throughout the universe, and since subsequent simulations have failed to get us much further towards living things, the significance of the Miller experiment needs to be reassessed. I suggest that Miller's and all later simulations might have been much more significant if they had *failed* to yield any of the simple chemicals from which we are all made. If it had proved completely impossible to re-create the formation of any of life's simple building-blocks under primordial conditions, despite many years of trying, then that really would have been a dramatic discovery. It would have suggested that life could not have originated on this planet.

The discovery that living things are constructed from chemicals that probably form spontaneously throughout the universe does not really tell us anything about how life 'learned to live'. It confirms that life *might* have originated spontaneously, on earth or elsewhere; but a religious person could justifiably claim that a divine creator might have used the most available suitable materials of his universe to construct its living things – as would any tinkering 'spacemen', beings from 'other dimensions' and so on.

Imagine some aliens investigating the origin of the cities which they could see from their spacecraft as they orbited the earth. Would the discovery that these cities are largely made of rocky minerals found widely throughout the earth's crust justify the conclusion that the cities were erected spontaneously from dust and dirt? Of course not. Similarly, the fact that amino acids, bases and sugars may have been present on the primordial earth does not justify the conclusion that living things were assembled spontaneously on earth from them. It really does nothing at all to resolve the mystery of the origins of life, other than keeping the possibility of such a spontaneous earthly origin open.

What is needed to give us confidence in scientific theories of the spontaneous origin of life on earth, is evidence that the simplest building-block chemicals could have reacted together to produce something – anything – capable of self-replication, variation and evolution. The origin of *replication* is the vital spark needed to trigger the evolution of life. Of all the essential steps on the way up from molecules to mankind, the origin of replication is the most fundamental; but before tackling the problems we face in explaining that origin, let's consider all the other essential steps. That will leave us well placed to assess the merits of the offered explanations.

Five essentials

It seems to me that there are a minimum of five essential steps that must be explained if we are to produce a satisfactory account of how *our type of life* could have originated on the earth (see figure 5.1). First we must account for the prebiotic synthesis of all the chemicals needed to build whatever organisms first arose.

Second comes the single most crucial step – the origin of replicators, or in other words, of things that could make more of themselves. There is no reason why we should restrict ourselves to considering creatures based on a similar chemistry to our own as the first replicators. That is what we did in chapter 4, but in doing so we made a very big and perhaps completely unjustified assumption – we assumed that the first life gave rise to all later life without any radical chemical changeovers or 'takeovers' on the way. As we will see in chapter 6, some scientists believe it is ridiculously simplistic to expect the first replicators to have been based on the same sorts of chemicals – nucleic acids – as are found at the heart of modern replication. But if we continue to make things as easy as possible, for the moment, then step two becomes the origin of the first replicating nucleic acids – or chemicals fairly similar to nucleic acids.

Step three is of course the origin of the link between nucleic acids and proteins (or perhaps initially merely peptides). All modern life works because nucleic acid genes direct the production of specific proteins. Regardless of which formed and replicated first – nucleic acids or proteins – or whether they somehow formed and began replicating together, the spontaneous origin of the gene–protein link is second in importance only to replication in the list of essential steps that our theories must explain.

Fourthly comes the problem of the first 'cells' composed of gene–protein systems cooperating together and competing with other

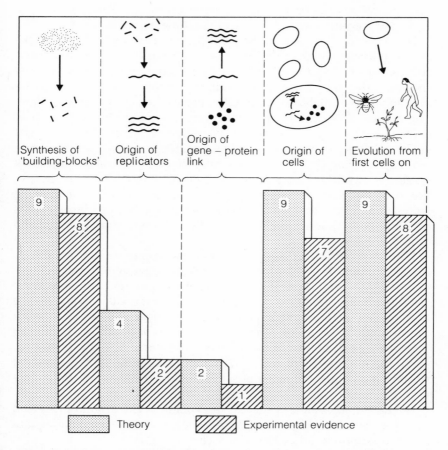

Synthesis of 'building-blocks'	Origin of replicators	Origin of gene – protein link	Origin of cells	Evolution from first cells on

Theory   Experimental evidence

Figure 5.1   Scores out of ten for the success of the theoretical and experimental work to explain five essential steps in the origin of life and evolution.

cells containing their own gene–protein cooperatives. How did the cellular way of life begin?

Finally we need to explain how the first very simple cells were able to evolve into such varied and complex organisms as mice and men and monkeys; insects, fish, lizards, worms and eels; amoebae, plants and fungi. . . . Let me briefly present my own very subjective assessment of our success in explaining these five essential steps so far. This assessment is summarized in figure 5.1, in which I have boldly given 'scores out of ten' for my estimation of the strength of current *theories* put forward to explain each step, and the amount of *experimental evidence* backing these theories up. This scoring is merely an imprecise little game, but it will illustrate a crucial point.

The prebiotic synthesis of the most simple chemical building-blocks of life (particularly amino acids, bases and various sugars) has been sufficiently explained and re-created in simulations for us to feel confident that they really were available on the early earth. They are probably also available in many other places throughout the universe. The scores of 9 and 8, for theory and evidence backing up our explanations of prebiotic synthesis, reflect my view that this first essential step presents us with few problems, always remembering that I am scoring simply on the basis of the presence of the necessary chemicals, without worrying about their likely abundance or purity. We obviously do not know all the details, nor can we ever be completely certain that we are on the right track, but this first step has certainly been much more satisfactorily explained than many of the others.

With step two – the essential one of the origin of replicators, things become much less satisfactory. Nobody has yet re-created the manufacture and replication of nucleic acids (or proteins) *under plausible prebiotic conditions*. Of course on paper it is easy enough to see how nucleic acids might have formed and replicated, so I can score the strength of our theories about the origin of replicators a bit higher than the dismal failure of our efforts to re-create it; but I cannot set even the theory score very high, because without experimental support it obviously remains possible that the theories are completely wrong.

We have had even less success in explaining the origin of the vital gene–protein link. The theories are woefully vague and inadequate and the experimental evidence is virtually nil.

The formation of cells is much easier to explain. We know that suitable lipids can form bilayer membranes spontaneously, and we suspect that such lipids may well have formed on the early earth. Even if the first cells were not contained within a lipid bilayer membrane, there are other perfectly feasible ways for the first gene–protein systems to have become cordoned off from one another until the conditions were just right for lipid–bilayers to form.

Finally we arrive at what might seem to be one of the biggest and hardest steps of all. The long evolution of the first simple cells all the way up to complex multicellular creatures such as ourselves. This is the stage at which the insights of Darwin's *Origin of Species* come into their own, and I will be looking at it in some detail in chapter 8. For the moment let me simply say that this actually appears to be one of the easiest stages to explain. Our theories of how cells could have evolved into many varied types of creature, and of the ways in which these creatures continue to evolve, are excellent in outline. Again, we will obviously never know the details, but possible mechanisms for such evolution are well described by modern evolutionary theory, and that theory is frequently confirmed by observations of evolution in action.

Despite the fact that scoring points like this is an imprecise little game, it does serve to illustrate a major gulf which remains to be bridged if we are to provide a satisfactory explanation for the way in which molecules could have given rise to mankind. It is a gulf presented by the origin of the first replicators and the origin of the gene–protein link. Scientists interested in the origins of life are well aware of this gulf – they think and talk and write at great length about the problems of the origin of replication and of the gene–protein link. Unfortunately, little of their puzzlement percolates through (or is allowed to percolate through) to the public at large, who generally remain happy to believe that science knows the answer to the mystery of the origin of life on earth.

Now that I have introduced you to the gulf separating the facts from that fantasy, we should go to the edge and look into it.

Replicators, replicators . . .

What has actually been achieved by the many attempts to re-create the formation of the first replicators – assuming for the moment that they were composed of nucleic acids or something very similar. Sadly, very little has been achieved. Many introductory biology texts will confidently tell you that simple nucleic acids have been shown to form and replicate themselves under prebiotic conditions, but such reports are simply wrong.

When challenged on this point, one celebrated author agreed with me that his confident assertion that

> under conditions resembling those on the prebiotic earth simple
> organic molecules actually form from elementary constituents
> . . . and assemble themselves into self-replicating nucleic acids
> which mutate and are altered in frequency by natural selection,
> all in the laboratory.

was completely mistaken. Endless similar assertions can be found throughout the literature of biology. They are all based on a great exaggeration of, and often misunderstanding of, the little that actually has been achieved. I can only presume that such false dogmatic assertions themselves become replicated, from textbook to textbook, because the authors so dearly want to believe that they are true.

The first problem facing anyone wanting to re-create the presumed formation of self-replicating nucleic acids, is to get *any* sort of nucleic acids to form, regardless of whether they replicate themselves or not. As we saw in the last chapter, modern nucleic acids are chain-like 'polymers' made when 'nucleotides' become linked together, and these nucleotides are themselves composed of linked bases, sugars and phosphates. Getting bases, sugars and phosphate groups to join together into nucleotides, *under plausible prebiotic conditions*, has itself proved extremely difficult. Nobody had yet come up with any obviously acceptable way for suitable nucleotides or nucleotide derivatives to form in any abundance on the primordial earth, but there are a host of suggested pathways for nucleotide formation, and simulation experiments have had some limited success (although many scientists dispute that the simulations were performed in plausible prebiotic conditions).

Casting aside the unsolved problems of nucleotide formation, what successes have been achieved in getting nucleotides to link up into nucleic acids? Few people have devoted more time to this problem than Leslie Orgel, of the Salk Institute in California, and Juan Oro at Houston University, and they have both had *some* success. For example, when nucleotide solutions are slowly evaporated under reasonable prebiotic conditions (to simulate the periodic drying up of rock pools or lakes), short nucleic acid chains containing up to eight linked nucleotides do appear. I should emphasize, however, that highly purified mixtures of preformed nucleotides have to be used to get such reactions to work, quite unlike the messy mixtures of many different chemicals likely on the early earth. The long nucleic acid chains that are so easily imagined while musing with pencil and paper, have so far never been formed.

One of the most plausible proposals for forming longer nucleic acid chains involves cycles of periodic flooding and drying of the sorts of rock pools in which short chains could have formed. Some short chains formed during each hot drying phase might have paired up in a staggered fashion during flood phases, due to chance sequence complementarities. This might have allowed some shorter chains to become linked into longer ones when the drying conditions returned (see figure 5.2). The problem with this neat idea, as with so many 'plausible' proposals about the origins of life, is that so far nobody has been able to get it to work under reasonable prebiotic conditions. If it did happen, then it would also have provided an early form of replication, especially if the double-stranded nucleic acids were more

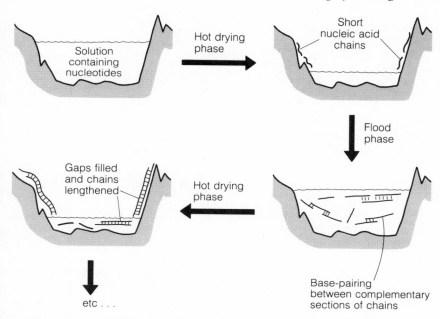

Figure 5.2 One way in which short chains of nucleic acids might have formed and given rise to increasingly longer chains. This has not yet been achieved in simulation experiments.

resistant than single strands to degradation during the flood phases (as our knowledge of modern nucleic acids suggests they would be). The process outlined in the figure would clearly let existing nucleic acids preferentially encourage the formation and survival of new nucleic acids complementary to themselves. These complementary nucleic acids would then themselves encourage replicas of the originals to form.

Nobody has ever been able to get nucleic acid chains to form and replicate within the same experiment; but if *purified, preformed* nucleic acids are used as starting materials for replication simulations, some limited success can be achieved. The most successful experiments to date have come from Leslie Orgel's laboratory. He added some long-chain nucleic acids to mixtures of chemical derivatives of the four nucleotides, and found that the first stage of replication occurred to a very limited extent (see figure 5.3). Only very short complementary chains were formed, but the major problem with the experiment is revealed by Orgel's admission that it 'is unlikely to correspond to anything that occurred in the primitive Earth, since

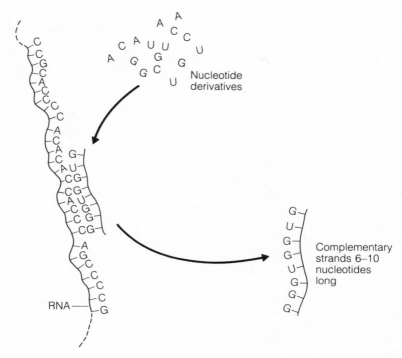

Figure 5.3   Leslie Orgel has managed to get the first stage of nucleic acid replication to occur without enzymes to a very limited extent. The second stage, getting the newly made short strands to produce replicas of short sections of the original long strand, has not been achieved. Unfortunately the nucleotide derivatives used by Orgel are unlikely to have been available on the early earth.

there is no easy way in which [the nucleotide derivatives he used] could have accumulated in the prebiotic soup'.

More recently, Orgel and his co-workers have been experimenting with various chemicals similar to nucleic acids, but considerably simpler; and their efforts are being complemented by many similar attempts throughout the world to get some sort of primitive replication to occur under prebiotic conditions and in the absence of enzymes. But the depressing truth about all attempts to get nucleic acids of specific nucleotide sequence to replicate without the help of enzymes is, again, that nobody has been able to get them to work under reasonable prebiotic conditions. Indeed, nobody has even been able to get nucleic acids containing a string of *identical* nucleotides to replicate under acceptable prebiotic conditions (something which should be much easier to achieve than the replication of nucleic acids of mixed nucleotide sequence), although there have been some successes when the reactions have been given assistance from chemicals that seem unlikely to have been available on the early earth.

I am not trying to convince you that the spontaneous origin of self-replicating nucleic acids on earth must have been impossible – it may have happened just as so many of the textbooks suppose; but as yet there is no hard experimental evidence to back that supposition up. The lesson provided so far by the many attempts to get nucleic acids to form and replicate spontaneously, is that it may be a very difficult process to get going.

In some ways the attempts to re-create the process so far provide good evidence *against* the idea of the spontaneous origin of self-replicating nucleic acids; and yet they are frequently presented as providing 'incomplete but significant' evidence supporting that idea. Most scientists assume that the failure experienced to date simply tells us that we have not yet hit on the right system, or the right conditions; or that they simply cannot be expected to re-create in a few weeks in a laboratory chemical processes that perhaps took millions of years. One or all of these excuses may well be valid, but it must also be possible that they have failed because they have been trying to re-create something which did not happen, and never could have.

Suppose that I am being unduly sceptical, and that eventually the sorts of simulations I have been describing eventually succeed in providing hard evidence that all the reactions needed to form self-replicating nucleic acids really could have occurred on the primordial earth. Even then, our theories about the origin of life would still face three major problems – those of 'selection', 'purification' and 'concentration'.

Select, purify, concentrate, select . . .

The perfect simulation of the origin of life would begin with a realistic mixture of simple chemicals resembling mixtures likely on the early earth, and would then be left to run. Obviously we would have to do some things to the mixture from time to time, in order to keep the simulation realistic. We would need to change the temperature and lighting to simulate the passage of night and day; we would add water at intervals, to simulate rainfall; we could slowly increase the concentrations of various salts that might have been produced by the weathering of rocks, or decrease them to represent sedimentary rock formation, and so on. Some of the changes we imposed might be very dramatic, such as the timely addition of molten 'lava' to our mixture, its occasional evaporation to complete dryness, or the sudden exposure of the mixture to new types of rock; but they would all need to represent plausible changes that could somehow and somewhere have occurred on the primordial earth.

This is not the way in which scientists have so far approached the problem of simulating the origin of life. The achievements of such 'single-run' experiments have so far been limited to the formation of simple building-block ('monomer') chemicals, such as the amino acids formed in the classic experiments of Stanley Miller. If more complex, and admittedly very ambitious, single-run experiments were ever to yield even a very short self-replicating nucleic acid, then that really would be cause for celebration and congratulations.

Instead of tackling large, complex, difficult and probably expensive single-run simulations, scientists have opted for a completely different approach. They try to re-create the origin of life in discrete and carefully controlled stages. First, for example, they discover that three separate experiments can successfully produce small amounts of amino acids, bases and sugars. Fine – those are exactly the components most needed to make life. So they then start another experiment by mixing, for example, *selected*, *pure* bases and sugars and various other 'plausible' prebiotic chemicals in *high concentrations* (much higher than the concentrations in which they were formed in the first stage) under a completely different set of conditions from those in which the bases and sugars were formed in the first place.

Sometimes such 'phase two' simulations (under questionable 'prebiotic conditions') have yielded nucleotides or interesting nucleotide derivatives; so once again our scientists say 'fine', and march on to phase three. Here they take pure and highly concentrated mixtures of the desired products from phase two, such as nucleotide derivatives, and mix them with further 'prebiotic' chemicals selected to encourage nucleic acids to form. I have already said that this sort of experiment can sometimes yield nucleic acids up to eight nucleotides long. So with another 'fine', phase four is set up, in which pure nucleic acid chains (usually much longer than the ones created in phase three) are added to high concentrations of purified nucleotide derivatives, this time under whatever conditions will most encourage the nucleic acids to replicate.

They do not replicate, even with all this artificial help, but occasionally they do allow a few short chains of nucleic acids that are complementary to small sections of the original chains to form (although not yet under plausible prebiotic conditions or using plausible nucleotide derivatives). Thus, the long serial argument proceeds, suggesting that if the newly formed chains were purified, then linked up into longer chains, then added afresh to high concentrations of nucleotide derivatives, they might eventually give rise to nucleic acids that were replicas of short sections of the original nucleic acid chains. These are the sorts of experiments which back up such confident assertions as 'nucleic acids have been shown to form and replicate themselves under conditions resembling those of the prebiotic earth'. They are woefully inadequate to justify such grand conclusions.

Figure 5.4 summarizes the approach to prebiotic simulations just outlined. From a series of separate experiments, each using certain selected, pure and concentrated products of the previous stage, it is argued that the whole process from start to finish could have proceeded spontaneously on the primordial earth.

Even if every stage on the way to self-replicating nucleic acids really had been re-created under plausible prebiotic conditions using this sort of approach (which is not yet the case), the relevance of that success would still be highly questionable. The selection, purification and concentration steps in such a sequence are obviously crucial, or else they would not be bothered with. Indeed, if they are not bothered with then a tarry chemical chaos is all that has so far been produced. So the 'long serial argument' approach inevitably begs the question: 'How did the necessary selection, purification, concentration (and periodic changing of the conditions) occur spontaneously on the primordial earth, or how was the need for it avoided?'

One popular answer is simply 'time'. We must obviously be careful not to expect too much of simulations that take only a few hours or at most a few weeks to run, but which are designed to re-create chemical changes that may have taken millions of years during the origin of life. Time may well help us over one of the problems listed above – that of concentration. It may well be fair to use unaturally high concentrations of the reacting chemicals in laboratory simulations, simply to speed things up. Much the same chemical reactions may occur in two flasks containing solutions of the same chemicals in the same proportions but in one case much more concentrated than the other. The reactions in the more dilute mixture often simply take a longer time, because the reacting chemicals bump into each other less often than they do in the more concentrated solution. So the concentration problem may not be such a problem after all; and in any case, it is fairly easy to think up ways in which solutions of chemicals on the early earth could have become greatly concentrated, by the drying up of rock pools and in other ways.

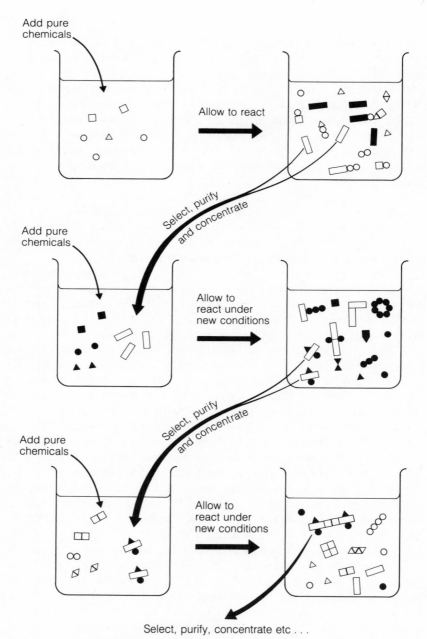

Add pure chemicals

Allow to react

Select, purify and concentrate

Add pure chemicals

Allow to react under new conditions

Select, purify and concentrate

Add pure chemicals

Allow to react under new conditions

Select, purify, concentrate etc . . .

Figure 5.4   Scientists try to re-create the origin of life by selecting certain products of some simulation reactions, purifying and concentrating them, then adding them to new reaction mixtures under new conditions, and so on. This long serial approach has yet to yield nucleic acids that replicate themselves in plausible prebiotic conditions; but in any case, it begs the question 'What did the selecting, purifying and concentrating, and how were the conditions changed as required?'.

The other problems, of selection and purity, are much more severe. Out of all the various chemicals being produced in various places throughout the earth, how did the ones that could form self-replicating nucleic acids (or self-replicating anything) come together in sufficiently pure form to allow each subsequent stage of the chemistry to proceed to significant extents? Chemical reactions are notoriously sensitive to the presence of 'impurities' – chemicals not involved in the desired reaction which can interfere with that reaction by promoting side-reactions, by reacting with the desired products, and so on. The reactions that take place in complex messy mixtures of many different chemicals are certainly not the same ones as occur when a few components of the mixtures are purified out and combined in isolation.

One major 'selection and purity' problem important to the origin of life is that many of the molecules used to construct living things occur naturally in two 'mirror image' forms, known as 'stereoisomers'. Your right hand and your left hand are clearly both 'hands', both able to do all of the things that hands can do, such as opening doors, unscrewing jars, lifting up objects and so on; but only the right hand will fit properly into a right-handed glove, and only the left hand into a left-handed one. This is because your hands are 'mirror images' of one-another – similar in many ways but with subtly though fundamently different three-dimensional structures.

Many molecules are also 'handed' in this way. Thus every amino acid occurs in a right-handed and a left-handed form, as do sugars and so on. Now for any given molecule, only one form – right-handed or left-handed – is ever found inside modern living things. So this is another selection and purity problem facing scientists trying to explain the origin of life. How were molecules of just one handedness selected, or purified, from the mixtures of both forms which would be likely to exist on the early earth?

Nobody has got anywhere near to providing plausible answers to all the problems of selection and purity involved in creating the very first forms of life. There are lots of suggestions and theories, but none have ever been convincingly tested in the laboratory.

This is an appropriate place at which to re-emphasize the crucial point that evolution does not 'know' where it is going in advance. The molecules of the prebiotic earth obviously did not 'know' that they were going to give rise to life (they presumably didn't know anything). Evolution does not proceed relentlessly towards specific goals (such as 'men' or 'monkeys' or 'mosquitoes' or even 'life') determined in advance. Instead, every step in the origin and evolution of life must be explicable simply in terms of the chemical and physical changes that were likely at any particular time. This may seem obvious, but it is easy to forget if we become careless with our reasoning. In saying, for example, that mechanisms 'had to be found' to select, purify and concentrate certain chemicals which could have given rise to future life, we should remember that these mechanisms had to arise and operate spontaneously, driven only by energy dispersal and the fundamental forces. We know where early evolution was heading, because we live with its results, but the molecules that brought about that evolution were neither able to know nor care.

One of the simplest possible answers to the problems of selection, purification and concentration invokes the wide variety of different locations and environments in which various prebiotic molecules could have found themselves. A great disservice has perhaps been done to the study of life's origins by the coining of the phrase – 'primordial soup'. It suggests that life emerged from one big chemical 'pot' such as the early ocean, while the truth is almost certainly far more complex. At the very least there must have existed a wide range of different primordial 'soups', each containing different ingredients exposed to different conditions. The oceans, for example, would have supported different chemical reactions from those proceeding in rivers, or lakes or rock pools; and the reactions occurring in different bodies of water would have varied depending on such things as the nature of the rocks they formed on, the types of mineral salts they contained, the extremes of temperature they experienced and their tendency to either dry out or flood.

This gives us many more environments to play with when we muse about the possible origins of life. For example, we can imagine occasions when two pools might have merged into one (as a result of rainfall or earth movement etc.), allowing their different harvests of chemicals to be mixed together in a new 'pot' under a new set of conditions. We can imagine new types of mineral suddenly being 'stirred into' various pools when they become linked by developing rivers that begin to wash down over many different types of rocks. We can imagine great upheaval accompanying earthquakes and volcanoes, perhaps spilling the contents of some pools onto hot rocks where they would bubble and hiss to dryness – maybe destroying some of the chemicals formed in the cool pools and allowing others to react together into new sets of products.

The possibilities are almost literally endless, and they may have solved many of the problems of selection, purification and concentration that we have been worrying about. Imagine, for example, a primordial ocean in which the formation of sugars and bases was taking place. Any phosphate-rich rocks at the edges of this ocean would have undoubtedly trapped samples of the ocean in little pools, which might occasionally have dried out – concentrating their solutions and perhaps encouraging the first nucleotides and simple nucleic acids to form. Later, perhaps many years later, volcanic upheaval might have poured boiling rock into some of the pools, destroying many of the nucleic acids by chemical reaction and heat. If nucleic acids able to pair up into double-strands were preferentially protected from damage, they would effectively be purified from a more chaotic nucleic acid mix. Repetitions of this process might have effected a crude form of nucleic acid replication, since at each cycle new nucleic acids complementary to existing ones would have better chances of survival. Eventually a stream diverted into the path of the rock pools by earthquake or eruption might have brought a supply of amino acids or simple proteins formed in another place. A few of the pools might then have been ready to forge the gene–protein link.

The details of this scenario are of course completely fanciful, but the point is that there might have been plenty of opportunity for different parts of the primeval landscape to have behaved overall like modern chemists – here, stirring one mixture together at a certain temperature; there, mixing the products into a new 'flask' with new ingredients; preferentially destroying some products in various places, mixing in new ones, changing the conditions, adding more starting materials and minerals, and so on.

So far I have said very little about the mineral compounds present on the early earth – the rocks and sands and clays which would form many of the 'pots' for prebiotic reactions and which would also yield up phosphates, carbonates, silicates, sulphates and so on into the reacting mixtures themselves. Modern chemists don't think much about the vessels in which their reactions take place – they are usually made of inert glasses or plastics, specifically chosen because they will leave the chemicals they contain well alone. This would certainly not have been true of the 'beakers' and 'flasks' of the early earth – the vessels of early chemistry may have participated directly in the chemical reactions taking place within them.

Many organic chemicals are adsorbed very strongly and sometimes quite selectively onto the surface of particular minerals such as clays, and this could have formed one of the most effective selection, purification and concentration mechanisms of the early earth. It seems quite feasible and fair to imagine rocky prebiotic reaction vessels producing chemicals which were then selectively adsorbed onto the vessel walls, or onto tiny pieces of clay and chalk and so on suspended in the solution. Once held on the mineral surfaces, the chemicals might have been able to undergo further reactions, perhaps catalysed by the minerals they were attached to (minerals can act as quite efficient chemical catalysts, although they do not approach the specificity and high efficiency of the enzymes). Sedimentary rocks formed from such suspended mineral particles could have held a cargo of organic chemicals, ready and waiting for new conditions and new possibilities to emerge.

The conditions in the rivers, lakes and seas above such sediments might often have changed, bringing new chemicals into the pores and spaces within the sediments where they could initiate further reactions of the organic chemicals within. When a river or a lake dried out, the sediments would be exposed to the energy of sunlight, which might have driven forward still more and different chemical processes until the waters flooded in again, bringing with them further supplies for yet more chemical reactions.

The potential of minerals as catalysts and the agents of prebiotic selection and purification has still not been fully explored. They might well have acted as the first 'organic chemists', allowing the potential of various chemicals in primordial 'soups' to actually be realized in the creation of life.

Other, non-mineral selectors, concentrators and purifiers might also have been at work. Suspensions of tiny clumps of simple proteins, lipids, nucleic acids, carbohydrates and so on (known as 'coacervates') may have formed and then played a similar role to that suggested for suspended mineral particles. Various specific chemicals of the 'soup' may have become stuck to the coacervates, effectively purifying these chemicals from the surrounding messy mixtures and perhaps promoting new reactions in a coacervate environment which could have been very different from the environment in the surrounding solution.

So there are a great many *ideas* concerning ways in which the emergence of life might have been assisted by various natural mechanisms which acted both to change the conditions from time to time, and to select, purify and concentrate various components of primordial 'soups', 'slurries' or 'slimes'. Lest everything might begin to seem 'too neat' we should remember that the vast majority of reactions and interactions would probably have got nowhere near to the production of life. The vast majority of pools and lakes, slurries and slimes, and the vast majority of the almost infinite combinations of events producing heating and cooling and mixing, purification and so on, may have yielded little more than 'tarry chaos'. But out of all the endless possible sequences of events in many millions of pools and rivers and lakes and muds, it might have needed only a few favourable sequences to arise for life to have been inexorably on its way.

Living things are often delicate and vulnerable creatures, but life itself is a tenacious resilient phenomenon which, once begun, may be very hard to stop. The essence of life is replication, and once anything on the earth started to replicate and gradually vary in ways that opened up new possibilities to make the replication more effective, evolution would have got going and the replicators would have begun to inherit the earth.

Have you been sufficiently inspired by the imaginative scenarios outlined above to cast aside all doubts and hail life as the inevitable child of the early earth? Many people are, and I often feel tempted. It is so easy to believe in 'plausible ideas' when there is no way to find out whether or not they really describe what happened. In the fight to keep our enthusiasm restrained we should always remember that we *know* the direction in which evolution was heading – it was heading our way, the way of nucleic acid genes that encode proteins which make us work. Naturally then, we manage to dream up ways in which evolution might have taken the first steps along that path; but what about alternative paths? Might it not be equally easy to devise alternative schemes by which the earth could have generated completely different forms of life? If you were sitting today composed of 'nylon'-based 'genes' encoding catalysts based on linked lipids, or whatever, would the fatty plastic scientists be telling you that it was always 'inevitable' that you should be constructed that way, given the chemistry of the early earth?

Imagine tutoring a group of chemists from birth, telling them everything we know about physics and chemistry while keeping them completely unaware of the chemistry of life or of our theories about where life has come from. If we provided these chemists with full details of the earth's formation and asked them to decide what would happen next, would they come up with creatures such as us? Would they even suggest that the origin of life was likely at all? If they were allowed to do experiments they might soon come up with primordial soups containing some amino acids, sugars and bases – but they would also contain lots of other things. Which components of the soups or of the earth as a whole would the chemists assess as the most likely generators of life?

Were there forces at work on the early earth that made creatures constructed of nucleic acids and proteins (and fats and carbohydrates and so on) by far the most likely to be formed and to survive? Could other types of chemicals have constructed equally successful life-forms, or were there good reasons for these particular chemicals to become the scaffolding and machinery of life, and these alone? One of the many scientists who believe that there may well have been good reasons for the 'choice' of the materials of life, is Professor John Scott of Manchester University. Unfortunately, he was not kept in the dark about the chemical nature of life from birth, but his suggestion is so simple, yet potentially powerful, that it deserves at least a brief discussion. The first and possibly major architect of the chemistry of our living world, according to John Scott, may have been about the simplest chemical entity of all – the electron.

The ravages of hydrated electrons

John Scott's vision begins with a primordial soup, or soups, containing amino acids, sugars, bases, phosphate groups and so on – all the usual mix. The harsh rays of the sun would have poured energy into the cooking soup, particularly in the form of ultra-violet radiation, which would have flooded down unhindered (the early atmosphere must have lacked the oxygen which now absorbs much ultra-violet radiation by forming a protective layer of ozone). The main component of any primordial soup would have been water, and when water molecules are energized by ultra-violet light free electrons can be ejected – one of the most reactive chemical species of all. Because they are so reactive, free electrons only survive for an instant, becoming surrounded almost immediately by a 'cage' of four water molecules to form what is known as a 'hydrated electron'. These hydrated electrons are also extremely reactive, usually surviving for less than a millisecond before undergoing further reactions; but that is long enough for them to diffuse quickly throughout a significant volume of the surrounding solution before hitting something they can react with.

So hydrated electrons are likely to have been abundant in all primeval surface waters, in which they would act as energetic little 'bullets' reacting with and often destroying any molecules that strayed into their paths. 'Guided missiles', is actually a better analogy than bullets because, like all negatively charged objects, hydrated electrons are attracted towards positive charge and repelled away from negative charge. So these 'positive-seeking missiles' would have preferentially destroyed the positively charged chemicals all around them, and veered clear of anything with a sufficiently large negative charge. In this selective destruction lay their ability to act as vital architects of life – according to John Scott.

Return to the modern world for a moment, to reconsider the nature of the chemicals we are made of. Those with an overall negative charge are much more common than the few that carry a positive charge. The sugar–phosphate backbone of DNA and RNA is studded with negatively charged phosphate groups; many modern carbohydrates are covered in negative charges; and many proteins that would otherwise be electrically neutral are rendered negatively charged by having appropriate carbohydrates attached to their surfaces (making them 'glycoproteins'). Even cells themselves carry a negative surface charge thanks to a covering of appropriate carbohydrates. On the basis of such suggestive observations, Scott has proposed the following scenario.

From the earliest days in the history of the earth, highly reactive hydrated electrons were darting about its surface waters. They reacted with and destroyed positively charged molecules more frequently than electrically neutral ones, and much more frequently than negatively charged ones, which they tended to veer clear of. So when the simple chemicals of the earth began to link up into longer chain-like 'polymers', only those polymers that were somehow protected from the hydrated electrons' attacks could be expected to survive and accumulate.

Thus, out of all the various polymers that might have formed, the primordial world became steadily enriched in those carrying a negative charge, and to a lesser extent in neutral polymers composed of whatever chemicals were least vulnerable to hydrated electron attack. The repeating sugar–phosphate backbone of nucleic acids is one obviously protected structure, as are many carbohydrates. The bases of nucleic acids would have been more sensitive, but they would have been protected from attack by being linked to the long negatively charged sugar–phosphate backbone. This protection would have been especially effective in nucleic acids that could pair up into double-stranded structures by virtue of complementary base sequences, holding the sensitive bases within a protective negatively charged molecular 'cage'. Thus the ravages of hydrated electrons may not only have enriched the primordial world in nucleic acids, but also have favoured the survival of nucleic acids that were complementary to pre-existing ones. This might have been the real driving force behind the origin of the first simple form of replication

So nucleic acids and carbohydrates are likely survivors of the earliest phase in the history of the earth – becoming ever more abundant not because their formation was selectively encouraged, but simply because they were destroyed less often than many other chemicals. They would be accompanied by any small molecules, perhaps including some amino acids, which were able to find shelter within the protective folds of the larger polymers. Perhaps the crucial gene–protein link was forged when amino acids accumulated within the protective folds of DNA and RNA, becoming linked up there into short proteins whose sequences depended on the sort of selective affinities between amino acids and nucleic acids discussed earlier. Of all the proteins made, the ones that survived might have been those able to react with carbohydrates in solution to provide them with a negatively charged carbohydrate coating.

Once large quantities of negatively charged polymers had begun to accumulate, then small positively charged ones might have begun to survive a little better if they were able to stick to or wind around negatively charged polymers such as DNA or RNA. This is just the sort of situation found in modern chromosomes, in which a central DNA double-helix is coated with small positively charged proteins (called 'histones' and 'protamines'). Modern ribosomes also contain various proteins 'wrapped up' in chains of negatively charged RNA.

So John Scott has offered a very neat answer for many of the problems of selection, purification and concentration; and also a potential driving force behind the origin of genes and chromosomes, ribosomes and possibly even proteins – all the most fundamental structures of life. But he suggests that the simple hydrated electron may also have played a major role in taking things further, towards the origin of the living cell.

While the scenario outlined above was unfolding, the waters of the earth would have become steadily richer in ionic salts washed down from the land by the early rains. The arrival of these salts could have drastically altered the hydrated electrons' effects. In sufficiently concentrated salt solutions, the selectivity of the hydrated electrons' attacks would have been much reduced. Positive ions would bind to and neutralize the protective negative charges, leaving all the previously protected polymers and larger aggregates of polymers and their smaller companions suddenly vulnerable to attack. If they were to survive much longer, the polymer systems would need to find shelter within a new outer covering – the electron-resistant lipid membranes of the first cells.

Membrane-bound sacs or 'vesicles' would probably have been forming haphazardly for many thousands or millions of years – they would not have suddenly begun to form just when they were needed! But with the arrival of the salts they might have begun to be *naturally selected*. Any emergent gene–protein systems that became entrapped within cells, or which could actively encourage cell membranes to form around them, would gain an increasing advantage over all their cousins still slopping about free in the increasingly hazardous outside world, because hydrated electrons cannot readily penetrate the barrier of a lipid-bilayer membrane. The most successful cells might have covered themselves further in a coating of negatively charged carbohydrate, resembling the similar coating found on the surface of most modern cells.

Modern cells are no longer threatened by the ravages of hydrated electrons, the build-up of oxygen in the atmosphere (due to plant photosynthesis) has seen to that. In the upper layers of the atmosphere oxygen reacts to form a layer of ozone (O_3), which absorbs most ultra-violet light, preventing it from reaching the sensitive living things below. Oxygen also reacts particularly rapidly with hydrated electrons. So with the evolution of photosynthesis (see chapter 8), the influence of the hydrated electron would begin to wane, but all modern life may be left with the legacies of its reign – nucleic acid genes that encode proteins; carbohydrates; glycoproteins; and even the negative charge surrounding all our cells. According to the appealingly simple vision of John Scott, the path leading the early earth from chemical sterility up to life was narrower but much clearer than we might at first sight suppose.

As with all appealingly simple ideas about the origins of life, we should caution ourselves to stand back and look for hard evidence. At the moment, there is not much hard evidence supporting a crucial involvement of hydrated electrons in the origin of life. Hydrated electrons would surely have been around in the surface waters of the early earth, but did they direct the origin of life and evolution along the path John Scott suggests? They might have done, but unfortunately the prebiotic simulation experiments needed to give us more confidence have yet to be performed. John Scott has provided the idea, but it now needs to be tested in conditions simulating those of the primordial earth.

Genes that encode proteins

As we contemplate the deep gulf separating us from an understanding of how 'mere chemicals' could have given rise to modern life, we find that the deepest trough within that gulf is presented, not by the origin of the first replicators, but by the origin of the gene–protein link. The origin of replication may be the most *fundamental* step in the origin of life, but the emergence of the gene–protein link is the one that has been least satisfactorily explained.

Many accounts of our origins skip jauntily over this deep trough as though it were a mere crack in an otherwise solid edifice of evolutionary theory. Many books dismiss it in just a couple of paragraphs, with self-assured statements such as 'somehow within the primeval soup the first self-replicating nucleic acids began to encourage amino acids to link up into proteins.' Occasionally you can find apologetic statements pointing out that 'the precise mechanism of this step remains to be determined', but only very rarely is the origin of the gene–protein link presented as the fundamental gulf in understanding which it really is.

I could easily spend the rest of this book, and probably several other volumes as well, telling you about the multitude of different ideas dreamed up to explain how genes might have begun to make proteins, and how the precise genetic code in use today might have first come into being. Unfortunately, none of the ideas are backed up by any hard experimental evidence, and none have proved sufficiently convincing to be accepted as the 'established view'.

The general outline offered in figure 4.7 is the closest I can get to identifying any favoured candidate for you, but it has certainly not achieved the status of accepted dogma. Let me give you a quick taste of some of the other ideas put forward to explain how nucleic acids first 'learned' to encode specific proteins.

Some scientists suggest that, rather than binding to specific tRNA precursors as shown in figure 4.7, amino acids were able to line up directly on the short strands of nucleic acid that formed the earliest genes, and then be linked up into a protein. For this idea to work, amino acids and the codons that encode them would need to have some degree of selective affinity for one another. The problem is that no such selective affinities have ever been found. The only hints of selective affinities between amino acids and nucleic acids that might explain the origin of the genetic code, are the ones between amino acids and their *anticodons*. This is the possibility which has prompted schemes such as the one offered in figure 4.7.

A few scientists have suggested that amino acids did not interact specifically with *either* their anticodons or codons, but rather that they became selectively trapped within some sort of 'codon–anticodon sandwich'.

Others suggest that the first proteins were not specifically encoded by nucleic acids, but that nucleic acids were somehow able to encourage proteins and peptides of random, or at least unspecified, amino acid sequence to form. The origin of specificity would come later, in some still mysterious way, perhaps because some of the unspecific proteins were happily able to act as the catalysts needed to make the whole process increasingly specific.

Still others suggest that there were selective interactions between the first genes and amino acids, but that they allowed distinction between only a few very broad classes of amino acids. For example, there might have been only two types of original codons – those encoding 'water-loving' (hydrophilic) amino acids and those encoding 'water-hating' (hydrophobic) amino acids. So the first proteins would have been 'specific', only in so far as they contained different arrangements of sections strongly attracted to water and others that would be repelled away from water into the interior of the folding protein. Roughly half of all the possible codons might have encoded *any* available hydrophilic amino acid, while the other half would have encoded any hydrophobic ones. Which particular amino acids were found in any protein would have been determined simply by chance and availability, provided they were of the right class – hydrophilic or hydrophobic.

Other suggestions are that the first proteins all contained only one type of amino acid, or that the first genes consisted of long stretches of nucleic acid containing just one type of base; and perhaps the first codons consisted not of three nucleotides, as in modern life, but of two, or four, or five, or of some vague region of a nucleic acid of indeterminate length. I could continue to list 'possible' and 'plausible' ideas almost indefinitely, but there would be little point. Instead I want to look briefly at one of the most promising developments of recent years – a discovery which may well have given us a major (if very general) clue not only to the origin of the gene–protein link, but also to the origin of replication itself.

RNA as chicken *and* egg?

The problem we have been considering, of the origin of nucleic acid replication and of the gene–protein link, is often referred to as the 'chicken and egg' dilemma of early evolution. In all modern cells nucleic acids are needed to make proteins, while proteins are needed both to replicate nucleic acids and to catalyse the process of protein manufacture itself. So modern nucleic acids and proteins are completely dependent on one another. The dilemma, then, is how could nucleic acids have first formed and begun to replicate without the catalytic assistance of proteins; or how could specific proteins have arisen without nucleic acid genes to encode them. Which came first – protein 'chicken' or nucleic acid 'egg'? Or did they somehow evolve together, interdependent from the start?

If life really did begin with self-replicating nucleic acids, then the problem boils down to the need for effective *catalysts* for that replication before there were efficient enzymes available. Before the advent of coded proteins there would certainly have been lots of simple alternative catalysts around, such as certain metal ions, small organic molecules, or perhaps the surfaces of minerals like clays. The problem is that these would all have been very *general* catalysts – catalysing a wide range of different (though broadly similar) reactions rather than the few specific ones needed for nucleic acids to form and evolve. These general catalysts may well have given some assistance to nucleic acid formation and replication, but they are unlikely to have been sufficient. The fact that nobody has yet been able to convincingly re-create nucleic acid replication without enzymes, suggests that it cannot be a very easy process to get under way.

One possible, and very neat, solution to this perplexing dilemma emerged in 1983, when a team of scientists at the University of Colorado, led by Thomas Cech, discovered that some RNA molecules were themselves capable of a form of catalysis. They discovered RNA molecules within modern cells that catalysed the removal of central portions of their own RNA strands. Strictly speaking these RNAs are not true catalysts, since a true catalyst emerges unaffected by the reaction it catalyses. Instead they are autocatalysts which act upon themselves and emerge from the reaction in an altered form.

A few months after Cech's discovery was announced, however, Sydney Altman's research team at Yale discovered the first true RNA catalysts – molecules of RNA which can chop up *other* RNA molecules at certain defined places on an RNA strand. The versatility of RNA as a catalyst was further demonstrated in 1985, when Thomas Cech and Arthur Zaug reported small RNA molecules that could catalyse the link-up of short chains of RNA into longer ones.

So two of the most basic requirements for significant evolution – replication and catalysis – may initially have been met by the one type of chemical – RNA. RNA molecules might have been able to catalyse their own replication, long before catalytic proteins arrived on the primordial scene. Thus, the chicken and egg dilemma could be avoided if RNA was both chicken and egg.

Imagine, for example, a population of short-chain RNA molecules being formed by the random linkage of nucleotides as discussed earlier. Eventually a few RNAs might arise whose base sequence allows them to catalyse a stumbling, inefficient form of replication, both of themselves and of other RNAs. An RNA population explosion would begin, perhaps generating many other forms of catalytic RNA able to catalyse other reactions that would help the RNAs to form and replicate. Simple 'cells' (really only spontaneously formed lipid vesicles) entrapping various catalytic RNAs that could help one another, would survive and multiply more effectively than those containing less 'clever' or less 'cooperative' RNAs.

The scope for RNAs to act as efficient and versatile catalysts is largely unexplored. Variations in the base sequence of RNA chains could certainly give rise to a wide variety of different structures, folded back on themselves by base-pairing in many complex ways. Now that the first RNA catalysts have been discovered, the catalytic potential of natural and synthetic RNAs, and other nucleic acids, will come under increasing scrutiny.

So the earth might have witnessed a long and complex phase of RNA-only evolution, with simple RNA-based cells evolving into ever more sophisticated forms of RNA-based life. It then becomes much more plausible that some of these RNAs might have begun to catalyse the linkage of amino acids into specific proteins – because they would already have been the products of millennia of evolution during which their replication and catalytic prowess had been perfected. With the invention of specific proteins, the earliest organisms would have suddenly blossomed into much more versatile creatures of more richly varied form (see figure 5.5).

The newly crafted proteins could be expected to have increasingly taken over the tasks that had previously been performed less efficiently by RNA; and they would have begun to perform many entirely novel tasks as well. With time, RNA catalysis would have slipped from prominence and then all but disappeared. At some point the RNA genes would have given rise to 'hard copies' composed of the more resilient nucleic acid, double-stranded DNA. Some central RNA components of the first forms of RNA-based life would have evolved into the messenger, transfer and ribosomal RNAs of modern cells – seemingly mere intermediaries in the flow of genetic information from gene to protein, but occupying a vital central position by virtue of having been in on the protein-making act first.

The apparently very small number of catalytic RNAs still remaining within modern cells might be the 'living fossils' that provide the vital clue to how life first began – molecular 'coelacanths' that have turned up unexpectedly in the cellular seas. Of course this is all wild speculation, unsubstantiated as yet by any convincing recreation of the processes involved; but catalytic RNA has been discovered only very recently, and scientists have not yet had the time to investigate its full potential.

As I write, it seems possible that the discovery of catalytic RNA might turn out to be the greatest single breakthrough in our attempts

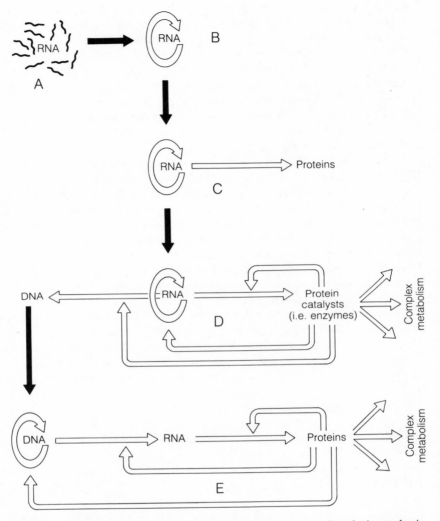

Figure 5.5   Catalytic RNAs might have allowed replication and evolution to begin without the catalytic powers of proteins. The generation of short RNA strands of random base sequence (A), might have generated some RNAs capable of catalysing RNA replication (B). Evolution of these first replicators could then have given some of them the ability to make proteins (C). Enzymes could then have evolved to catalyse RNA replication, protein synthesis, complex cellular metabolism and the copying of the original RNA genes into double-stranded DNA (D). When DNA took over the task of storing and replicating genetic information, the molecular relationships of the modern cell would have been forged, with RNA as an intermediary between the interdependent genes and proteins it gave rise to (E).

to understand the origins of life; or alternatively, it could prove a great disappointment. Experiments to investigate the potential of catalytic RNAs as creators of life are easy to devise, but they have yet to be performed. Given time and money, scientists may yet build prebiotic 'RNA-generators', in which replicating and evolving catalytic RNAs will take the first spontaneous steps towards new life, in conditions that truly resemble the likely environment of the primordial earth.

The question of money is a very pertinent one. Research into the origin of life is not considered an area in which important industrial advances or great fortunes are to be made (perhaps wrongly, as we will see later), so finance to support the many obvious experiments waiting to be done can sometimes be hard to find. Due to this scarcity of financial resources the study of the origins of life has been forced to become a most efficient and cost-effective industry – from just a thimble-full of facts the scientists engaged in that study manage to generate a virtually endless supply of theories!

A case not proven

Many laymen and students think that science and scientists are wonderful, if a bit frightening. They see the scientists of the world as calm and logical seekers after the truth – collecting data, dispassionately standing back and assessing what it might mean, ruthlessly rejecting ideas that cannot survive the cold blade of reason and all cooperating together to unravel the secrets of a mysterious and sometimes very obstinate universe. Alas, however, scientists suffer from the same failings of bigotry, vanity and greed that afflict us all in varying proportion. Science is often a highly competitive game with fame and sometimes fortune as the prizes. The cold blade of reason is often honed to perfection to attack the ideas of rivals, while left to rust unused when scientists advertise ideas of their own. Despite such failings, science as a whole still makes worthwhile progress, because there are usually enough rivals to cut away the nonsense before too long. The path of scientific progress is constructed out of occasional planks of truth overlying a much thicker foundation of rubbishy undergrowth.

But what if the vast majority of scientists all have faith in the one unverified idea? The modern 'standard' scientific version of the origin of life on earth is one such idea, and we would be wise to check its real merit with great care. Has the cold blade of reason been applied with sufficient vigour in this case? Most scientists *want* to believe that life could have emerged spontaneously from the primeval waters, because it would confirm their belief in the explicability of Nature – the belief that all could be explained in terms of particles and energy and forces if only we had the time and the necessary intellect. They also want to believe because their arch opponents – religious fundamentalists such as creationists – *do not* believe in life's spontaneous origin. It is this combative atmosphere which sometimes encourages scientists writing and speaking about the origin of life to become as dogmatic and bigoted as the creationist opponents they so despise.

Personally, I consider fundamentalist creationism to be a far sillier idea than the craziest of all the crazy notions which scientists have ever proposed; but as scientists gloat over the deficiencies of non-scientific accounts of our origin and evolution, they should not ignore the considerable deficiencies in their own account. At the moment scientists certainly do not know how, of even if, life originated on earth from lifeless atoms. They do have a few plausible ideas on the subject, but many more rather implausible ones.

Given an appropriate early atmosphere, we have good reason to believe that some of the simplest chemical building-blocks of life could have formed on the early earth. We have no convincing explanation of how they accumulated in sufficiently pure and concentrated form to give rise to the nucleic acids and proteins needed for life's origin and evolution. We have no satisfactory account of the origin of replication, although there are a few rough but probably simplistic ideas. The origin of the link between nucleic acids and proteins is one of the deepest and most important mysteries of all; and while we can certainly see how the first cells *might* have formed and evolved, nobody has got anywhere near to re-creating the origin of even the simplest evolving cell.

With all these uncertainties around, the case presented by the standard scientific version of the origin of life on earth remains 'not proven' and in parts deeply suspect, a sceptical verdict which applies to even the very general belief that 'somehow' the organic chemicals of the early earth spontaneously gave rise to life. The true story of the origin of life on earth, if there ever was such an earthly origin, may well be very different from the simplistic tale of the modern textbook and classroom.

Graham Cairns-Smith of Glasgow University is one scientist who thinks that the current version of our origins lacks its entire first chapter. Over the past 20 years he has developed an intriguing alternative tale which will hopefully come as a refreshing novelty as you read about it in chapter 6.

6   Crystalline life

You do not have to use stones as the scaffolding for a stone arch.
A. Graham Cairns-Smith

Earlier in the book we imagined some inquisitive aliens surveying the cities of the earth and pondering on their origin. Let's now imagine another set of aliens examining our mysterious world some time in the future, but this time unable to see through the earth's atmosphere due to some inadequacy of their alien 'eyes'. They can, however, see various orbiting unmanned 'space stations' hurtling around the globe high above its concealing atmosphere. Examining these objects, they discover some quite surprising complexities. They find a labyrinth of interconnecting rooms and passages and tubes and compartments all filled with various surprisingly pure chemicals which move about and interact in certain seemingly organized ways. There are pumps and heaters and coolers which directly manipulate the chemicals, but these are themselves controlled by complex computers in communication with all parts of the orbiting craft.

From time to time some of the end products of all the chemistry are carefully packed up and jettisoned to the planet below, leading our little green aliens to suspect that these might be unwanted wastes. Other packages of chemicals appear to be transported up through the atmosphere from time to time – presumably supplies. And most intriguingly, one or two of the orbiting craft are seen to be busy assembling other similar structures alongside themselves – they are building more of themselves, or 'replicating'.

Our aliens would be faced with a mystery not dissimilar to the one faced by scientists trying to explain the origins of life. Presented with seemingly purposeful complexity they have to explain how it could have originally arisen. What might they make of it all? If they adopted the strategy favoured by many of our own (green?) men, their reasoning might go something like this: 'These self-replicating orbiting objects are composed of chemicals such as iron and nickel, silicon and tin and so on, which our instruments tell us are abundant on the planet below. So presumably they are derived from simpler structures which formed spontaneously from these materials as a result of all sorts of chemical reactions; but how did they manage to give rise to such impressive descendants, and how did the descendants come to be up there and moving at such high speed?

'Well everything seems to be controlled by the central computers, so maybe originally there were *only* computers, much simpler ones of course (let's not be ridiculous!), but computers of some sort that could somehow encourage the manufacture of other similar computers. So somehow, presumably on the planet below, the first computers must have spontaneously formed and begun to replicate and evolve.

'Now what are the computers made of again? Hmmm, lots of silicon in there. That's neat! Our instruments tell us silicon is one of the most abundant elements on the planet! Things are becoming much clearer! Somehow the silicon of the earth gave rise to very simple structures that could reproduce and evolve. This evolution produced the first simple computers. Further evolution gave rise to ever more complex computers which became surrounded in complex outer structures that began to look a bit like the ones we now see orbiting above the atmosphere. There may be lots more similar structures on the surface below, but somehow natural selection has crafted computers that can build rockets to send themselves into orbit. What sort of selection pressures would favour such events? Well of course the business of constructing new computers and their associated structures will be much easier in the zero gravity of orbit.

'Great! I think we've identified the broad outline of events. It's still a bit of a puzzle why they should send so many pure chemicals back to the surface again – perhaps they are in cooperation with other structures on the planet that send up the supplies. Well, we can leave these details to sort out later – it's time to publish our discoveries!'

Our happy aliens would, of course, be completely mistaken. Any such space stations will be created by us – more natural things who have begun to make computers and robots in the hope, for example, that they might one day produce pure drugs and other chemicals in the zero gravity of orbit, then send them down for our own benefit. Since we already use robots to build cars, maybe we will one day use them to 'replicate' space stations as well. The aliens' mistaken central assumption was that, since computers lay at the heart of the space stations, they must *always* have lain at the heart of all the self-replicating things of the earth. They were also happy to assume that computers could have arisen spontaneously on earth, simply because there was lots of silicon available down there!

Now you might think that I have conjured up a rather stupid bunch of aliens to sustain the fantasy related above, but Graham Cairns-Smith, a chemist at Glasgow University, believes that most scientists have been equally stupid in their musings about the possible origins of life on earth. His arguments suggest that our 'stupid' aliens might actually have come closer to the truth about life's origins than the scientists of today. Although they completely missed an essential link in the chain of events – intermediate creatures such as us – they may at least have arrived at the right sort of materials as the basis of the very first forms of 'life'. Graham Cairns-Smith suggests that replicating and evolving *mineral* crystals, perhaps containing lots of silicon, are much more likely to have formed spontaneously on the early earth than the 'self-replicating naked genes' favoured by most scientists.

We have already seen that the spontaneous formation of self-replicating genes that encode proteins is a very difficult process to re-create or explain. Nobody has got anywhere near a realistic re-creation of such events, and I have tried to point out that even the various 'plausible' explanations may be much less plausible than their advocates suppose. Cairns-Smith goes further. He argues that the sorts of problems highlighted in the previous chapter (of purity, selection, concentration and so on) make the spontaneous origin of self-replicating life based on nucleic acids quite inconceivable.

Cairns-Smith is probably the most prominent 'dissident' among the ranks of scientists interested in the origins of life – he has certainly produced the most radically different alternative. His approach was to try to identify the *easiest* way in which replicating and evolving structures could have arisen on the early earth, *regardless of what they were made of*. I have already explained that in seeking the origins of life we are essentially seeking the origins of replication and evolution. Hopefully that search will also reveal the origins of life based on nucleic acids that encode proteins, but it may be very naive to expect such complex modern systems to have arisen directly.

Once the replication and evolution of *anything* had got under way, then the earliest creatures (whatever they were made of) might have created the conditions required for more complex life-forms such as ourselves to arise. The first 'low-tech' creatures (as Cairns-Smith calls them) would not have made nucleic acids and proteins for *our* future benefit – they would have made them for good evolutionary 'reasons' of their own. But having assisted in the creation of 'high-tech' life, the first organisms might have been replaced when that high-tech life began to multiply out of control. Thus there might have been one or more fundamental 'takeovers' during the long history of life, similar to the possible takeover of the earth by computerized robots so beloved of the science fiction writers of today.

There are two main aspects to Cairns-Smith's imaginative scenario. Firstly, there are his assertions that the standard version of our origins is wholly implausible; that first life must have been low-tech and very different from the high-tech biology at the heart of living things today; and that at least one major takeover has occurred in which simple early forms of life created the conditions for more complex and very different life-forms to arise and inherit the earth. Secondly, there is his contention that the early low-tech life was crystal life, based on crystalline minerals that could replicate and evolve. Personally, I find his criticisms of the standard tale very convincing, but feel that he takes his own 'crystalline life' proposal to rather fanciful lengths considering it is still woefully lacking in experimental support. But let me introduce you to his ideas, leaving further scepticism and criticism until later.

The crystal genes

Any population of things that can replicate themselves in a reasonably faithful manner, while varying occasionally due to chance errors or novelties in the replication process, should be able to evolve by natural selection – as long as the variations affect the ability of the things to survive and replicate further. In modern creatures, genes made of DNA are the things that replicate with occasional variation, and what they *do* to affect their chances of surviving and replicating further is largely to encode protein molecules (they also encode some functional RNAs such as transfer and ribosomal RNAs). All scientists acknowledge that the first genes may not have been identical to the DNA, or the RNA, of modern cells. Many envisage simpler, less precisely organized nucleic acid-like structures from which our modern nucleic acids evolved. Graham Cairns-Smith believes that the first genes bore absolutely no resemblance to nucleic acids at all, indeed that they were not even organic compounds. He suggests they were inorganic crystalline materials such as tiny lumps of clay.

He arrived at the idea of crystal genes while trying to imagine any sort of simple chemical system that might be able to evolve by natural selection. He was not thinking about the origin of life at the time, so his vision wasn't blinkered by the need to aim towards the chemicals involved in the replication and evolution of modern life. The possibilities for crystal genes to prepare the way for nucleic acid genes only occurred to him later. But why did he settle on crystals?

Crystals of all sorts would certainly have formed on the early earth – nobody doubts that. There must have been endless different places in which the early rains washed rich solutions of inorganic salts (weathered from the first rocks) down into cooling pools or drying lake beds where crystals could form and grow. Alternatively, groundwater percolating up through porous rocks might have brought mineral solutions to the surface ready to crystallize elsewhere.

Simple school chemistry teaches us the *highly idealized* basics of crystal growth in which ions, atoms or molecules become packed together in a stable and very specific repeating pattern (see figure 6.1). As it is laid down, each layer of a growing crystal provides a new surface on which further growth can occur; and the growth is very controlled and specific, because only the 'right' chemicals can fit onto the surface of a growing crystal in a stable and self-perpetuating manner. Thus millions of 'rhombic' crystals of copper sulphate or 'cubic' crystals of sodium chloride are grown each year in countless school chemistry classes throughout the world. The controlled selectivity of crystal growth is also used as one of the most powerful and routine tools for the purification of wanted chemicals from impure solutions.

Suppose you manage to make some wanted drug or other chemical using an appropriate chemical reaction. At the end of the reaction

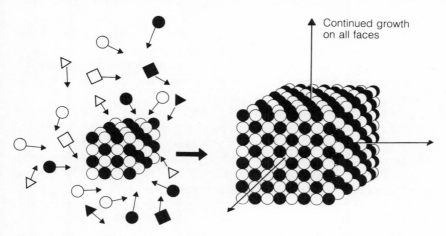

Continued growth
on all faces

Figure 6.1   Idealized crystal growth (see text for details).

your flask will not contain the desired chemical alone, perhaps dissolved in some solvent – chemistry is not that simple. Instead, there are always going to be impurities and contaminants, the products of unwanted 'side reactions' or some of the original starting materials remaining stubbornly left behind. You will be very lucky if 90 per cent of the molecules dissolved in the solvent are the ones you want. 'Yields' of 80 to 60 per cent are much more common, and still pretty good – in many reactions the yields are 50 per cent or less. The hardest part of many chemical reactions is getting the desired product out of the reaction mix in reasonably pure form, and crystallization is often a very effective way to do it.

Under the right conditions of solvent, temperature, concentration and so on, you may be able to get the substance you want to begin to crystallize out of the messy mixture of the solution. Once crystallization has begun, it usually continues at a rapidly accelerating pace. All the various molecules in the solution will be constantly bumping and bouncing into and and around the crystal surface, but only those that can fit snuggly and stably into the existing crystal structure will stick to form a new surface on which further crystallization can occur. Very soon your flask may be filled with a horde of visible and often very beautiful crystals composed of the desired chemical in almost completely pure form. You will then only have to separate the solid crystals from the solution left behind, and perhaps wash them with fresh solvent or maybe dissolve them in the solvent and recrystallize them once more, to be left with a pure sample of the desired product free of all the unwanted 'muck' associated with the initial reaction.

So crystals can certainly 'grow', and they can also multiply if they shear along the natural crystal planes – just like splitting slates or wafers. Crystal growth and multiplication are some of the easiest things in the world to get to happen. It is impossible to imagine an early earth on which crystals did not form and grow and multiply – both certainly happened, but could they have allowed crystals to *evolve*?

Apart from multiplication, the next essential requirement for evolution is *variation* in a self-propagating manner. At first sight the story of crystal growth just given would seem specifically to exclude the possibility of variation; but what you have been told so far is not the real story of crystal growth (sorry!), it is simply the ideal 'broad outline' version given at school or in elementary texts. Crystal growth certainly *approximates* to the neat perpetual assembly of endless identical crystal layers, just as nucleic acid replication approximates to the endless perpetuation of identical unchanged genes; but in both cases no evolution would be possible if the true situation matched the

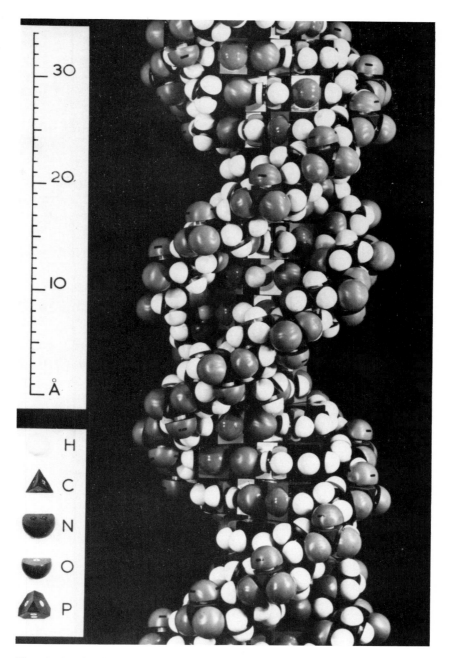

Plate 1   Model of the DNA double-helix, with plastic shapes representing individual atoms. One Angstrom (Å) = 10^{-10} metres

(By courtesy of the Biophysics Department, King's College, London)

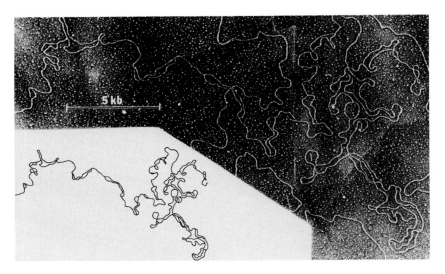

Plate 2   A tangled thread of double-stranded DNA visualized using an electron microscope. At various points the partial replication of the double-helix has led to the formation of 'eyes'. The scale bar indicates the length of a stretch of DNA containing 5000 base-pairs

(By courtesy of D. S. Hogness, Stanford University Medical School)

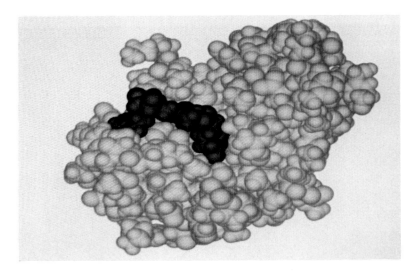

Plate 3   Computer representation of an enzyme (light shading). A molecule which can participate in a reaction catalysed by the enzyme is also shown (dark shading) attached to the enzyme surface. Each sphere represents an atom

(By courtesy of R. J. Feldmann, Division of Computer Research and Technology, US National Institutes of Health)

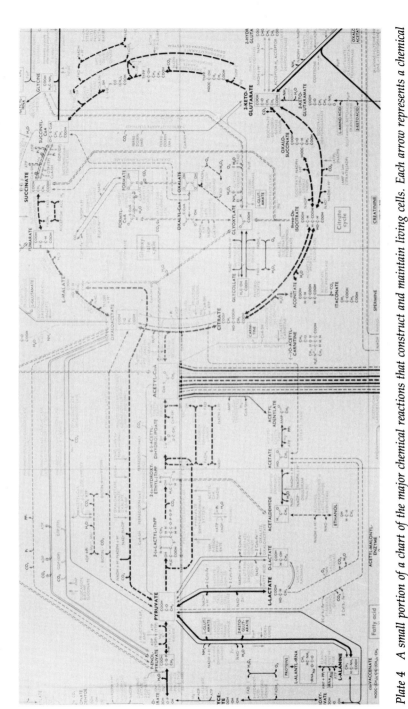

Plate 4   A small portion of a chart of the major chemical reactions that construct and maintain living cells. Each arrow represents a chemical reaction catalysed by a specific enzyme, and long sequences of such reactions form many complex interconnecting 'biochemical pathways' (Reprinted from 'Biochemical Pathways' (1974), Boehringer Mannheim GmbH)

Plate 5   A mixture of clay crystals showing complex patterns of grooves and shearings. Other clays can form tubes and spheres and membranes. Could such structures have formed the architecture of the first simple, inorganic forms of life?
(By courtesy of W. D. Keller, University of Missouri-Columbia)

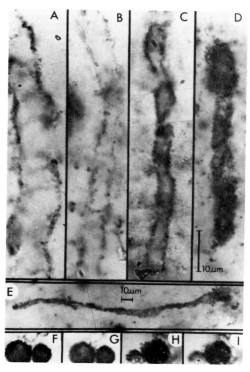

A   B   C   D

E

F   G   H   I

10μm

10μm

Plate 6 (left)   Remnants of some of the earliest cells. Microfossils from rocks laid down about 3500 million years ago

(By courtesy of J. W. Schopf, University of California)

Plate 7 (below)   What may be an alien solar system forming around a star 50 light years from earth (Beta Pictoris). The central star has been masked out to reveal the presumed solar system as a bright disc seen edge on. Our own solar system may have looked much like this in its youth, over 4000 million years ago. Planets may already have formed by accumulation of the material of the disc, or may form more fully in the future. Life might arise on these planets, or colonize them; or it may already have begun

(By courtesy of R. J. Terrile, Jet Propulsion Laboratory, Pasadena)

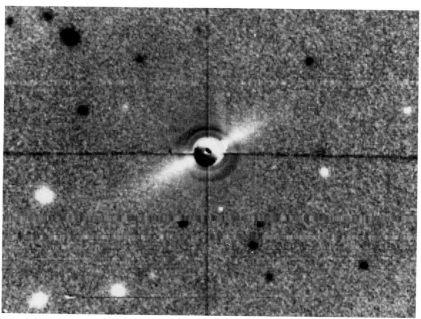

Plate 8   *Two superb views of the Martian landscape taken by the Viking 1 Lander.*
The spacecraft performed a complex series of experiments to search for signs of life in
the Martian soil, but found none. A boom belonging to the spacecraft cuts across the
lower image
(By courtesy of R. J. Terrile, Jet Propulsion Laboratory, Pasadena)

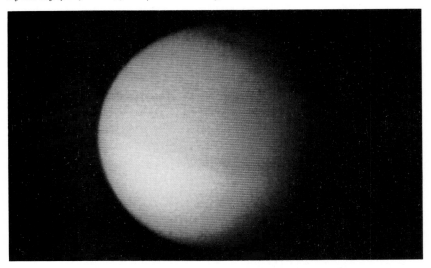

Plate 9   *Titan, the largest satellite of Saturn, photographed by Voyager 2. The thick*
atmosphere may shroud a world containing all the chemical raw materials for life, but
currently locked in deep freeze. Scientists might one day warm up a bit of it, or all of it,
to give rise perhaps to simple life
(By courtesy of R. J. Terrile, Jet Propulsion Laboratory, Pasadena)

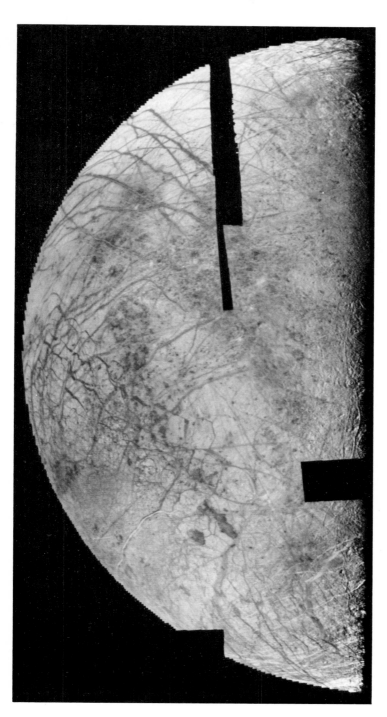

Plate 10 A composite view of Europa, a satellite of Jupiter, photographed by Voyager 2. Some scientists think there may be life beneath its fissured crust of water ice

(By courtesy of R. J. Terrile, Jet Propulsion Laboratory, Pasadena)

Plate 11 (above) A spiral galaxy, somewhat similar to our own. This alien galaxy of countless millions of stars is about 10 million light years from us and many thousands of light years across. What sort of living things and civilizations might it hold, and do they ponder over similar photographs of our own galaxy? (By courtesy of The Royal Observatory, Edinburgh)

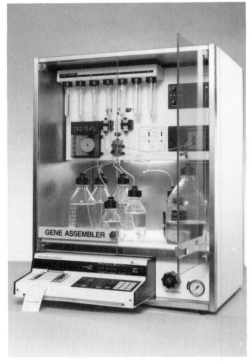

Plate 12 (right) DNA molecules of any desired sequence can now be made automatically by bench-top machines such as this 'Gene Assembler' from Pharmacia. They allow mankind to write new messages in the 'code of life' (By courtesy of the Division of Molecular Biology, Biotechnology Group, Pharmacia)

simple textbook ideal. Just like nucleic acid replication, crystal 'replication' may have great scope for the generation and then reasonably, but not totally, faithful perpetuation of chance mistakes and variations.

How could crystals vary in a self-perpetuating manner? One of the simplest possibilities is in physical shape. You may think that any given type of crystal must always have the same shape – salt crystals always being cubic, copper sulphate ones rhombic, and so on; but things are certainly not that simple. Growth on different faces of a crystal can occur at different rates, and different 'domains' of a crystal can form, separated by regions of slight mismatch or misalignment of the crystal atoms, but each still growing to the same overall plan. Take a look at figure 6.2 to see what I mean. Crystals with many different complex shapes can be composed of many domains all adhering to the same basic plan. If you look closely at a pile of copper sulphate crystals grown from a saturated solution you will find few perfectly formed rhombi – most of the crystals will have much more complex shapes composed of various domains and faces of preferential growth or shearing, but all based on an underlying rhombic symmetry.

Now suppose the three variant structures at the top of figure 6.2 arise together by chance. Structures b and c will be novel variants of the original basic form, a, and all three might replicate as indicated by growth in one preferred dimension accompanied by the occasional shearing off of progeny crystals (real crystals can certainly do this, see plate 5). Now suppose that one structure encourages faster, more efficient, replication than the others. It might, for example, be retained more effectively in the pores of the rock from which the crystal 'nutrients' are being washed out. This most efficiently replicating form will obviously be 'naturally selected' and may soon come to dominate the crystal population.

Of course new and alternative variant forms could be arising all the time, many probably worse replicators than the currently most successful form, but a few perhaps better. Whenever a more efficient replicator arises it can be expected to increase in numbers and perhaps come to dominate the crystal population in its turn. Thus crystals might evolve by Darwinian natural selection, with the crystal population becoming progressively dominated by ever more efficiently growing and replicating forms. At least that is what Graham Cairns-Smith believes.

Even if they can evolve, crystals might not seem to have much scope to evolve very far, but Cairns-Smith thinks they could hold much more complex and versatile forms of 'genetic information' than

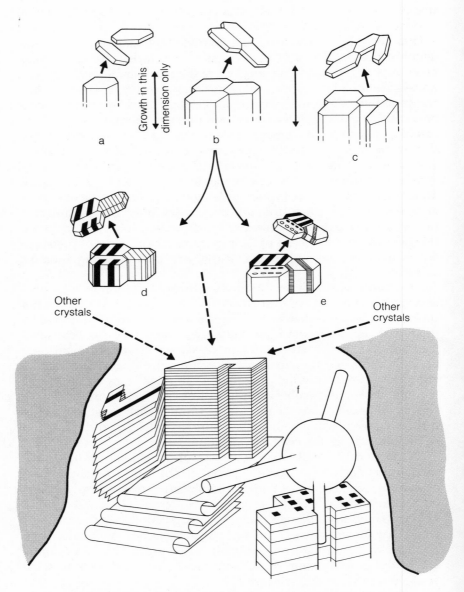

Figure 6.2 Crystals may be able to replicate, hold complex structural information and evolve (a–e). This might have led to the evolution of crystal 'organisms' capable of performing the chemistry that created organic life (f).

held by the simple examples considered above. This is because crystals can vary in lots of more subtle ways than mere variations in shape.

Most clays, for example, basically consist of layers of oxygen ions with layers of positively charged ions sandwiched in-between. These might be ions of silicon (Si^{4+}), or of aluminium (Al^{3+}) and so on. They may even be positively charged organic molecules. Now in many clays, one type of ion can become replaced or 'substituted' by another type, without destroying the clay's ability to grow, so complex patterns of substitution could be built up to make the surface of a crystal a very complex chemical structure indeed (see figure 6.2 d and e).

You can see from the figure that I have assumed that once a particular substitution pattern has arisen, it will tend to generate the same pattern in the new layers of crystal laid down during further growth. There is some very limited experimental evidence to suggest that this sort of precise crystal replication can happen, although things may not be quite so simple. Instead of encouraging identical layers to form on top of one another, such substitution patterns might cause some sort of matching or 'complementary' layer to form. This complementary layer could then encourage the original pattern to re-form in the next layer. Of course this would be very similar to the process of complementary nucleic acid chain formation which drives the replication of DNA – are you beginning to see why Cairns-Smith feels able to consider the possibility of 'crystal genes'? Crystals may be able to contain and perpetuate the genetic information needed to give rise to endless generations of complex and gradually varying crystal patterns and forms.

Even if you have been prepared to accept Cairns-Smith's arguments so far, I suspect you are still feeling that crystal evolution would be unlikely to allow 'crystal life' to ascend the ladder of organized complexity very far. Let's accept that crystal shapes and substitution patterns (and other sources of variation) might power the evolution of crystals best able to form in various environments and to be retained in these environments. Could crystals possibly exert sufficient control over their environment to be considered as worthwile 'forms of life'?

According to Cairns-Smith, crystals may well be able to *do* quite a lot to their environment, and to evolve into complex cooperating structures to a much greater extent than you might at first suppose. It is well known that crystal surfaces can act as efficient catalysts for many chemical reactions, including many involving the organic chemicals of modern life. The catalytic abilities of crystalline clays and other minerals are often recruited into conventional versions of the origin of life, to catalyse the reactions that supposedly created the first self-replicating nucleic acids able to encode proteins. Cairns-Smith's ideas about the involvement of clays and other crystals are radically different from those more traditional tales. He suggests that populations of 'living' (i.e. replicating and evolving) crystals began to make various organic chemicals *for their own benefit*. The takeover by these organic chemicals which gave rise to modern life came much later.

Why should living clays have begun to make the organic chemicals that would eventually kindle the fire of organic life? Obviously the chemicals would have to help the clays to survive and multiply in some way, otherwise the ability to make them would not be preserved by natural selection. Cairns-Smith imagines populations of quite complex, *cooperating* clays making organic chemicals that might act as useful 'glues' holding various parts of 'crystal organisms' together; or making small organic chemicals that could bind to various inorganic ions and either assist their incorporation into growing crystals, or perhaps remove ions that might interfere with crystal growth. Other organic molecules might have controlled the size and structure of various parts of crystal life, by inhibiting or encouraging the growth of particular crystal faces. And in all cases, crystals able to make organic chemicals that helped the crystals to survive and multiply would be naturally selected and would serve as the raw material for further evolution.

From a simple beginning of crystals that could replicate and evolve, Cairns-Smith builds up a picture of a primeval world populated by complex, cooperating living crystal organisms all making various organic chemicals which help the crystal life to survive and multiply. These 'organisms' would consist of aggregates of different types of crystals – plates, blocks, membranes, spheres, tubes, spirals etc., all cooperating for their common chemical good (see figure 6.2f for an impressionistic schematic view of what a simple crystal organism might look like, with all the organic chemicals omitted).

Living crystals might have been the 'chemists' that solved all the problems of purity, selection and concentration considered in chapter 5. They might have trapped the energy of sunlight and used it to power the organic chemistry taking place in complex assemblies of crystal plates and spheres and tubes and membranes. These 'organisms' would not have looked anything like the organisms of today. They would not have been composed of cells or have been able to run, or jump or fly. They may have consisted of variable assemblies of crystals looking little different from a random crystal mess; but by encouraging other similar assemblies to form, and by slowly evolving into new and ever more versatile forms, they would be well entitled to the status of 'living things' – extremely simple living things, nowhere near as complex as even the simplest of modern cells, but living nonetheless.

The takeover by organic life would come when some organic chemicals within crystal life began to replicate themselves with a speed that outpaced the crystal organisms which first made them. Imagine, for example, a crystal organism making RNA-like polymers which served to hold various parts of the crystal creature together. Any such crystal creatures making RNAs *that could replicate themselves* might have had a great advantage over those with RNAs incapable of self-replication, since their supplies of RNA would be more secure. But we saw in the previous chapter how self-replicating RNAs might evolve into much more versatile catalytic RNAs that may become able to make other RNAs and proteins to assist *their own* survival and multiplication, rather than that of any crystals. Once crystals had made self-replicating and possibly catalytic RNAs, crystal life might well have been doomed. It would have created a much more versatile and powerful genetic material than the 'low-tech' crystal genes. New life-forms based on nucleic acids would be expected to thrive and multiply and become increasingly independent of the crystal life which first made them.

I can barely do justice to Graham Cairns-Smith's intriguing ideas in one short chapter of a book such as this. If the brief outline given above has fired your imagination then I suggest you consult the books and articles listed on page 205 – they all contain stimulating and often surprisingly easy reading. In the meantime, we should return from the fantasy land of wild speculation to the harsh realities of evidence and plausibility. What chance is there that Cairns-Smith's dissident ideas are any closer to the truth than the conventional tale which he rejects?

According to Cairns-Smith, the great advantage of his idea of crystal life is that it makes the origin of life much easier. He arrived at the idea of crystal life because he felt it must be the easiest sort of life to get under way. This assertion prompts some obvious questions: 'If it arises relatively easily, then where is it? Why isn't there crystal life all around us today, or is there?'

He offers various answers to such queries. Firstly, he suggests that there might well be populations of living crystals on the earth today – we simply have not conducted a proper search for them. They might actually be rather difficult to spot, because we do not really know what a crystal organism would look like. As I have already said, it certainly would not have legs, or eyes or ears or wings. It could simply be a rather loose collection of interacting crystals whose boundaries and components could be both variable and indistinct.

We should conduct a search for 'odd-looking' crystal structures doing unexpected things, while being careful not to destroy their integrity by the brutality of our collect and search techniques. If someone gathered together a pile of people with a bulldozer, then reached down with a mechanical grab, scooped up a few unfortunate individuals, squashed them together and then dropped them onto a hard surface to look for signs of life, they probably wouldn't find any! Similarly, trowels and spades and drills and scoops might be inappropriate tools in the search for crystal life.

Secondly, Cairns-Smith suggests that complex living crystals making lots of organic chemicals might be unable to survive on the modern earth. The organic raw materials needed for their replication and survival would probably be nutrients to bacteria, protozoa, fungi and so on, making it impossible for complex crystal life to live and grow in the face of microbial competition.

Alternatively, he suggests that crystal life might be around on the modern earth, but very rare; or absent because the conditions on earth today are inappropriate. He is also fair enough to acknowledge that crystal life might not be around today because it never has been and never could be. His faith in his ideas appears to be firm but not total.

Leaving aside the quest for crystal life on the earth today, the supposed ease with which it could arise and evolve suggests that it should be relatively easy to create it in the laboratory. In answer to the query: 'Could mineral crystal genes evolve?' Cairns-Smith confidently asserts 'Yes, they could hardly help it'; to which you might reasonably respond: 'well let's see them do it'.

Sadly, nobody has got anywhere near to re-creating the sort of crystal evolution which forms the basis of all of Cairns-Smith's arguments. One reason may be that nobody has yet *tried* very hard, or been able to try. As I have indicated already, it is not easy to attract funds for studies into the origins of life. I am sure Cairns-Smith would like nothing better than to be able to test and develop all his ideas in the laboratory, but someone would need to give him the money to do so. He does claim that 'we should be able to make a primary [crystal] organism', but until he or someone else does so, and until crystals have been shown to replicate and evolve in the ways he claims they could, then his ideas will undoubtedly be treated with great scepticism and caution.

We will be returning briefly to the experiments Cairns-Smith might perform, if he had the money, in chapter 10. For the moment, it is time to take stock.

Graham Cairns-Smith is certainly not the only person to suggest that the origins of life may lie in quite different directions from what is usually supposed, but in recent years his has been the loudest, most persistent, and most radical voice declaring that, in searching for our origins, we should perhaps be looking for living things completely different from the nucleic acid and protein-based creatures of today. His insistence that we should be seeking the simplest and easiest routes towards replication and evolution, rather than routes that lead directly to modern life, is surely valid.

His idea that evolution might have seen one or more *takeovers*, in which 'low-tech' life-forms were supplanted by very different 'high-tech' forms is an important suggestion regardless of whether the low-tech life was crystal life or not. The standard version of our origins assumes that life was based on organic chemistry, and probably nucleic acids and proteins, from the very start – that there may have been many transitions but no dramatic takeovers. Cairns-Smith sees life based on nucleic acid genes that encode proteins as equivalent to a stone arch. Nucleic acids and proteins depend on each other as much as the individual stones of an arch, and just as an arch must originally be built on some sort of scaffolding, so life based on nucleic acids and proteins must have been erected on a scaffold of simpler forms of life. The 'scaffolds' used to construct some of the first arches may have been mounds of earth which could be dug away once the arches were in place. Similarly, the 'scaffolding' of life based on mutually dependent nucleic acids and proteins might have been living crystalline clays.

Personally, I am quite prepared to accept that crystals may well be able to replicate and evolve by natural selection, to some extent, and may well have done so on the early earth. Like most scientists, I am well convinced that the catalytic powers of crystals may have played a crucial role in the origins of life; and I would also accept that crystal evolution *might* have extended and perfected these powers. But when Cairns-Smith waxes lyrical about complex crystal organisms performing a multitude of chemical reactions in the service of crystal life, then waves of scepticism begin to rise. That is largely a subjective reaction, and it may be quite wrong.

Deep down I feel that the origin of life could not possibly have been as neat and tidy a process as either the standard tale or the dissident vision offered by Cairns-Smith suggests. Both may give us a very simplified glimpse of a part of the truth – 'primeval soups' and 'living clays' may both have played a role, in addition to other mechanisms and systems that remain unknown to us. The real truth is of course lost for ever, no matter how successful our simulations and re-creations may become. Whatever that truth was it remains a deep mystery, despite what some schoolbooks, textbooks and encyclo-paedias may suggest.

7 An infected world

It is quite conceivable that the living beings on all planets are related, and that a planet, as soon as it can shelter organic life, is soon occupied by such organic life.
Svante Arrhenius

Are we perhaps being ridiculously parochial, crazily short-sighted and narrow-minded, when we assume that our earliest ancestors arose upon this little planet of ours? The night sky reveals a galaxy of countless millions of stars, many perhaps surrounded by planets upon which life might have originated; and the galaxy that we can see – our own 'milky way' galaxy – is in astronomical terms merely our own 'back yard'. We already know of many millions of other galaxies and still we haven't seen to the universe's edge (if it has one).

The vast number of alternative environments out there in which life could have originated makes the possibilities of the primeval earth shrink into puny insignificance. If life really does arise easily, as many scientists contend, then it may well have originated spontaneously on earth; but in that case the rest of the universe must also be teeming with an unimaginable variety of different life-forms. If life does not arise easily, even if it is an extremely unlikely event, the entire universe must surely have offered somewhere suitable for its spontaneous origin.

The only alternative to a spontaneous origin is to suppose that 'life' is some spiritual or supernatural phenomenon breathed into lifeless matter by some living God; but even then the problem of the origin of life remains unsolved – it simply becomes the problem of the origin of God. If neither God nor life ever originated, but simply are, and always were, then explanations or at least descriptions of that strange state of affairs become our problem.

Rather than slipping any further down an endless philosophical spiral, let's address a simple and very relevant question: Assuming that life did originate as a spontaneous result of the fundamental forces interacting with matter and energy, why should we suppose that it originated on earth, when the entire universe was available?

It used to be believed that life arose spontaneously on earth all the time: that meat began to rot due to the spontaneous origin of bacteria and maggots within it; that insects were constantly created out of inorganic nothingness; and even that mice could leap miraculously and spontaneously to life from piles of dusty grain, or frogs from weedy ponds. In 1862 the great Frenchman Louis Pasteur received honours from the French Academy of Sciences for experiments which discredited such theories of spontaneous generation. With great care and patience he had demonstrated that life always comes from other life. Bacteria and maggots arise within meat from pre-existing infection and infestation; and insects, mice and frogs certainly do not arise spontaneously from the non-living world, but from the living fertilized eggs of their forebears.

In telling us that life always comes from other life, Pasteur turned the ultimate origin of life from no problem at all, into a very great problem indeed; but this has had little long-term impact on the belief that *long ago* life really did originate spontaneously on earth. But if life on earth nowadays comes only from other life, might it not always have been so? What goes for meat might also go for mother earth – we may be living on an infected or infested world which carries life only because that life has come to earth from somewhere else.

Obviously, if the earth received its life from somewhere else, then that goes no way towards solving the problem of life's ultimate origin. If we live on an infected globe, then we still need to explain the origins of the creatures that did the infecting. The origins of replication, of nucleic acids and of genes that encode proteins would remain unresolved, although we would have many more worlds to choose from in our search for environments in which these origins could have occurred; and we would have considerably more time (10 000 to 20 000 million years instead of just under 5000 million) in which all the various steps could have taken place.

The time advantage might not be very significant, and should not be overstated. In the first place, 20 000 million years is only four times longer than 5000 million years; and secondly, it probably took several thousand million years for stars to make the carbon, nitrogen, oxygen (and other) atoms essential for our sort of life to work. The great expansion in physical horizons may be much more significant. If the life now on earth originated 'somewhere out there', rather that 'down here', then we may have countless millions upon millions of planets to choose from as its cradle, rather than only one. Before troubling to think about all these opportunities, we should satisfy ourselves that life really could have reached the earth from somewhere else, and then see if there is any evidence to suggest that it did.

Panspermia

Svante Arrhenius, a great Swedish physical chemist, was one of the people who felt that Pasteur's experiments had something important to tell us about the ultimate origins of life. In a short paper published in 1903 he outlined his theory of 'panspermia' (which means 'all-seeding' in Greek), suggesting that life came to earth as tiny micro-organisms or spores 'blown' through interstellar space by the pressure of light rays from the stars.

Electromagnetic radiation, such as starlight, exerts only a tiny pressure on anything it hits, but if the objects are small enough this pressure may be sufficient to push them away from the stars into the void of interstellar space. Arrhenius envisioned radiation pressure overcoming the force of gravity which held tiny micro-organisms suspended in the atmosphere of their native planet. Alternatively, microorganisms may have been impelled upwards from the planet's surface by the impact of comets or meteorites, to then be caught by starlight and driven away before they could fall back. The microorganisms (or their 'spores') would thus be scattered through the wastelands of interstellar space like dandelion seeds on the wind. The incredibly low temperatures of space would have slowed down the metabolism of these seeds of life, allowing them to remain viable for the thousands of years it would have taken them to reach the vicinity of other stars. There, if the combinations of starlight and gravity were appropriate, they may have gently settled into new homes such as the early earth, or have been carried downwards by passing meteorites.

Arrhenius did not suggest how the microorganisms or spores would have been protected from the damaging effects of ultra-violet radiation and other cosmic rays on their long journeys, but others have offered possible answers and tried to test their validity. One possibility is that they could have acquired a protective coating of interstellar dust, or of the various organic and inorganic molecules shown to be present in interstellar molecular clouds; or perhaps they somehow became protected within the body of meteorites.

Peter Weber and J. Mayo Greenberg of the University of Leiden in The Netherlands have subjected bacterial spores to intense ultra-violet radiation, vacuum and extreme cold to simulate the environment of interstellar space. They found that if carried within the molecular clouds which roam around space, a significant fraction of spores may well be able to remain viable for many millions of years – certainly long enough to travel from one solar system to another. So panspermia powered by starlight is certainly not a crazy idea. It may be the way in which life first colonized the earth, and the life of the present-day earth may now be being driven out to new homes and frontiers far above our heads.

In one form or another the picturesque cause of panspermia, with its 'seeds of life' drifting endlessly around the universe, has been championed by a series of the most successful and celebrated scientists of recent times. Shortly before the great Arrhenius wrote down his thoughts on the subject, Lord Kelvin (immortalized in the 'Kelvin' scale of absolute temperature) suggested that life was first carried down to earth within a meteorite. More recently, Francis Crick (codiscoverer of the DNA double-helix) and Sir Fred Hoyle (who has made a major contribution to our knowledge of how elements are synthesized within stars) have both developed their own variations on the panspermia theme. Panspermia seems to be the accepted territory of scientists who have made such a name for themselves in other fields that they need not fear exposing themselves to ridicule by suggesting they have come from other worlds!

Francis Crick suggests that the earth may have been infected *on purpose* by some alien technological society, rather than falling victim to some random star-blown infection. Along with Leslie Orgel, one of the most prominent of the scientists involved in more conventional studies into the origins of life, he has constructed a tale in which purpose-built rockets were packed with microorganisms or their spores and sent out from their native planets on journeys which lasted thousands, millions or even billions of years. The rockets are supposed to have been designed to home in on planets surrounding other stars and then release their vital cargo into the atmosphere and oceans of worlds such as our earth. It is not suggested that they were sent specifically to earth, but once here, some of the microorganisms could be expected to have thrived and multiplied, priming the evolution of an entirely new technological society – us – which might, in its turn, send its own seeds of life out to new generations of stars.

We can certainly understand the motivation our ancient alien forebears might have had for their act of cosmic fertilization. The desire to perpetuate life is one of the strongest driving forces of all living things, one which could be expected to be retained by natural selection regardless of the types of organisms involved. Many of us yearn for immortality, but failing that we wish to leave children and grandchildren to carry on from where we must leave off. The desire to seed the universe is a natural extension of procreation which some of our own species are already beginning to ponder wistfully upon. So far, we have restrained ourselves to simply sending out messages, on radio waves and on spacecraft such as the Voyager probes, but soon we may decide to send life.

If we wanted merely to send *any* life, then microorganisms and their spores would be the obvious choice. They can survive the longest, be carried the furthest (because they are so small and may survive so long), and are sufficiently variable and adaptable that at least a few would surely stand a good chance of setting up home on various alien worlds.

Francis Crick and Leslie Orgel urge caution on scientists tempted to infect the rest of the universe with life from earth, but I wonder if they will be listened to. The fact that we ourselves clearly could, and perhaps will, attempt to send life to other worlds, argues strongly in favour of the idea that other peoples, many thousand million years ago, may have broadcast the living seed that gave rise to us. If they did, then we are very unlikely to ever meet them or their 'stay at home' descendants. They are probably long dead, perhaps roasted to extinction by their expanding or exploding sun, or frozen when it quietly died. Maybe they tried to reach new worlds themselves (just as our descendants may one day need to seek a new solar system if they are to have any hope of survival), perhaps they even succeeded; but any microorganisms sent out as part of their attempts to keep the flame of life alive would undoubtedly have been able to spread much further.

Of course if we are the products of panspermia, then we are almost certainly surrounded by close cosmic cousins living on planets orbiting stars in our own galaxy – any attempt at panspermia would be unlikely to have infected only the earth. Any such cousins are of much greater importance to us than the common and very ancient ancestors we would share. These cousins may be at a similar stage in evolution to ourselves as they orbit on planets surrounding similarly aged stars. They may right now be busy building radiotelescopes, searching the skies for signs of life and sending out signals and space probes which might reach us at any moment, or may already be here.

Evolution from space

Fred Hoyle and his colleague Chandra Wickramasinghe suggest that infections from space are as relevant to living things now as they may have been to the first origins of life on earth. In a series of controversial and oft-ridiculed books and articles they have developed the thesis that life was not only sent to earth by intelligent civilizations elsewhere, but that it continues to arrive. They suggest that much of the evolution of life on earth is directed, not by the natural selection of chance mutations, but by the arrival of entire new genes from space at regular intervals, either as naked nucleic acid or carried within bacteria, viruses and possibly even insects.

According to Hoyle and Wickramasinghe, interstellar space is teeming with life, in the particles of 'dust' clouds, or 'molecular' clouds of interstellar space, or trapped within meteorites and comets. Every now and then the earth is showered with a new batch of these creatures, causing everything from new pandemics of diseases such as influenza, to dramatic leaps forward in evolution.

Anyone with a reasonable grounding in the modern theories of biology and evolution will find much to shake their heads sadly at as they venture through Hoyle and Wickramasinghe's writings. These two physicists have a breathtaking ability to misunderstand completely the biological arguments they seek to demolish, leading them triumphantly (and correctly) to denounce as nonsense ideas that no biologist has ever been crazy enough to propose. But we should beware! Diamonds come from piles of rocky rubbish; and of course, almost all the current tenets of science have in their time been dismissed as laughable, or even dangerous, drivel.

Fortunately, Hoyle and Wickramasinghe's controversial version of panspermia is one of the most testable of all the ideas concerning the origins of life. If Hoyle and Wickramasinghe are correct, life is arriving on earth from space virtually all of the time. So all we need to do is look for it.

Hoyle and Wickramasinghe base much of their argument on 'absorption spectra' that record which frequencies of starlight are absorbed as it passes through interstellar dust. By comparing the spectra of starlight that has passed through interstellar dust with the spectra of important biological compounds, they claim that interstellar dust contains large amounts of living things based on a similar biochemistry to our own. Most other astronomers could hardly disagree more violently. They contend that the spectra Hoyle and Wickramasinghe so proudly display are simply what would be expected from interstellar dust grains containing ice, or amorphous hydrocarbons, or various inorganic minerals.

The poor layman or other outsider does not know who to believe, but the argument seems very soluble. Wait a few more years as the resolution of our radio-telescopes and other instruments improves, and we shall surely know whether Hoyle and Wickramasinghe are startlingly correct or hopelessly wrong. There may well be lots of unexpectedly complex organic chemicals out in space, but are they a part of living things, or are they simply the universal precursors that can only give rise to life when they alight upon some suitable planet such as the early earth? If, over the next few decades, exploration of the depths of space continues to reveal only a barren lifeless wilderness, then the search for life's origins will become focused increasingly down upon the earth we know so well.

Clues from biology

Even if space does turn out to be completely barren, the advocates of 'directed panspermia' such as Crick and Orgel, who suggest that life may have been sent out from elsewhere only once and long ago, are unlikely to give up. In the absence of any evidence out in space, they turn to the living world of today to support their unorthodox ideas. Consider, for example, the fundamental 'uniformities' at the heart of all forms of life on earth today. Every creature on earth uses nucleic acids to store its genetic information, and they all appear to use the same basic genetic code (although a few fairly trivial variations have turned up quite recently). That genetic code directs the production of proteins using the same set of 20 amino acids in all organisms, and the amino acids are always in the 'left-handed' form, while the sugars in the backbones of all genes are always 'right-handed'. There are no creatures using right-handed amino acids and left-handed sugars, or left or right-handed forms of both these basic constituents of life, although organisms built along such lines could possibly function perfectly well.

These are just the most central of many such biochemical uniformities. Whenever we look deep into the workings of the great diversity of living things on earth, from dandelions to dragonflies, barracudas to bacteria, we find that all life adheres to the one basic biochemical plan. Evolution has certainly garnished the basic plan with many rich embellishments, but in essence we are all machines based on genes that encode proteins and use them to achieve different ends in remarkably similar ways.

This remarkable uniformity is usually attributed to the presumed descent of all modern creatures from one common ancestral form. This common ancestor need not have been the first or only form of life around on the early earth, indeed it almost certainly was not; but it would have been the most successful, a success that allowed its progeny to drive all competing lines of descent to extinction (see figure 7.1). According to this tale, the most recent common ancestor of all modern life might have itself been quite a sophisticated and highly evolved form. It may have been a particular type of cell that had to compete with other cells using different genes, different genetic codes, differently 'handed' molecules and so on. But of all the alternative solutions to the fundamental problems of life, only one survived to father the life on earth today – presumably because it was much better at surviving and 'fathering' than all the rest.

This might sound a nice neat and plausible tale, but many scientists retain lingering doubts. If there is one lesson that our investigations into biology should teach us, it is the scope for *diversity* within the living world. Viable ecological 'niches' exist for millions upon millions of different creatures, even though some might seem rather 'useless' or very 'inferior' compared to most others. In many ways we are pretty feeble and helpless creatures ourselves, compared to plants which can harness the energy of the sun directly to make virtually

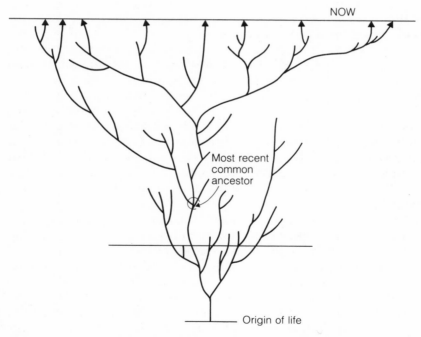

Figure 7.1   All life on earth today may be derived from a common ancestral species of cell in which the major aspects of modern biochemistry had already been perfected and fixed.

everything they need. Of course plants might be considered inferior because they can neither move nor think (presumably). When it comes to reproductive success, then all higher organisms are hopeless compared with bacteria or viruses.

So is it really feasible to imagine that only the one basic biochemical plan could have had such an advantage over all others that it drove them all to complete extinction? Is it not more likely that the astonishing uniformity of modern biochemistry indicates that there only ever was the one plan available, because we are all derived from the one type of microorganism which reached the earth from space? Since this initial invader would already be the product of a lengthy evolution, its way of doing things would already be both efficient and firmly set. So further evolution from that stock would be restricted to exploiting the possibilities of the invader's own basic biochemical plan.

We could argue about such questions for ever (and perhaps people will), but it is certain that if modern biochemistry *was not* quite so uniform then we might be able to rest more contentedly with our ideas about the origin of life on earth. The fact that the biochemistry of all sorts of living cells is so uniform keeps alive the suspicion that it might never have had any choice.

Francis Crick, Leslie Orgel and others have also pointed to a few other features of modern biochemistry which might support the idea that life on earth is derived from the living things of somewhere else. For example, living things on earth use molybdenum – a very rare element on earth – to assist certain key enzyme reactions in ways which other more common elements might manage just as easily. So does this indicate that our ancestors lived on planets rich in molybdenum, in orbit around molybdenum-containing stars which we might be able to identify by sophisticated spectroscopy? Most scientists find this argument rather unconvincing, but it deserves a mention.

A more convincing piece of evidence in favour of panspermia would be the discovery of fossilized and fairly complex cells dating from a very early stage in the earth's history. The fossil record certainly tells us that any life that did 'seed' the earth from space must have been very small and simple. As we examine rocks of increasing age we find the fossils within them become increasingly small and simple. This is one of the major pieces of evidence supporting the idea that all modern life-forms have evolved from simpler forms over the ages. The earth is about 4600 million years old, and the earliest generally accepted fossilized cells are currently estimated to be about 3500 million years old. That leaves around one thousand million years for the first cells to arise, which many scientists think should have been quite sufficient. But if fossils of earlier and perhaps more complex cells could be found, then the established version of our origins might be in serious trouble. If fossilized cells continue to be discovered dating from earlier and earlier times, then it may begin to look as if there was insufficient time for life to originate all by itself on earth.

This is an area of great uncertainty and contention. In the first place, how can we possibly estimate how long would be sufficient for the first cells to arise? If a fossilized complex cell were discovered dating back to 4500 million years ago, there would probably be no shortage of scientists claiming that the 100 million years separating that fossil from the birth of the earth would have been plenty of time for cells to originate – after all, 100 million years is a very long time. A few scientists, such as Fred Hoyle, think that even the entire 4600 million years of the earth's history was insufficient time for the simplest of living cells to evolve by natural selection. Since we have failed so dismally to re-create the essential steps involved in the origin of cells containing genes that encode proteins, we have no objective way of resolving such disagreements.

Another problem in this area is that it is very difficult to be sure that 'cellular fossils' really are fossilized cells. A fossilized early single cell cannot be expected to look very different from bubbles or spherical crystals in rocks. We can get some assistance by examining and dating organic chemicals found associated with the 'fossils', but it may not be easy to distinguish traces of organic chemicals produced by living things from remnants of a non-living organic 'soup'. Many supposed 'fossilized cells' have later been dismissed as 'pseudofossils' such as bubbles or crystals. I doubt if we will ever get much certainty from the examination of the earliest fossilized 'cells', and the arguments will surely continue.

So where have we got to, at the end of this short chapter of colourful speculation? We have come nowhere near to reaching any firm conclusions, but hopefully it has introduced you to yet more ideas at odds with the conventional story of our origins, some of which are very hard to dismiss. Personally, I see no reason for assuming that life must have originated on the earth we now live upon. We must surely keep our minds open to all possibilities, at least until someone has convincingly re-created the spontaneous origin of life on earth, or until many more decades of searching allow the rest of the universe to be pronounced as definitely dead.

Since we are trying to keep our minds as open as possible, we certainly should not dismiss some other even more 'weird' ideas.

Many weird ideas of the past have become the 'self-evident common-sense truths' of the present. I have said nothing at all of the possibilities of life on earth coming from, or being overseen by, life that lives in places completely unknown to us, such as other unseen 'dimensions'. If there really are other dimensions to the universe which our humble 3-D selves can neither experience nor see, then our progenitors or our masters may be living right on top of us (as far as they are concerned). Imagine a totally flat two-dimensional microscopic creature living upon a (perfectly flat) laboratory bench. We could constantly peer down at it through our microscopes from the unknown heights of the third dimension, ready to casually destroy it in an instant. The creature itself would feel much more secure than it ought to – believing itself to be surrounded in all of *its* dimensions by only the interminable empty space of the surface of the bench.

We should not dismiss the possibilities of extra dimensions or other 'hidden spaces' simply because we have no experience of them – that would be like living in a desert and denying the possibility of sea. We live in a universe which we do not really understand, so how can we possibly be dogmatic about its nature?

When faced with such outlandish ideas as extradimensional 'gods' which made us and perhaps watch over us with interest, or mirth, or growing disdain, the idea that we might have originated from spores carried from elsewhere in our homely old 3-D world suddenly becomes one of the most comfortingly parochial possibilities of all!

8 From proteins to palaeobiologists

Nothing in biology makes sense except in the light of evolution.
Theodosius Dobzhansky

Most things are harder to get started than they are to keep going. This may also apply to life, and to all the major revolutions in the structure of life which have occurred between life's origin and the present day. It may well have taken hundreds of millions of years for the first replicating life-forms to arise on earth; but once here, they were here to stay, and their descendants now occupy almost every conceivable location on the surface of the planet.

The first living cells may have taken longer to arise than the first simple replicators, but once cells had arisen they must have multiplied at a pace which swamped non-cellular life to quick extinction. Multicellular creatures, made of groups of cells cooperating together, took much longer to appear (see figure 8.1). For about 80 per cent of the time that life has lived on the planet, it has been as only simple single cells; but when multicellular life did arise (perhaps about 1000 million years ago) it multiplied and diversified into ever more complex forms at astonishing speed. After 4000 million years of either lifeless or single-celled calm, the earth suddenly burst forth with massive creatures that swam and ran and flew across its surface, or noisily rustled and swayed as the wind disturbed the first grasslands and towering forests.

The story of life on earth (regardless of whether it originated here or arrived as interstellar spores) is a tale of explosive expansion and diversification. All the unbelievable complexity of the living world today has flourished from the simple seed of replicators which occasionally changed. Mindless evolution, driven by natural selection from a pool of undirected change, has generated the living minds

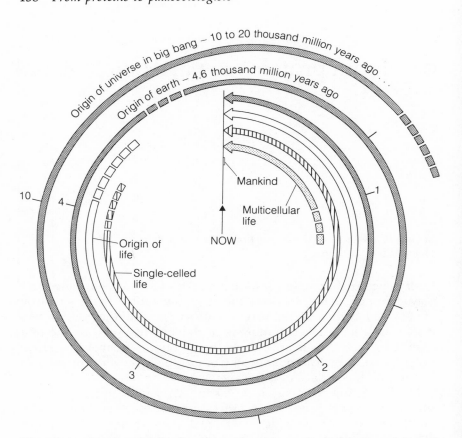

Figure 8.1   An approximate chronology of major events during the origin and evolution of life on earth. Figures indicate thousand million years ago.

which now ponder over the meaning and mechanism of it all. What further revolutions might these minds be about to begin? Perhaps not the minds of humans, who may be remembered as a first 'attempt' which failed; but the minds of something may soon (in evolutionary terms) set life on earth along a new and radically different course.

That is a topic for us to keep in mind for later. For the moment, the problem is to examine and explain the development of the diverse creatures of modern life from the earliest living forms. We are going to leave the origins of life on earth behind us, and examine how the simplest of cells containing genes that encoded proteins could have evolved into such complex multicellular, thinking, seeing and speaking beings as you and I.

In briefly considering the final step on the way up from chemicals up to us – the *evolution* of the earliest cells into modern life, I will largely abandon assessment and criticism to quickly relate the main features of the 'standard' tale. This is partly because this is a book about life's origin, rather than its evolution, but also because I personally accept that in general terms the standard tale about this stage is convincing and fairly secure.

The fossils' tale

Much of the material covered in this book is pure speculation about events which occurred an unbelievably long time ago, and which left no direct evidence for us to examine. As we turn away from life's origins, however, to examine its progressive evolution, things become steadily easier and more tangible. The rocks of the earth beneath and around us contain the remnants and traces of past life in the form of fossils, and the fossils have a clear and very stirring tale to tell. The clearest message of the fossils is that the history of life on earth has been one of slow progression from small and simple to bigger more advanced forms of life. The oldest rocks are the ones which contain the simplest, most primitive fossils. As we examine ever more recent rocks we find increasingly complex forms of life emerging. Single cells give way to sponges and multicellular algae and ferns; these become accompanied by small worms and jellyfish and shellfish; then fish appear, and amphibians, seed plants, trees, dinosaurs, birds and mammals such as man.

Regardless of what explanation you favour for the origin and development of life on earth, you must accept that as time has passed the earth has become populated with increasingly large and more complex organisms. Of course, this is precisely what would be expected if life has developed by evolution driven by natural selection, starting from some very simple ancestral forms. This first message of the fossils certainly does not prove that evolution was the mechanism that crafted modern life – it is possible to dream up all sorts of alternative tales, from a God who gradually stocked the earth with his increasingly complex creations, to extraterrestrials (or Gods) who 'planted' the fossil evidence just to tease us – but the fossil evidence is admirably consistent with the idea of evolution, and evolution is the only explanation of the fossil record that seems to make any sense.

It has been claimed that the theory of evolution is 'unscientific', because it could never be proved wrong. This is nonsense. The discovery of a single fossilized fish, or human or any other advanced creature in rocks laid down 4000 million years ago would demolish the evolutionary explanation of life overnight. There are infinite ways in which the theory of evolution could be proved wrong, by the discovery of fossils in rocks dating from times when scientists say these fossils could not possibly be – but no such fossils are found.

So where does the record of the fossils begin, and what does it tell us? I have already mentioned some of the problems met in trying to identify fossil evidence of the earliest single-celled forms of life (see plate 6). No doubt a few of the 'accepted' fossil cells of today are really 'pseudofossils' such as suggestively shaped bubbles and crystals in no way produced by life; and no doubt a few genuine cell fossils will be found but never properly identified as such. The oldest generally accepted fossil evidence of life is the layered structure of fossils known as 'stromatolites'. These date from about 3500 million years ago, and are believed to have been formed by mat-like colonies of single cells which gradually built up on top of one another, layer upon layer. Structures similar to this can be seen forming on earth to this day, and no non-living inorganic processes are known which could form similar structures.

So stromatolites suggest there were at least simple living cells around 3500 million years ago, just over 1000 million years after the origin of the earth. Many claims have been put forward for cellular fossils dating from earlier times, and a few are probably valid, but none have ever been convincingly proved. Living cells either originated on (or arrived on, or were put on) the earth within the first 1500 million years of its history.

As figure 8.1 illustrates, the fossil record tells us that life on earth consisted of nothing but single cells until about 1000 million years ago, so for around four-fifths of its history the earth has been populated by either nothing or tiny single cells, but during the later part of that lengthy single-celled era something very significant did happen, which probably paved the way for the evolution of multicellular life. The first cells were probably similar in size and structure to the modern bacteria. So they would have been very small and would have consisted of just one compartment in which everything was found together – DNA, RNA, proteins and so on. Cells like this are known as 'procaryotes'.

The cells from which you and I and all other 'higher organisms' (including plants) are constructed, are quite different. In the first place they are usually much larger, but more importantly they contain several membrane-bound sub-compartments or 'organelles', such as the nucleus, floating about inside the cytoplasm almost like 'cells within the cell'. Cells with this more complex, compartmentalized structure are known as 'eucaryotic' cells, and they cannot be found in the fossil record until just under 1500 million years ago

Very shortly after the appearance of the first eucaryotic cells, the fossils of simple multicellular organisms begin to be found. All of the multicellular organisms on earth today are composed of eucaryotic cells, and combined with the appearance of multicellular life so soon after the first eucaryotic cells, this suggests that the origin of eucaryotic cells was the crucial step needed to set multicellular evolution on its way.

The earliest fossil evidence of multicellular animal life comes in the form of 'traces' of their activity, such as the burrows and trails left by simple worm-like creatures, dating from around 700 million years ago. Next, in rocks just over 600 million years old, we begin to find fossilized jellyfish and worms; and around the time that these fossils were being formed a major step forward in evolution which would greatly assist the fossil hunters was taking place – hard skeletons were appearing. Skeletons make much more obvious and durable fossils than those left by the soft-bodied earlier forms of life, so from the date of their origin our knowledge of the evolution of life (or at least of the life-forms that had skeletons) becomes much more detailed and secure.

The first marine vertebrates (i.e. animals with backbones) such as fish began to appear about 550 million years ago. By 350 million years ago these had given rise to the first amphibians able to crawl across the surface of the land. In the meantime, that land had become colonized with large multicellular plants, which first appear in the fossil record about 400 million years ago. The land's first amphibian animal invaders gave rise to reptiles, about 300 million years ago, and then true land-dwelling mammals about 200 million years ago. The mighty dinosaurs came and went between 175 and 75 million years ago, and during their reign they saw the first flowering plants.

With the end of the dinosaurs, the mammals became dominant among the larger creatures of the land, although still far outnumbered by the insects; and then in only the last few million years of over 3500 million years of continuous evolution, primates and eventually humans arrived on the scene. Human history is just a very few million years old – a mere fraction of the time for which the dinosaurs were dominant.

During the long course of evolution from the first life through to us, a series of major novelties have transformed the life that possessed them. The first novelty was probably the cell itself, then the eucaryotic cell, then the ability of eucaryotic cells to multiply by sexual reproduction and to cluster together into multicellular life. Next comes the specialization of the cells of multicellular life into different types, each performing a different function. The development of a body cavity or 'coelom', and of skeletons or shells, and muscles and nerves. The ability to swim and to bite, and to see and hear, then to walk and give birth on land rather than in the sea, are all further major developments. As animals were acquiring all these new complexities, plants (which had inherited the vital 'trick' of photosynthesis from far back in the earliest days of single-celled life), were beginning to produce seeds and pollen and flowers. And gradually, throughout it all, the first simple forms of chemical 'sensitivity' were giving rise to nerves and complex nervous systems which eventually became endowed with those intangible complexities we call consciousness and thought. How all this happened through the natural selection of chance variations in the structure of genetic materials is what biologists must try to explain, or at least describe.

Mechanisms of change

The living creatures of the earth are alive because they contain genes that encode proteins, which make each organism into what it is – a man, a fish, a mouse, a bacterium, or whatever. The mechanisms which power the evolution of one type of creature, such as a human, from a different earlier form, such as an ape, must work largely by changing the protein molecules which the organisms possess. Of course the complement of protein molecules possessed by any one organism is determined by the genetic material it receives from its ancestors. So the mechanisms that power evolution work by changing genetic material.

Any change in genetic material can be described as a 'mutation', and if that mutation is handed on to future generations then these generations will consist of 'mutant' individuals, relative to the previous form. From the 1950s onwards, scientists have discovered an increasingly wide range of ways in which genetic changes can be generated, and they continue to uncover new ways to this day. I want to quickly show you some of the most important mechanisms of genetic change known to be at work within modern cells (see figure 8.2). Some of these would not have been available to the very first cells, but many of them would. In any case, you will soon realize that there must have been plenty of opportunity for the very first cells to evolve into new and ever more complex and efficient forms of life.

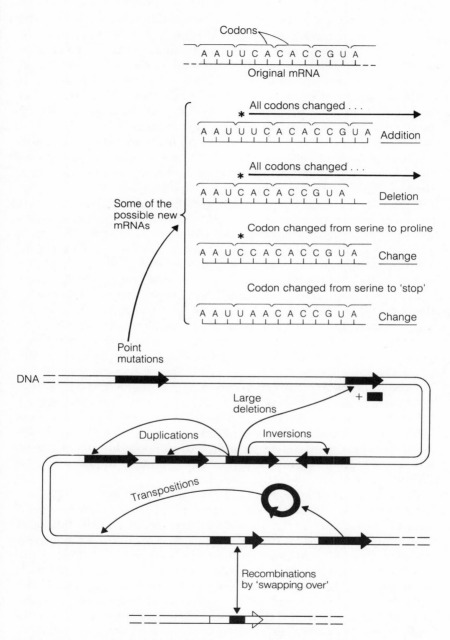

Figure 8.2   Some mechanisms of genetic change (see text for details).

The simplest sort of genetic change, and therefore one likely to have been important during the first days of life, is known as a 'point mutation', bringing about a single change in the base sequence of DNA (or RNA, or any other nucleic acid) at one particular point. The simplest mechanism by which point mutations can be generated involves chance mistakes in the process of nucleic acid replication, mistakes which can be encouraged by various chemicals able to act as 'mutagens', or by various forms of radiation. Nothing in life or chemistry is perfect, and every so often a nucleotide carrying the 'wrong' base can be incorporated into a replicating nucleic acid chain. This can give rise to a 'daughter' DNA molecule that differs by one base from its progenitor. That might not seem to be much of a change, but it can be very significant indeed.

Obviously a single base change like this could change a codon encoding one particular amino acid into one encoding a quite different amino acid (the mutation would occur in the DNA of a modern cell, but its effect on protein manufacture would obviously be expressed through the mRNA which the DNA gave rise to). The codon 'UCA', encoding serine, for example, might change into 'CCA', encoding proline. This might drastically alter the activities of the protein encoded by the gene containing the mutation, especially if the changed amino acid appeared at a critical site. Proline, for example, is an amino acid which tends to induce a sharp bend in a protein chain, a bend which would not have been present in the original form.

More dramatically, the serine codon 'UCA' might be changed into UAA, which does not encode an amino acid at all, but indicates the point on a gene at which protein coding should stop. The appearance of this new 'stop' signal in the middle of a gene would at a stroke generate a new gene coding for a protein composed of only the first half of the original one. This truncated protein might act quite differently from its full-length progenitor.

Both of these examples have involved the replacement of one base for another, but mistakes during the replication or maintenance of genes can also lead to the addition or deletion of a nucleotide (and therefore of a base). This can have a very drastic effect on the protein encoded by a gene, because it alters all of the codons following the mutation. Genetic information consists of a series of codons, each composed of three bases which encode a particular amino acid. If a nucleotide (and its carried base) is either added or deleted at some point in a gene, then all of the bases following the mutation, up to the end of the gene, will be read as an entirely new sequence of codons as the ribosome marches blindly along the mRNA copy of the gene.

Such changes are known as 'frameshift' mutations, since they alter all subsequent codons by changing the 'frame' in which the corresponding mRNA is read (see top of figure 8.2 for clarification). So despite being caused by the addition or loss of only a single nucleotide, frameshift mutations can drastically change a gene into another form encoding a protein that is completely different from the site of the mutation onwards.

Many of the other changes that can be inflicted upon genetic material are catalysed by various proteins, although some of them could probably happen to a lesser extent without any help from proteins. The fact that they are often catalysed, does not necessarily mean that they are beneficial or 'desirable' from the point of view of the cell. Many might best be regarded as occasional mistakes brought about by the activity of proteins that can cut and reseal genetic material. Thus whole sections of DNA can become duplicated, deleted, or 'inverted' (see figure 8.2). Sometimes long sections of DNA can break loose or be copied from a cell's genetic material, to wander free for a while before becoming re-incorporated elsewhere, a process known as 'transposition'. And sections of DNA, especially those with broadly similar base sequences, can often change places with one another in a process known as 'recombination' or 'swapping over'.

The mechanisms of all these possible changes in genetic material are often quite complicated and not always well known. There is no point in us troubling about them here. For our purposes the important point is that there are lots of ways for pieces of DNA or RNA to change, grow larger, grow smaller and recombine to form an infinite variety of different sequences which could code for an infinite variety of proteins. Once nucleic acids had begun to replicate and code for primitive proteins, the way would have been open for them to give rise to increasingly larger and more diverse nucleic acids encoding an increasingly large battery of different proteins. And remember, the changes which drove this diversification forward would not have been *directed* in any way towards the production of ever more complex and efficient forms of life. The direction would have been imposed by natural selection – selecting only those changes that happened to produce more efficient forms of life, and rejecting all the rest.

Nucleic acids are coded molecular messages which can replicate and gradually change. Their messages are deciphered into a molecular language which uses an alphabet of 20 letters, since nucleic acid codons can code for any one of 20 amino acids, and the messages can be several hundred 'letters' long (i.e. proteins can be composed of hundreds of amino acids strung together). Our own alphabet, of a similar number of letters, can be used to construct a virtual infinity of sentences and phrases all hundreds of letters long, so perhaps you can appreciate how the genetic alphabet also manages to 'say enough' to construct all sorts of different and sometimes very complex living forms. Let's look at some major events in the evolution of the molecular messages of life.

The first proteins

Nobody will ever know what went on within the first cells, but we can certainly identify some of the problems they might have faced and how they might have been solved. I am now assuming that simple cells have somehow formed, containing nucleic acids that can not only replicate, but have also learned the 'trick' of encoding proteins of defined sequence. This advanced state of affairs may well have been preceded by an extended phase of evolution in which nucleic acids such as RNA were the only biological catalysts, assisted by the catalytic effects of various ions and small organic molecules.

The most vital jobs performed by living things involve the replication, maintenance and decoding of their genetic material. So some of the earliest proteins may well have acted to improve the efficiency of these processes: perhaps catalysing gene replication and protein synthesis to make them quicker and more precise. Many of the other main problems faced by the earliest cells might well have involved keeping their membranes intact, well maintained, and able to enlarge and divide in two during cell division. Some of the earliest proteins might have served a rather uninteresting structural role, perhaps forming a scaffold-like framework to keep the contents of the cell together in a neat bundle for the membrane to surround. The membrane would also have acted as a barrier to the entry of some needed chemical supplies, so ways would have been required to transport such supplies into the cell, and transport waste products out. 'Transport proteins' could be expected to have evolved and been found embedded in the cell membrane, from where they could bind to wanted supplies, and bring them in, and bind to unwanted wastes and send them out. Modern cells are equipped with a diverse battery of such proteins which exert constant and very precise control over the chemical environment within a cell.

As cells became more complex and acquired genes encoding an increasing diversity of proteins, it would have become increasingly important for these proteins to be made at appropriate times and in

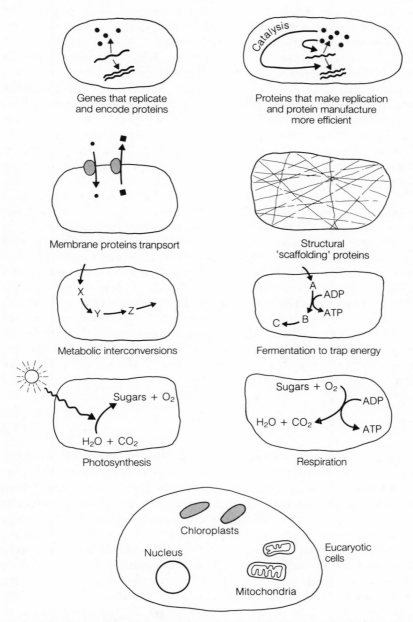

Genes that replicate
and encode proteins

Proteins that make replication
and protein manufacture
more efficient

Membrane proteins tranpsort

Structural
'scaffolding' proteins

Metabolic interconversions

Fermentation to trap energy

Photosynthesis

Respiration

Eucaryotic
cells

Figure 8.3   Some of the major novelties that have changed the first cells into the complex cells of modern life.

appropriate amounts. Thus the first gene-regulating proteins would have arisen – proteins that allowed a battery of different genes to serve a common end (the 'good' of the cell), by switching the available genes on and off as appropriate.

I have been assuming that the very first forms of life were able to find all of their chemical supplies in the surrounding 'soup'. It is often assumed that such supplies (amino acids, bases, sugars, nucleotides etc.) must have originally been quite abundant, but this may well be an unsound assumption. There is no obvious geological record of the legendary 'primordial soup', in the form of seams of primordial 'coal' or wells of prebiotic oil. If it did exist, it may have been extremely dilute, or concentrated in only a few small and scarce locations, or have existed for a very short time.

Regardless of how plentiful or poor the initial source of chemical supplies was, there must undoubtedly have come a time during the first flourishing of life when the supplies would certainly have been scarce. Living things will always multiply until the supplies needed for that multiplication become scarce. So cells would begin to evolve proteins that catalysed the formation of chemicals needed by the cells, using more abundant, or more basic or less directly useful natural chemicals as their raw materials. In other words, cells would gradually acquire the proteins needed for 'metabolism' – the interconversion of chemicals within a living cell. As the abilities of early metabolism developed, and cells became able to perform an increasing variety of useful chemical interconversions, so the very first 'energy crisis' would probably have arisen.

Getting the energy

In many of the chemicals found in living things, atoms are arranged in ways that are not the 'most stable', lowest energy configurations. Up till now, I have assumed that the dispersal of radiant energy from the sun (or the energy of volcanism, lightning storms, meteorite impact etc.) served to drive these atoms up into the higher energy configurations of some of the molecules needed for life. Relying so directly on the effects of such energy sources would have been very inefficient and restricting. Any cells that became able to trap and store chemical energy in some way, so that it could then be used to drive useful but energetically unfavourable reactions forward as and when required, would have had a great advantage over their competitors.

We can draw an analogy with a man using a water wheel driven by a fickle stream to power some task, and worrying about the days when the stream is dry, the power that is wasted as he lies asleep at night, and his inability to control the rate of supply. If he constructed a pump and linked it up to the water wheel to lift some of the water up into a raised storage tank day and night when the stream was full, then a considerably increased and more adaptable power supply would be assured. The water in the tank could be allowed to run down at a controllable rate and drive another wheel as and when the power was needed.

The first cells might have 'tried out' lots of different ways of trapping chemical energy in a reusable form, but one system seems to have been better than all the others, because all energy capture and supply problems are nowadays met by a chemical known as ATP, or occasionally by its close chemical relatives.

The chemical structure of ATP (adenosine triphosphate) is well worth looking at, because as you can see in figure 8.4 it is one of the nucleotides found in RNA, with two extra phosphate groups

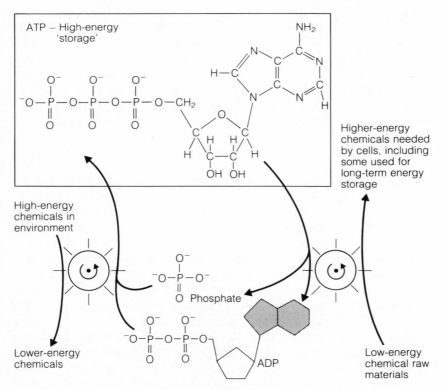

Figure 8.4   Cells can capture energy in the form of ATP.

attached. This is only one of the many clues which suggest that RNA might have been intimately involved in the origin of life, not only as a candidate for the first genetic material, but in other ways as well.

ATP corresponds to the cell's initial 'storage tank' of metabolic energy, because its sequence of three linked phosphate groups is rather a high energy configuration. An ATP molecule can react with water to form ADP (adenosine diphosphate), and a free phosphate group, which together comprise a lower energy configuration for the atoms involved. Remember that what I am really saying here is that the electromagnetic forces between electrons and protons are less resisted or 'violated' overall in ADP plus a free phosphate, than they are when these two are joined together into ATP.

Evolution has provided cells with enzymes that can exploit this energy difference between ATP and ADP in the following way. Relatively high energy chemicals taken in from the environment can be allowed to rearrange themselves into different lower energy forms. Instead of letting all the energy released in these reactions dissipate away as heat, the enzymes can use some of it to manufacture ATP from ADP and phosphate ions (this is like using the energy of running water to pump some water up into a storage tank – see figure 8.4). The energy captured by ATP can be kept within a cell until energy is required to drive some desired reaction forward. Enzymes have evolved which can couple the breakdown of ATP to the manufacture of a wide variety of desired high energy chemicals. Thus as the ATP is degraded back into ADP and phosphate, some of the energy released is used to convert low-energy raw materials into higher-energy chemicals needed by the cell.

ATP has been called the 'energy currency' of living cells, because it can be made at certain times and places by reactions that give out energy (just as we make money at work), and then used to make energy-requiring reactions happen as desired (just as we use money to get other people to work for us as desired). The evolution of enzymes able to generate ATP during the breakdown of plentiful high-energy chemicals in the environment, and then couple the later breakdown of that ATP to the manufacture of high-energy chemicals needed by the cell, was one of the greatest ever advances in evolution. It began the process of freeing cells from their dependence on an unreliable source of natural supplies. As long as they could find sufficient chemicals to power the production of ATP, they could then use that ATP to manufacture virtually anything they required. They soon began to store the energy of ATP by using it to generate high-energy chemicals that could be degraded to regenerate ATP when required. The starch of rice and potatoes, or the fat around your waist, are two present-day examples of such energy storage in action. Starch and fat are long-term high-energy 'deposits' that cells can convert their ATP 'currency' into, to be converted back into ATP when the need arises.

For a detailed example of ATP energy capture in action, we can turn to the yeast cells which convert grape juice into wine. The yeast cells produce enzymes which convert the plentiful sugar of the grape into alcohol, by catalysing a series of reactions which give out energy. Rather than all the energy being lost to the environment as heat, yeast enzymes ensure that some of it is used to convert ADP into ATP.

The involvement of one of the most important enzymes is illustrated in figure 8.5. The enzyme concerned catalyses the transfer

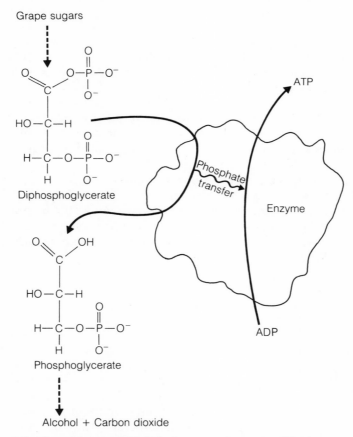

Figure 8.5   One of the steps by which, in yeasts, the energy of the grape can be used to generate ATP, plus alcohol and carbon dioxide 'wastes' (see text for details).

of a phosphate group from one of the breakdown products of the sugar ('diphosphoglycerate') onto ADP. If the conversion of diphos-phoglycerate into phosphoglycerate took place freely in water, then the energy difference between these two compounds would be given out as heat. By catalysing the transfer of the phosphate onto ADP rather than letting it escape into the surrounding solution, the enzyme ensures that some of the energy is trapped as ATP. It acts a bit like a water wheel, trapping some of the energy of the passing water. The ATP made in this and other reactions during the conversion of sugar into alcohol, is used by the yeast cells to power all of the energy-requiring reactions involved in their growth and multiplication. To the yeast, ATP is the prize of its exploitation of grape sugars, while the alcohol which the sugars are eventually turned into is an unwanted waste. To us, of course, the alcohol is the prize! (Or the carbon dioxide gas if we are bakers.)

Enzyme reactions such as the one we have just looked at would have been a tremendous help to the earliest cells, but they still would have left the cells dependent on supplies of some fairly complex raw materials from the environment. There would not have been any vines around to manufacture abundant supplies of high-energy sugars, for example. Instead, the cells would depend on sufficient supplies of such chemicals being formed spontaneously by the action of the sun's heat and light, or by other sources of energy such as volcanoes.

The next great step forward in the evolution of the first proteins, would have been the gradual refinement of proteins that allowed cells to trap the sun's energy directly and use it to power the manufacture of all the cells' chemical needs from very simple raw materials. The next great step, in other words, would have been the origin of 'photosynthesis'.

Plugging in to the sun

The green plants of the modern earth can use the light energy flooding down on them from the sun to power all of the chemistry that keeps them alive. This ability to 'plug in' directly to the sun, makes plants and photosynthetic bacteria the most self-reliant creatures on the planet. Given enough sunlight and suitable temperatures, plants can survive and flourish on only water, carbon dioxide, and a few simple inorganic minerals. They do this largely thanks to various 'pigment' molecules, especially the 'chlorophyll' which makes plants green, and a series of proteins. The pigments, such as chlorophyll, are chemicals that can absorb the radiant energy of the sun in a way which briefly kicks an electron out of the molecule to form an energized (or 'excited') complex consisting of an electron and the remainder of the chlorophyll (now positively charged due to the loss of the electron – see figure 8.6).

If the chlorophyll molecule is floating about free within a watery solution, the electron will soon settle back into place and the energy absorbed from the sunlight will be released again as heat and light (in the form of 'fluorescence'). In photosynthetic organisms, however,

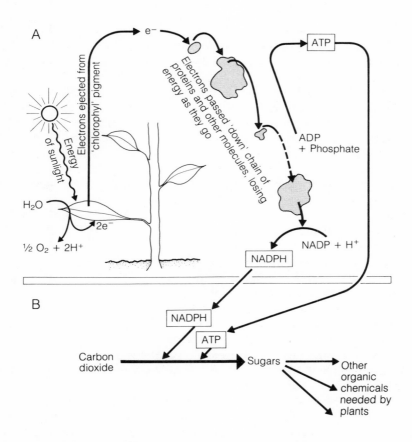

Figure 8.6   A much simplified summary of photosynthesis, in which the energy of sunlight powers the manufacture of ATP and NADPH (and the release of oxygen from water). The ATP and NADPH is then used, along with carbon dioxide gas, to generate sugars – the organic raw material of all plant life.

such electrons are not allowed to fall back. Instead, proteins and other, simpler, molecules are arranged around chlorophyll molecules to channel the electrons away (see figure 8.6A). They eventually end up in a type of molecule called NADPH, which is basically a carrier of hydrogen atoms. NADPH is another important chemical related to the nucleotides found in RNA.

As electrons pass along the chain of proteins and other molecules towards NADPH, they gradually settle down into less energetic arrangements. As they do so, the energy they previously held is trapped in the form of ATP. The details of how all this happens are rather complex, and have been much simplified here to highlight the general principle. Energy from the sun simply energizes electrons, kicking them out of chlorophyll into a high-energy state. Proteins and other molecules catch hold of the freed electrons and allow them to fall back down to a low-energy state, trapping some of the energy as ATP in the process.

From what has been said so far, it is obvious that ATP and the hydrogen carrier called NADPH are two of the products of plant photosynthesis. Figure 8.6A shows you that another product is oxygen gas (O_2), formed when water molecules are split to provide the electrons that recharge chlorophyll molecules and make them ready for another round of excitation. So far then, the net effect of photosynthesis appears to be the release of oxygen from water and the production of ATP and NADPH, all powered by the light energy of the sun. The ATP and NADPH are then used to drive forward the manufacture of all the organic chemicals needed for a plant to survive and grow.

The basic raw material for this next stage is carbon dioxide gas (see figure 8.6B). This is combined (rather indirectly) with the hydrogen atoms carried by NADPH, using the energy supplied by ATP, to produce various sugars, which then serve as the organic raw material to construct all the other chemicals of the living plant. Other required types of atoms, such as nitrogen and sulphur, are supplied by the mineral nutrients taken in through a plant's roots, and the energy-requiring steps of all this complex metabolic activity are powered by the ATP formed during the first stage of photosynthesis.

Figure 8.6 shows that the overall effect of photosynthesis is to use water and carbon dioxide to form sugars (i.e. carbohydates) and oxygen gas, all powered by the energy of sunlight. The very first photosynthetic cells are actually believed to have used hydrogen sulphide (H_2S) in place of water, but eventually some cells turned to the abundant supplies of water and began to release large amounts of oxygen gas as an unwanted waste. The generation of free oxygen gas by the first water-using photosynthesizers initiated great changes in the chemistry and biology of the earth. Oxygen is a very reactive, high-energy, chemical. At first it would have reacted with various other chemicals in the primordial waters, such as iron ions, various organic chemicals, and many others; but eventually it would have begun to accumulate in the waters, and then eventually as free oxygen gas in the atmosphere.

Reacting to oxygen

Oxygen gas currently accounts for about 21 per cent of the volume of the earth's atmosphere, and virtually all of that oxygen is believed to be released by the activity of photosynthetic organisms. The free oxygen first began to accumulate in significant amounts about 1800 million years ago. One if its most dramatic effects on the earth's chemistry would have been the production of the 'ozone' layer at the outer limits of the atmosphere. Ozone (O_3) is formed from oxygen by the action of ultra-violet light, and once formed it absorbs that ultra-violet light and so prevents it from reaching the earth below. So with the arrival of photosynthesis, the supply of ultra-violet radiation to the primordial waters would have steadily diminished. Since many of the chemical reactions taking place in these waters might previously have been driven by the ultra-violet energy, the arrival of oxygen might have drastically altered the chemical environment of the earth's surface, not simply by reacting with various chemicals directly, but also by putting an end to reactions driven by ultra-violet radiation.

Living things which depended on ultra-violet-generated chemicals as raw materials might thus have been put in great jeopardy by the origin of photosynthesis, but a much more direct threat to life would have been the oxygen itself. We are used to thinking of oxygen as a life-supporting chemical, because we are descended from organisms that survived the arrival of oxygen on the planet and which put it to good use, but to many of the earliest living cells oxygen would have been a highly reactive and deadly poison. So the origin of photo-synthesis and the release of oxygen would have posed a great threat to all forms of life other than the cells that actually released the oxygen – by acting as a poison directly, by reacting with many organic and inorganic chemicals to alter the chemical environment around living things, and by forming an ozone layer which prevented most of the sun's ultra-violet radiation from reaching the earth's surface.

A great many of the earlier types of cells were probably driven to extinction by this major global revolution, while the survivors must have adapted to the arrival of oxygen by acquiring proteins that protected them from its harmful effects and allowed them to circumvent the chemical changes the oxygen brought about. Some survived simply by retreating into the few parts of the environment that the oxygen couldn't reach.

The history of evolution reveals that most great environmental changes bring both threats and opportunities to the creatures of the earth. The threats posed by the arrival of oxygen have been outlined above, and they no doubt led to the disappearance of many branches of the tree of early life, but an opportunity lay in the very chemical reactivity which made oxygen such a threat. We have already seen that some energy can be extracted from chemicals such as sugars by coupling their degradation into lower energy forms to the manufacture of ATP. The arrival of oxygen presented much greater energy-yielding possibilities, because the reaction of oxygen with organic chemicals, such as sugars, releases much more energy than the 'non-oxidative' reactions living things would previously have utilized.

Sugars can react with oxygen to yield carbon dioxide and water. This is essentially a reversal of what happens during photosynthesis, and since the sun's energy is needed to drive photosynthesis forwards, energy is *released* when the reaction is allowed to move in reverse. So when some cells began to use the sun's energy to produce sugars and other organic chemicals from carbon dioxide gas and water, other cells became able to reverse this process and trap the energy released at ATP. This is not achieved by a literal reversal of all the steps of photosynthesis, but is catalysed by a whole new battery of enzymes which would have been acquired and perfected by gradual evolution. The process they catalyse is known as 'respiration', and the organisms that performed photosynthesis also learned to catalyse the reverse process of respiration when required. Thus, photosynthesis could be used to produce the sugars and other chemicals needed for growth; but if they were made in excess, some could be converted back into carbon dioxide and water to provide energy when required.

Figure 8.7 can be used to distinguish between the two main types of cell and organism present on the earth today, as far as their energy transactions are concerned. The most versatile are the plants, which can perform both photosynthesis and respiration. This allows them to make the organic chemicals they need from water, carbon dioxide and various simple minerals, all powered by sunlight; but they can also degrade the excess products of photosynthesis by respiration, to

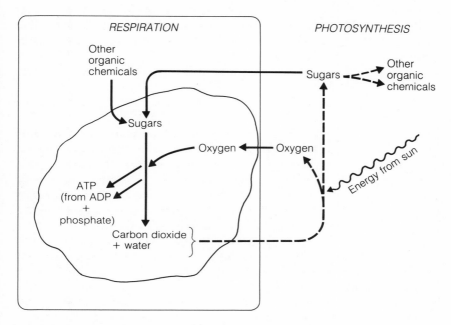

Figure 8.7   In photosynthesis, the sun's energy is used to make sugars and release oxygen (dashed lines). In respiration, sugars are reacted with oxygen to release energy, which is trapped as ATP (solid lines).

make the ATP that serves as a more controllable and adaptable source of energy than direct sunlight. Animal cells, such as our own, are much less versatile. They are able to catalyse respiration alone. This allows them to survive and multiply provided they can obtain plentiful supplies of sugars and other chemicals by eating plants (or by eating other animals that live off plants). Animals are entirely dependent on plants to initially harness the energy of sunlight and produce the chemicals they need both for growth and the production of energy.

Animals (and other non-photosynthetic forms of life) might in one sense seem 'smarter' than plants, since they get the plants to do the energy-trapping chemistry for them, but this has made them totally dependent on plants to power their own lives. Plants could survive on earth without animals, but animals are totally dependent on the photosynthetic plants.

The modern earth also carries some simpler cells that continue to get their energy from the ATP-generating processes utilized before photosynthesis and respiration evolved. These include many microorganisms which degrade organic chemicals into lower energy forms without combining them with oxygen, a process which has become known as 'fermentation', of which the alcohol-producing activities of yeasts is only one example.

Cellular cooperatives

The origin of photosynthesis was undoubtedly one of the great revolutions in the history of life, allowing living things to 'plug in' directly to the energy of the sun and use it to power the chemistry of life. Two of the other major revolutions seem to have come very closely one after the other. Firstly, eucaryotic cells containing a nucleus and other internal 'organelles' arose, and then very quickly were found clustered together into multicellular organisms.

The most important compartment or organelle of the eucaryotic cell is the nucleus – a membrane-bound vesicle containing the vast majority of a eucaryotic cell's genetic material (see figure 8.8). In modern eucaryotes the DNA is split into several distinct bundles known as chromosomes. The other major organelles carried by eucaryotes are the 'mitochondria' (several or many per cell), whose main function is to perform the process of respiration which yields most of a cell's ATP. During the degradation of sugars in a eucaryote, the simpler, more ancient process of fermentation takes place first of all in the cell cytoplasm, and then the end products are passed into the mitochondria where they are completely degraded by respiration to carbon dioxide and water with the production of ATP.

Plant cells also contain organelles known as 'chloroplasts' in which photosynthesis takes place. The radiant energy of sunlight is trapped by chlorophyll and other pigments embedded in an internal membrane of the chloroplasts, and used to drive the production of ATP and NADPH, with the accompanying release of oxygen from water. The ATP and NADPH are then used to incorporate carbon dioxide into sugars, and then on into various other chemicals (such as amino acids) needed by the cell.

There were always two clear alternative explanations for the origin of eucaryotic cells. Firstly, they could have formed quite independently of the simpler 'procaryotes' (i.e. cells lacking a nucleus or any other intracellular organelles). Secondly, they might have formed when two or more procaryotes 'came together' to form larger cellular 'cooperatives'. This last explanation is now very much the vogue, and there are various strong clues suggesting that it is probably correct. Both mitochondria and chloroplasts show very close

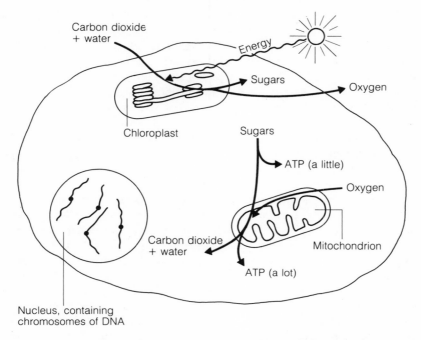

Figure 8.8 The three main organelles of eucaryotic cells – the nucleus, the mitochondrion and the chloroplasts (plant cells only).

resemblances to simpler 'free-living' procaryotes such as bacteria. They both contain a little of their own DNA, encoding a few proteins; and they both reproduce by dividing in two, just like cells. Also, chloroplasts share many subtle similarities with modern free-living photosynthetic bacteria, while mitochodria share similarities with some non-photosynthetic bacteria which get their energy by respiration.

Clues such as these have led scientists to believe that eucaryotic cells arose in the following sort of way: With the origin of photosynthesis many of the pre-existing species of cell would have died out, while some must have slowly adapted to survive the effects of oxygen, and then to use it in respiration. Some of the simpler, more ancient cells (which perhaps survived by living in regions where the oxygen concentration was low) may eventually have gained some protection from oxygen by engulfing smaller cells capable of respiration. The respiring cells would be protected and nourished by their larger hosts, while mopping up the oxygen which would damage these hosts. Thus a stable and mutually beneficial 'symbiotic' relationship could have arisen. The small respiring cells would have evolved into mitochondria, while any photosynthetic cells that were later engulfed and added to the 'cooperative' could have evolved into the chloroplasts of plants. The accumulated evidence makes it seem almost certain that events something like this must have brought about the origin of the eucaryotes, although obviously the precise details will never be known.

At the same time as mitochodria and chloroplasts were evolving, the emerging eucaryote cells were presumably beginning to package their DNA into separate chromosomes and enclose it within a membrane to form the nucleus.

In a sense then, the earliest eucaryotic cells might have been the first 'multicellular' forms of life, composed of small cells *contained within* larger ones. That is not what we mean by 'multicellular' now, referring instead to aggregates of many individual cells bound together to form a larger living thing; but since all modern multicellular organisms are composed of eucaryotic cells, and since multicellular life appears in the fossil record very soon after the first single-celled eucaryotes, it seems that something about eucaryotic cells enabled the evolution of multicellular life to get under way. What could it have been? One of the favourite possibilities is the ability of eucaryotic cells to multiply by sexual reproduction rather than simply by dividing in two. So what is sexual reproduction, and why might it have initiated the evolution of multicellular life?

Sex – for variety or stability?

You were created by the sexual union of your father and your mother, a fact which immediately demonstrates one of the major differences between sexual reproduction and asexual forms of reproduction such as splitting in two – organisms produced by sexual reproduction have two parents, rather than only one, and they inherit genetic information from both. When a cell (or any organism) reproduces asexually by splitting in two, the daughter cells will have identical genomes apart from the occasional changes induced by mutations that affect only one of them. Asexual reproduction produces endless generations of virtually identical organisms which can only evolve by the slow accumulation of new mutations. The offspring of sexual reproduction, on the other hand, are always very different from their parents, partly because their genomes contain genes drawn from two unrelated individuals. Consider what happened when you were made . . .

You are derived from a single fertilized egg cell which formed when a sperm cell produced by your father fused with an egg cell from your mother (see figure 8.9). Each of these single cells contained one full copy of the genetic information needed to make a human being, distributed between 23 separate chromosomes. So the fertilized egg cell from which you are derived contained *two* sets of the human 'assembly manual'. For every chromosome derived from your father, there was an equivalent chromosome from your mother; and each member of the 23 pairs of chromosomes contained genes specifying similar characteristics. This duplicity of genetic information was maintained as the original fertilized egg cell divided into two, then four, then eight cells, and so on. So each cell of your body still carries two copies of the human genome – one from your father and one from your mother.

This state of carrying two copies of each chromosome (and therefore each gene) is known as the 'diploid' state. The simpler state of carrying only one copy of each is the 'haploid' state. Sperm and egg cells are haploid, while the cells from which you are constructed are diploid.

You might think that since you carry one genome from your father and one from your mother, you should therefore be a perfectly equal 'blend' of your father's and mother's genetic characteristics. That is not the case, however, partly because for many genes one version (it can be either your father's or your mother's) will be 'dominant' over the other. As a result of this dominance only the protein encoded by the dominant gene has an effect on your own make-up, the other 'recessive' gene remains 'silent' and inapparent. There is not always a clear-cut division between one dominant gene and another that is recessive, so some of your characteristics probably are a bit of a blend between those of your father and mother, but these are complexities I do not want to go into. Having established that your cells carry two copies of the human genome, let's look at what happens when you yourself reproduce.

If you are male, you will obviously reproduce by making and releasing sperm cells; if you are female, by making eggs. Both of these types of 'germ' cells are haploid, containing only one copy of each chromosome, so somehow the diploid cells of your body must give rise to haploid germ cells. This takes place in the testes or ovaries by a rather complicated process of cell division known as 'meiosis' (see figure 8.9).

The first event in meiosis is that the entire genetic material of a

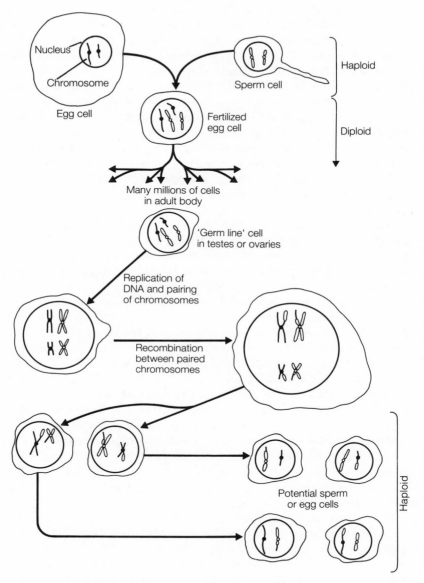

Figure 8.9   The genetic mechanics of sexual reproduction (see text for details).

diploid cell becomes replicated, each chromosome yielding two identical 'sister' chromosomes still joined together somewhere near their centre. Next, the pairs of similar chromosomes derived from your father and mother all become paired up along the centre of the cell. This is illustrated in figure 8.9, using only two pairs of chromosomes for clarity. At this stage the maternal and paternal chromosomes are held close together and are able to swap corresponding sections of DNA to give rise to completely new 'hybrid' chromosomes containing genes derived from both your father and your mother. This is the process of 'genetic recombination', which allows the two parental chromosomes to generate to an endless variety of hybrid chromosomes for transmission to the next generation.

Following a bout of recombination, the cell divides in two, during which contractile proteins latch on to the chromosomes and pull *one member of each replicated pair* into each newly forming cell. Importantly, whether a chromosome is largely paternally or maternally derived is not distinguished in this process, so the meiosis of large numbers of cells can form a great variety of different daughter cells, all containing different mixtures of maternally and paternally derived genetic material, which will have been previously mixed up somewhat by the process of recombination. The two cells produced so far then undergo another division, in which the two replicated chromosomes are pulled apart from one another to yield a total of four haploid germ cells – sperm cells or egg cells, depending on whether you are a man or a woman. If you are a man, each of your sperm cells can fuse with a woman's egg to produce a new diploid individual. If you are a woman, each of your eggs can receive a sperm.

In either case your children will receive 23 chromosomes from you and 23 from your partner, but these chromosomes will not be identical to any inside the body cells of either yourself or your partner. The chromosomes you pass on will be hybrids formed by recombination between the chromosomes you received from your parents, followed by the 'independent segregation' of these chromosomes into separate sperms or eggs regardless of which of your parents they are mostly derived from.

So sexual reproduction produces organisms which can be very different from their parents for two main reasons. Firstly, it yields organisms which are the offspring of two unrelated parents, and which receive equal amounts of genetic material from each; and secondly, during the formation of sperm and eggs it allows the chromosomes of one generation to be mixed up and recombined to produce an infinity of different chromosomes for the next generation.

You are a bit like a 'genetic mixing machine' which has received various genes from both your parents, and then mixes them up in new combinations to pass on to your offspring. Your parents did the same job of genetic mixing for you, just as your children will for your grandchildren.

With sexual reproduction, evolution invented a radically new and more subtle type of replication. Its most obvious difference from simpler forms of replication is that it constantly *mixes* genetic material derived from different individuals, to produce offspring which always contain significantly different genomes from either of their parents. Why should such subtle complexities have originated and been maintained?

Sexual reproduction may often allow evolution to proceed much more speedily and efficiently than the evolution of asexually reproducing species, because it provides a mechanism for many new and beneficial mutations to be brought quickly together in one organism, rather than waiting for them all to accumulate in a single asexual line. By endlessly creating variety, it may make species more resilient to the rigours of environmental change, ensuring that at least a few variants always exist that can thrive, or at least survive, in any new environment; and allowing the genes of successful new variants to spread quickly throughout the population.

Of course it could also serve to bring many harmful mutations together to produce weak or sickly variants, but in such cases the individuals concerned will simply die or reproduce themselves less successfully. The brute force of natural selection can be relied upon to gradually but continually rid the world of bad combinations of genes and preferentially exploit good ones for further breeding.

For years, the standard answer of biologists faced with queries about the origin of sexual reproduction has been to point to the 'advantages' which sex offers as a source of genetic diversity; and the origin of sex is often placed quite late in the history of life, around the time that the first eucaryotes were evolving. But no generally accepted version of the origin of sex exists, and it is becoming an increasingly contentious issue.

At least one alternative explanation for the origin of sex turns the standard explanation on its head, arguing that sex arose not as a source of genetic diversity, but in order to *protect* the first cells against the damage caused by genetic change. This argument has been championed recently by Harris Bernstein and his colleagues at the University of Arizona. They argue that the main problem facing the first cells would be the struggle to keep their existing genes intact in the face of many sources of error and change, rather than the generation of new genes to face future challenges. In response to this problem cells might have been selected which contained several copies of each piece of genetic material, rather than having to rely on only the one, and which were able to compensate for a defect in one copy by the increased activity and duplication of the others. Thus the diploid (or 'triploid' or 'tetraploid') state might have originated as a means of protecting genetic material against change.

Any cells that remained permanently in the diploid form, however, would also suffer disadvantages, because they would need to find a larger supply of raw materials in a given time than the haploid cells they could be expected to be in competition with. So in those early days the best compromise might have been a life-cycle which was predominantly haploid, but which included the periodical fusing together of two similar cells into the diploid state. The periodical fusions would allow any genetic defects and damage to be made good by mutual replacement and recombination. Such a life-cycle, of haploid cells fusing every now and then into diploid cells, might have been the first form of sex. In some modern organisms, such as ourselves, the diploid state has become predominant, with the haploid state being retained simply for our sperm and eggs; but the sexual reproduction which now generates great variety and change might have evolved from a system selected for its ability to do just the opposite – to make the genomes of the earliest cells resistant to change.

This unorthodox idea is fascinating simply because it is so unorthodox. It illustrates the great uncertainties which remain concerning the fine details of evolution. Whatever the truth about its ultimate origin, sexual reproduction appears to be a great source of new variety and change in modern eucaryotes, and may well have been for the first eucaryotes. It might have generated the speedy evolution needed for the first single-celled eucaryotes to quickly evolve into large and complex multicellular forms of life

To many laymen, the idea of single cells giving rise, over countless generations, to such 'grand' and 'intelligent' multicellular creatures as themselves seems, at best, hard to understand, and at worst, utterly ludicrous. I suspect that many people are intuitively more willing to grant that single cells could have arisen from some primordial soup or slime, than to grant that they themselves are descended from such single cells. Yet it is the first process, the origin of life, that is the harder to explain. Once cells had arisen containing genes that encoded proteins, then the gulf separating 'mere' chemicals from ourselves may have largely been bridged.

Although we may look and feel very different from single cells, both single cells and ourselves are essentially chemical machines based on genes that encode proteins. The differences between different forms of life on earth apparently depend on the different genes, and therefore different proteins, they contain (and the ways in which these genes and proteins interact both with themselves and with the rest of their environment). To help you to believe that single cells could have evolved into humans during the course of evolution, you should remember that you yourself were a mere single cell nine months before you were born (although a much more complex one than those of 1000 million years ago). The fact that I was a single cell in 1954, makes it hard for me to deny that creatures like myself could have evolved from much simpler single cells over thousands of millions of years of evolution.

So the steps leading from single-celled life up to complex multicellular life are ones I have not discussed in great detail. This is essentially a book about life's *origins*, rather than its further evolution. Suffice to say that over a great many millions of years genomes that made single cells have evolved into the genomes that make creatures such as you and I, thanks to the natural selection of genes encoding proteins that help organisms to survive and multiply. That is a conclusion backed up by an impressive battery of experimental and observational evidence. To convince you of it, if you need convincing, would take another book, such as one of those listed in my suggestions for further reading. The evidence I have alluded to can be found in them.

Making minds

As the first eucaryotes evolved into sponges, jellyfish and ferns; and into reptiles, dinosaurs and men; the catalytic activities of proteins introduced countless novelties of form and function. Different cells of multicellular creatures became specialized to perform different tasks, yielding such different tissues (groups of similar cells) as muscle tissue, liver tissue, skin tissue and the 'nervous' tissue within our brains.

Nervous tissue, and its apparent ability to give rise to thought and consciousness, deserves at least some short consideration. At one time most people thought that the phenomenon of 'life' involved some clear-cut distinction between the animate and inanimate world, but life has been exposed as a hazy intuitive concept with no really precise meaning at all. In its place, 'consciousness' and 'thought' remain to many people as clear-cut concepts or phenomena which obviously distinguish a human from an amoeba, or a stone. Modern science does not know how thought and consciousness arise or what they are. It does know that both are dependent on the chemical structure and activity of the brain, and that both can be altered or abolished by chemical reactions; but it has no clear idea of what 'a thought' is in terms of atoms, molecules, energy and fundamental forces.

When we examine nervous tissue we find it is composed of nerve cells along which electrical signals travel, in the form of waves of electrical charge. These signals depend upon protein molecules in the cell membrane (see figure 8.10), which open and close to let various charged ions flood across the membrane in different directions. Nervous signals are carried *between* nerve cells by chemicals known as neurotransmitters (made by enzymes), which are released from one nerve cell to stimulate or inhibit the transmission of signals along another. The assumption is made that consciousness and thought are somehow the result of these electro-chemical signals travelling around the complex interconnecting network of nerve cells which we call the brain. If that is true, then consciousness and the ability to think are ultimately products of genes that encode proteins, because genes and proteins construct the nerve cells and allow the transmission of the electrical signals which integrate into thoughts. But nobody knows for sure that this assumption is true.

Let nobody persuade you that modern science has explained or even described the chemistry of consciousness, because it has not. Consciousness may simply be the pinnacle (so far) of what the evolution of genes that encode proteins enables chemical reactions to do. It may be some totally aphysical 'principle' breathed into us by 'God'. There might be some clear-cut point separating cells and tissues capable of conscious thought from other cells, or 'mere chemicals', that are incapable of such wonders. Or perhaps everything is conscious to widely differing extents, with no boundary between the 'high ground' and the 'low'.

Ruskin has said: 'A grey rock is a good sitter. That is one type of behaviour. A darting dragon-fly is another type of behaviour. We call one alive and the other not. But . . . to make "life" a distinction between them is at root to treat them both artificially.' Perhaps we should also say: 'A grey rock is a poor thinker. A grey-haired man is a good thinker. But to make "consciousness" and "thought" a distinction between them is at root to treat them both artificially'? I don't know, and neither does anyone else, yet.

So let us tentatively include consciousness and thought in the category of things that genes that encode proteins can do, remember-

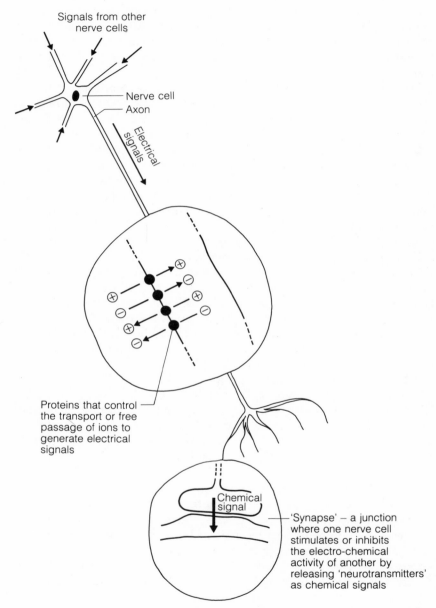

Signals from other
nerve cells

Nerve cell
Axon

Electrical
signals

Proteins that control
the transport or free
passage of ions to
generate electrical
signals

Chemical
signal

'Synapse' – a junction
where one nerve cell
stimulates or inhibits
the electro-chemical
activity of another by
releasing 'neurotransmitters'
as chemical signals

Figure 8.10   The nervous system is a complex three-dimensional network of nerve cells, which pass electro-chemical signals within and between themselves.

ing that the detailed chemistry of thought remains to be uncovered. If evolution is capable of blindly crafting molecules into minds, what other wonders might it achieve given a few more thousand million years? What other wonders might it already have achieved elsewhere? And what wonders might be generated by the thinking beings it has made already, if they set their minds to the creation of new forms of life? These are some of the topics for the final chapters of this book.

9 Worlds such as this one

For this world was created by Nature after atoms had collided spontaneously and at random in a thousand ways, driven together blindly, uselessly, without any results, when at last suddenly the particular ones combined which could become the perpetual starting points of things we know – earth, sea, sky, and the various kinds of living things. Therefore, we must acknowledge that such combinations of other atoms happen elsewhere in the universe to make worlds such as this one, held in the close embrace of the aether.
Lucretius c. 70 BC

The most exciting, and threatening, scientific mystery of all is surely the mystery of life elsewhere in the universe. Every single human who has gazed upwards to the stars and planets must have wondered what and who might be up there. After millions of years of wondering we might at last be about to find out, as the explosive development of science and technology opens up vast new horizons to our scrutiny.

Of course some people say they already know a bit about who is 'up there', claiming to have seen and met and sometimes even talked to strange creatures from (presumably) other worlds. Many such claims can easily be dismissed, but it may be foolish to dismiss them all. Anyone who troubles to wade through the 99 per cent of nonsense found in the annals of 'UFOlogy' will find a troubling 1 per cent or so that is hard to dismiss. But even that troubling 1 per cent is not the subject of this chapter, because it is composed of individual experiences that can never be properly verified. If any of these experiences are genuine, then our visitors from other worlds are obviously very shy, or selective, or both.

This chapter is concerned with the attempts of mainstream science to discover life on other worlds, or simply to evaluate the likelihood of such life existing. If scientists do eventually find life elsewhere, then we will all share in the discovery as it is reported in our papers and flashed up on our television sets.

Any life on other worlds will of course have had its own origin, perhaps the same as ours, but possibly very different. Perhaps the puzzle of the origins of life will soon become a complex cosmic jigsaw in which the origin of life on earth will be merely one small piece. Or perhaps, as Arrhenius, Kelvin, Crick, Orgel, Wickramasinghe and Hoyle have suggested, things may be much simpler, since we might live in a universe seeded by life derived from only one or very few origins.

The mystery of extraterrestrial life can be broken into three smaller questions. Firstly, are there really other worlds on which replicating life-forms could live and possibly originate? Secondly, if there are such worlds, what would their life be like? And thirdly, which of these worlds really do harbour life? As yet we have no answers to the third question, while the first two have initiated a long-running and sometimes heated debate.

We are all aware of some of the fantastic proposals about other life-forms offered to us by the authors of science fiction. These writers do a good job in generating endless ideas without having to worry too much about the fine scientific details. They mine the rocky rubbish which can be sifted in search of occasional gems. They tell us of creatures based on silicon – an element with certain close similarities to the carbon which lies at the heart of life on earth. They tell of vast balloon-like creatures floating high in the atmospheres of planets such as Jupiter or Saturn, or of 'thinking fishes' swimming through seas of liquid ammonia, or conscious clouds of interstellar dust and gas. The ideas go on and on . . .

In order to count as 'forms of life', the creatures of science fiction must simply be able to replicate themselves and to evolve. Just how 'alive' we would consider them to be, and whether or not we have any chance of ever meeting and perhaps communicating with such creatures, depends largely on how *far* they have evolved, or how far they might evolve in the future. We could speculate endlessly about possible weird forms of life very different from our own, but there is one argument to suggest that such speculations might be mis-founded. It is an argument suggesting that any other life present in the universe now, or in the past, would be based on similar chemical foundations to our own.

The case for common chemistry

The atoms of the universe consist essentially of a big pile of hydrogen with a little helium mixed in, along with tiny amounts of other elements – amounts which would certainly escape a 'casual glance'. Hydrogen is believed to account for about 92.7 per cent of all the atoms in the entire universe, and helium for around 7.2 per cent. This leaves a tiny 0.1 per cent for all the other types of atoms, of which there are 90 known to occur naturally. After helium, the most abundant atoms in the universe appear to be oxygen (at 0.05 per cent), neon (at 0.02 per cent), nitrogen (at 0.015 per cent) and carbon (at 0.008 per cent). So the six most abundant elements in the universe are hydrogen, helium, oxygen, neon, nitrogen and carbon, which together account for about 99.99 per cent of all the atoms in existence.

As every schoolchild learns, helium and neon are examples of 'noble' gases, which are extremely stable and unreactive, and so will not participate in any chemical reactions unless the conditions are very special and extreme. So these two noble gases seem completely unsuitable as components of living things, since the essence of living things is that they replicate and evolve as a result of chemical reactions.

If we remove the unreactive elements helium and neon from our list, we find that the most abundant elements that seem suitable components of living things are hydrogen, oxygen, nitrogen and carbon. We could have worked that out without knowing anything about the chemistry going on inside ourselves, and if we had then turned inwards to consider our own atoms we would have discovered a startlingly suggestive coincidence. There are 36 different types of atoms found inside the living things of earth, but only four types account for 99 per cent of living matter. These four types are hydrogen, oxygen, nitrogen and carbon – the four most abundant types of atoms in the universe that seem suitable components of life!

So life on earth is essentially made up of hydrogen, oxygen, nitrogen and carbon atoms, with trace amounts of other elements; and (disregarding unreactive helium and neon) these are the four most abundant types of atoms in the universe. The conclusion that seems to scream out at us from these figures is that our type of life, based on hydrogen, oxygen, nitrogen and carbon, is probably the easiest and most likely type of life for the universe to give rise to. So if there really are other worlds such as this one, supporting other living things, they may well be based on a hydrogen, oxygen, nitrogen and carbon chemistry very similar to our own.

Of course few would suggest that alien life must be identical to life on earth, but deep down at the chemical level there may be very strong similarities. Certainly, it may well be based on 'organic' chemistry involving hydrogen, oxygen, nitrogen and carbon atoms. Chemicals similar to earthly nucleic acids may form the alien genes, and amino acids may well be linked up into proteins to form the catalysts that accelerate alien life. So any aliens, or at least *many* aliens, may well be based on genes that encode proteins all surprisingly similar to our own. The discovery of amino acids, bases and so on in meteorites, and of the simpler precursors of such building-blocks in interstellar space, serves only to support this conclusion.

The universe is composed largely of the atoms that make us work, and is widely sown with compounds such as hydrogen cyanide, ammonia, formaldehyde, amino acids, bases and sugars which might act as seeds for the origin of our sort of life. Armed with this information, the aliens most of us dream and worry about suddenly don't seem likely to be so alien after all. Some have taken this argument much further. The biologist Cyril Darlington has argued that

> there are such great advantages in walking on two legs, in carrying one's brain in one's head, in having two eyes on the same eminence at a height of five or six feet, that we might well take quite seriously the possibility of (an alien) pseudo man and a pseudo woman with some physical resemblance to ourselves.

The famous Italian physicist Enrico Fermi once asked that if alien beings can arise as easily throughout the universe as some scientists suggest, then 'where are they?', a query echoed by sceptics everywhere. His friend Leo Szilard, a Hungarian scientist, apparently replied 'They are among us, but they call themselves Hungarians!'. If we take the argument of basic chemical similarity to its ultimate conclusion, then maybe the aliens really are among us – they simply don't want us to know. That's something else to worry about next time you meet a stranger at a party!

Various complications disturb the neat simplicity of the argument related above. Although hydrogen, oxygen, nitrogen and carbon atoms are the most abundant reactive atoms in the universe, they were certainly not the most abundant types of atoms in the newly formed earth. One of the four, oxygen, is the most abundant element of the earth, but the other three all come some way down the list. Silicon, iron, magnesium, aluminium, sulphur, nickel, sodium, calcium and phosphorus atoms are all more abundant on the earth than hydrogen atoms; carbon follows shortly after, while nitrogen appears considerably further down the list. So the reason life on earth is composed mainly of hydrogen, oxygen, nitrogen and carbon atoms is not because these were the most abundant atoms of the early earth – they were not. This might suggest to us that life on earth really did originate elsewhere, but that conclusion would be based on very simplistic reasoning. Hydrogen, oxygen, nitrogen and carbon atoms may have been by far the most abundant types in the *waters* and the *atmosphere* of the early earth, where life is presumed to have originated (as opposed to the main solid bulk of the planet). They would certainly have come much further up the list.

A second complication is that the 'big four' are present in living things not in the order – hydrogen, oxygen, nitrogen and carbon; but in the slightly different order – hydrogen, oxygen, carbon and nitrogen. Most of a living thing is water, which is why hydrogen and oxygen are so abundant, while all of the 'organic' chemicals of life are based on chains of carbon atoms which have other types of atoms attached, or occasionally incorporated into the predominantly carbon chains. This explains why carbon is more abundant in living things than nitrogen atoms. Despite such complications, the general point that life on earth is constructed out of the most abundant and seemingly suitable atoms that were available, and which may be similarly available elsewhere, is a strong argument to suggest that alien life might not be as 'alien' as is sometimes supposed.

The calculating approach

Assuming, for the sake of simplicity, that alien life may be based on a similar biochemistry, involving hydrogen, oxygen, nitrogen and carbon, as life on earth; can we say anything about the likelihood that such alien life really exists, or has existed in the past? The short and honest answer is probably 'no', but that has certainly not stopped some scientists from trying.

One of the most celebrated attempts was made by Frank Drake, an astronomer at Cornell University. In his book, *Intelligent Life in Space*, he published an equation which he felt would give us an idea of the likelihood of alien life – if only we could find suitable values for various parameters to be put into the equation. Drake was actually most interested in calculating the likely number of *intelligent* civilizations that might be sufficiently advanced to communicate with us by electromagnetic radiation (such as radio signals), even if the civilizations became extinct long before we received their messages. Here is one of the simpler versions of his equation:

$$N = R \times f_p \times f_e \times f_1 \times f_i \times f_c \times L$$

which all looks very rigorous and scientific, but of course means nothing until you know what all the symbols represent. The reasoning behind the equation is actually very simple to understand.

N is the number of advanced civilizations *in our galaxy* that might be sending out signals at any one time. So basically it is the answer Drake was after. If it works out at much less than one, then there are probably no other civilisations as intelligent as us in the galaxy. If it runs into thousands, then we probably have a large number of neighbours all wanting to talk.

To calculate the value of N, the first thing Drake does is to introduce a figure 'R', indicating the rate at which new stars have formed in our galaxy per year, averaged over the galaxy's entire lifetime. The current best estimate for the value of R is about 20.

Next, Drake assumes that life can only be expected to originate *on planets* orbiting stars at some suitable distance. Science fiction fanatics would criticize this as an unjustifiable restriction, but if we are estimating the likelihood of life based on similar chemical principles to our own, then it seems fair. This is where the big unknowns begin, because we have yet to directly detect a single true planet orbiting any star other than our own sun. This is not necessarily because they are not there, but probably because we do not yet have the means to reliably detect such planets. We do have indirect evidence of possible planetary systems around other stars, and telescopes both on earth and in orbit have recently photographed what may be alien solar systems caught in the act of formation (see plate 7). Astronomical theory certainly predicts that planets will quite commonly be found orbiting other stars. A conservative estimate suggests that at least one-tenth of all stars in the galaxy may have planets, an estimate which leads to 0.1 for the value of f_p – the proportion of stars with planets.

So one-tenth of the stars formed each year throughout the history of the galaxy may have had planets around them, setting the value of N so far at 2 (i.e. 20 × 0.1).

The next parameter in the Drake equation – f_e – represents the fraction of planetary systems containing planets that might provide suitable environments for the origin of life. Obviously we are getting deeper and deeper into the realm of pure speculation, especially in view of all the uncertainties that still surround the origin of life on earth. If we restrict ourselves to life based on a similar chemistry to ourselves, involving reactions occurring in liquid water solutions, temperatures somewhere between 0 and 100°C, and so on, then many planets are obviously going to be unsuitable. A common estimate assumes that at least one fifth of all planetary systems might possess a planet on which some sort of hydrogen, oxygen, nitrogen and carbon-based life might be feasible, but let's be extremely cautious and set f_e at one-hundredth, or 0.01.

The parameter f_1 represents the fraction of such suitable planets on which life actually does originate. Many scientists boldy set this figure at 1 (i.e. 100 per cent), reasoning that in any conditions in which life *can* originate and evolve it surely will. But let's again be extremely cautious, and set the figure at one out of every hundred possible planets, i.e. 0.01. At this point we can forget about the remainder of the Drake equation for a moment. It is intended to calculate the likely number of intelligent civilizations that might be sufficiently advanced to communicate with us. If we merely wish to know how many alien planets may currently carry life of any sort, regardless of how 'intelligent' it is, then we nearly have all the figures we need.

The figures so far allow us to estimate the average rate at which planets that will eventually carry life are formed in our galaxy. That rate is 20 (the number of stars formed per year) × 0.1 (the proportion that will have planets around them) × 0.01 (the proportion of planetary systems that might have planets suited to the origin of our sort of life) × 0.01 (a very conservative estimate of the proportion of these suitable planets on which life might actually originate). The answer to this calculation comes out at 0.0002, but this is merely the number of planets destined to carry life that are formed in the galaxy *per year* (0.0002 means one per 5000 years). To find out how many planets may actually be carrying life at any one time, we must multiply this figure by the number of years we expect life to survive on each of the planets. We know that life on earth has survived for at least 3000 million years, and life of some form will probably survive on earth for many thousands of millions of years more. So if we multiply 0.0002 by a conservative 3000 million years, we find that at any one time around 600 000 planets *in our own galaxy* may be carrying replicating life based on similar chemical principles as we are!

Of course none of the figures put into the equation were very reliable, although in places I have used much more conservative estimates than is usual. Maybe some of the figures should have been still smaller, but many scientists would suggest that most should be much bigger. Whatever the truth, this whole imprecise little exercise should not really be taken very seriously. Many people dismiss it as a ludicrous nonsense, but personally I feel it does illustrate a worthwhile and important point. It seems to tell us that there are two possibilities: either we are utterly alone, or else our galaxy and the entire universe is absolutely teeming with life (although each form of life may be separated from all the others by enormous and possibly unbridgeable distances). If life can originate spontaneously anywhere in the universe (such as on earth) then, unless the earth is a unique special case, it must surely have originated in countless other locations as well.

In principle, the number of alien biologies could be anything from zero to virtual infinity, but the Drake equation suggests that the real number is either zero or a great many indeed. Personally, I find it impossible to prefer the first choice. Until we have searched hard and far, and still found nothing, it must surely remain most likely that we are merely one tiny isolated fragment of a vast universal biosphere. The discovery of just one thing we could all accept as 'living' on a planet around one other star would surely resolve the issue. If there is one abode of life outside our solar system then it would be very difficult to deny that there must be many millions overall – the numbers of available stars are so great. One alien implies a multitude of aliens.

Drake, however, was not interested in just any old aliens. He was trying to calculate the likely numbers of intelligent civilizations capable of communicating with us. To do this he continued his equation with three more terms – f_i, f_c and L. f_i is the proportion of planets on which, after the origin of life, some form of 'intelligent life' (by our standards) arises. This is usually set quite high, since intelligence is assumed to be extremely beneficial for survival, and so it is perhaps an inevitable result of any extended process of evolution by natural selection. We may blow ourselves to extinction because we have too little intelligence, leaving the stage free for more sensible insects (or whatever) to arise in the burst of evolution powered by the mutagenic radioactivity released by our spectacular demise. I will set f_i at a conservative 0.1.

f_c represents the proportion of intelligent civilizations that reach a sufficient state of technological advancement to send radio signals towards the stars. This is again usually set conservatively at 0.1.

Finally, L represents the average lifetime of intelligent civilizations capable of radio communication, before they either destroy themselves or are frazzled or frozen by their ageing suns. We have been capable of radio communication for less than 100 years, and for over 30 years we have had the capacity to destroy our civilization completely. How long will we remain capable of generating radio waves before the nuclear holocaust, and will any residual human population survive to begin transmitting once more while avoiding the mistakes of its forebears? Obviously, nobody knows, so a suitable value for L could be anything from just a few to many thousands of millions of years.

If we set L at 100 years, then our final Drake equation (*using unusually conservative figures*) becomes

$$20 \times 0.1 \times 0.01 \times 0.01 \times 0.1 \times 0.1 \times 100 = 0.0002$$

This figure is much less than one, so it suggests that if intelligent civilizations remain capable of radio communication for only 100 years on average, then there are unlikely to be any around in our galaxy at the moment. The universe, however, consists of many thousands of millions of galaxies, so even with an average life-span of 100 years the universe must contain an enormous number of civilizations capable of sending out radio signals to other worlds, according to the Drake equation. If civilizations remain capable of radio communication for many thousands or millions of years on average, then there might be a great many such advanced civilizations in even our own 'tiny' galaxy.

Although it is easy to ridicule, the Drake equation is at least a useful way to illustrate how easily we could be merely a tiny part of a vast universal living horde. Unless life occurs on earth and nowhere else, then a universe composed of at least many thousands of millions of galaxies, all composed of many thousands of millions of stars, must surely contain an unbelievable variety of different living forms.

You may, like Fermi, be tempted to ask 'where are they?'. The vast distances between the stars and galaxies provide a ready explanation for their presumed absence on and around the earth, but what about their radio waves, and other forms of emitted electromagnetic radiation. *They* really might be here already, passing unnoticed through yourself and the pages of this book as you sit reading. Nobody has detected them yet, perhaps because they are extremely weak and diffuse after spreading throughout great volumes of space since their departure; but perhaps because we have not yet had much of a look.

Searching the cosmic haystack

By early 1986 mankind had spent about 125 000 hours searching for signals from extraterrestrial civilizations. That might sound like quite a long and hard look, but it actually represents only a momentary glimpse since the volume to be searched is so vast and the range of ways of 'looking' so great. So far there have been lots of false alarms, a few unconfirmed possibilities, but no clear successes. Searches are being performed at an ever accelerating pace by a technology which is improving in leaps and bounds. Since the most sophisticated searches are automatic and under way all of the time, we could discover clear evidence of alien life at any moment – perhaps we just have.

Looking for signals from other civilizations is often likened to searching for needles in a cosmic haystack – a haystack in which there are many complex ways and places for the needles to hide. Obviously, any signals from other worlds, whether beamed to us on purpose or having escaped accidentally like the radio, television and radar transmissions escaping from the earth today, may be very weak by the time they reach us. We do not know in what direction we should point our receivers in order to gather and amplify them, we do not know which frequencies to tune into, which bandwidths to search or even what would constitute a meaningful signal to alien beings.

Despite such difficulties the first search was begun in 1960 by Frank Drake, author of the 'Drake' equation. For 200 hours the telescope of the National Radio Astronomy Observatory at Green Bank, West Virginia, searched for signals from Epsilon Eridani and Tau Ceti – two sun-like stars 10.7 and 11.9 light years from earth respectively. There was a false alarm, but no success, but at least the search had begun.

After Drake's initial look, further searches came slowly at first, and then with rapidly accelerating frequency. Searchers in the United States were joined by others in the Soviet Union, Australia, Canada, France, Germany and Holland. As I write, at least two observatories are devoted full-time to the search for the signals of alien life. These are based at Ohio State University, and the Oak-Ridge Harvard–Smithsonian Observatory near Boston. Others are planned.

Most of the searches conducted so far have gathered radio signals at selected single frequencies. Many of the frequencies chosen have been the so-called 'magic frequencies' at which universally common atoms and compounds such as hydrogen and water emit radio waves. The logic behind concentrating on such frequencies is that any civilization trying to communicate with others might choose universally significant frequencies, rather than any chosen at random. More recently, however, searches have begun in which signals over a wide range of frequencies are all searched for at once. This strategy is more likely to pick up signals leaking unintentionally towards us, just as other civilizations may now be 'listening' to the radio and television (or military radar) signals we have unintentionally sent to them (although such unintentional messages would be extremely weak by the time they reached either them, or us).

Although nothing convincing has been found so far, there have been a few 'suspicious' events. The Parkes radiotelescope in Australia has recorded a single very short (1 millisecond) unexplained signal from a nearby star, which has so far never been repeated. Other similar 'one off' events have been recorded from time to time, but unless we eventually find them to be repeated over long periods of time we must assume they were due to natural phenomena or were created by faults in the instruments. Scientists are searching for any unusual electromagnetic signals, by virtue of being very short, or of narrow frequency range, or pulsating in unnatural patterns, or having an artificially imposed polarization, or whatever. Although they do not really know what they are looking for, they hope it will be obvious when they find it.

Searching for electromagnetic signals is not the only thing we can do to try to identify life around other stars. American scientists have searched for evidence of tritium (a very unstable radioactive form of hydrogen), as evidence of the activity of alien nuclear fusion plants. Soviet scientists have used optical telescopes to search for evidence of laser beams used by advanced civilizations for long-range communications systems; and American scientists are building new equipment to undertake a similar search. Other scientists, especially in the Soviet Union, are searching for evidence of giant 'astroengineering' projects in which whole planets are artificially formed or destroyed, or otherwise manoeuvred around.

So the search for evidence of life around other planets is well under way, and as we wait for the first positive results we should ponder on what our next moves should be once we discover that we are not alone. It is of course possible that the aliens will arrive before we have found their signals or other evidence that they exist – in which case events may well be taken out of our command. If they get to us before we get to them, then they will undoubtedly be 'smarter' than us. We can only hope that they will not treat us in the same way as we treat the less intelligent creatures with whom we share this earth.

But what about the possibilities of life nearer home, in our own humble little solar system? The American 'Apollo', 'Pioneer', 'Mariner', 'Viking', and 'Voyager' programmes have demolished the notion of 'little green men' on Mars, the moon, or any of our sister planets; but can we yet be sure that the solar system harbours no life other than ourselves?

Looking nearer home

If there is any other life in the solar system, then it is certainly not very active or obvious and is probably plant-like or microscopic. But although few scientists would place bets on us finding such life, it is a possibility which still cannot be ruled out.

The places that must be searched for life in the solar system are quite numerous. Firstly, there are the eight planets other than earth – Mercury, Venus, Mars, Jupiter. Saturn, Uranus, Neptune and Pluto. Next there are the large number of satellites of these planets – the Moon of earth, Europa of Jupiter, Titan of Saturn, and so on. There is also the asteroid belt, comets and meteors.

For a long time many scientists and others felt there might be life on Mars, a possibility taken sufficiently seriously for NASA to spend considerable money, time and effort equipping their 'Viking' spacecraft with a suite of complex experiments designed to detect that life. Some of the experiments yielded results which their designers would have initially considered as positive, but these are now regarded as 'false positives' produced by unexpected but 'dead' chemistry. The Vikings sent back beautiful pictures of the surface of another world, a few ambiguous results, but no hard evidence of any Martian life (see plate 8).

From Mars, interest turned outward towards Saturn – not the vast gaseous bulk of the planet, but towards its largest moon, known as Titan. Titan is the only moon in the solar system with a substantial atmosphere, largely composed of nitrogen. On 12 November 1980, the 'Voyager 1' spacecraft shaved past Titan at a distance of just 7000 kilometres (see plate 9). Its optical cameras did not 'see' much, because the moon's surface is hidden by an opaque aerosol layer in the atmosphere, but Voyager's instruments suggested a world covered in a liquid methane (CH_4) or ethane (C_2H_6) sea, and with a thick atmosphere (denser than the earth's) containing a little methane, hydrogen and various hydrocarbons and nitrogen compounds, in addition to the bulk of free nitrogen; but there is no free oxygen.

This atmosphere is similar to some which have yielded many of the simple chemical precursors of life in prebiotic simulation experiments; and Voyager also discovered evidence of hydrogen cyanide (a central compound in most versions of the prebiotic chemistry of the earth) and some larger chain-like hydrocarbons. Deep beds of accumulated hydrocarbons and various nitrogenous compounds may well cover large parts of Titan and be lapped by its methane or ethane sea. There is water on Titan too, although it is trapped as ice within the moon's solid 'land', because the problem with Titan is that it is very very cold.

The temperature on Titan is estimated at around minus 179 degrees Celsius. It may well be the germ of a living world in 'deep freeze'. It may have all the necessary starting materials to give rise to living things based on very similar principles to ourselves, but the temperature seems far too low for life to have yet begun. This may make Titan a vast 'prebiotic reactor' waiting to be warmed into life. Perhaps one day we will warm it up, or at least warm a little bit of it, in the largest and grandest prebiotic experiment of all. If we do, what life might Titan give rise to, and would we be wise to apply the warmth for its creation? Many will say Titan is a 'seed' we should leave well alone, but the temptation to observe at first hand a non-living world give rise to life may be hard to resist. It is assumed that there is no life on Titan already, largely because of the cold, and Voyager certainly found no evidence of life, but further probing of this fascinating moon is planned and who knows what surprises may lie in store?

Another fascinating world is the moon of Jupiter known as Europa (see plate 10). This is also a very cold place, with a surface of sulphurous water-ice. Beneath the icy surface, however, there may be a watery ocean warmed by the moon's internal radioactivity, by sunlight, and by electric currents generated as the moon sweeps through Jupiter's magnetic field. Some scientists think that this hidden ocean might contain life. In a highly speculative paper in the journal *Icarus*, Ray Reynolds, Steven Squyres, David Colburn and Christopher McKay of NASA's Ames research laboratory have mused about the possibility that Europa would be able to support some of the living things found on earth, and therefore might carry life of its own. The possibility of life on Europa is not backed up by any hard evidence, but hopefully spacecraft will return some day to take a closer look.

There is a temptation to speculate endlessly on about the possible details of alien life in the solar system and elsewhere, but it is a temptation I intend to resist. I see little point in burdening this short book with *too much* wild speculation that remains unsupported by any hard evidence (we have had enough of that already!). There is an equal temptation to *dismiss* the possibility of life in various places, simply because living things similar to the ones of earth could not survive in them. Thus it is often stated that life seems inconceivable without some sort of liquid for its chemistry to occur in, or at very high temperatures, or within mixtures of gases. These are some of the reasons why life is not expected on Mercury, Venus, Mars, Jupiter, Saturn, Uranus, Neptune, Pluto, and on most of the many moons orbiting some of these planets. These places are largely dismissed as being too hot, or too cold, or too dry and barren, or too poorly supplied with the 'likely' chemicals of living things.

Most scientists forced to place a bet on a location for alien life in the solar system would probably plump for Europa, at the moment; but most would probably prefer to bet that our own solar system does not contain alien life at all. If asked to bet on the possibility of other forms of life in the entire universe, there would be heavy betting that such life really does exist. If asked to bet about the chemical nature of that life, I doubt if any clear betting pattern would emerge. I have concentrated on the possibilities of life based on hydrogen, oxygen, nitrogen and carbon – because we know most about that sort of life and there is a reasonable argument to suggest that alien life may be of that sort as well. Others have speculated about life based on silicon chains, rather than carbon ones; or life which exists in the gaseous or solid phase, and so on. For the moment such ideas remain pure speculation, while at least we do know that hydrogen, oxygen, nitrogen and carbon-based life really does exist.

Of course this is a subject which it would be crazy to be dogmatic about. All sorts of 'weird and wonderful' alien life-forms might exist, some of which might be very difficult to detect. Would we notice the activities of living things whose generation times were much longer or shorter than ours? Life that takes thousands of years, or only a few microseconds, to reproduce, might be very hard to spot.

The discoveries of astronomy and biochemistry have placed the current generations of humans in an unsettling position. They make it likely, some would say virtually certain, that worlds such as this one really do exist and really do support living things which may be like, or completely unlike, ourselves. Yet we have no idea of where these worlds might be, of what life might scurry about them, or whether or not we would recognize it as life if we saw it. After millennia of simply thinking and philosophizing about the possibility of life elsewhere, we are at last settling down to the task of trying to find it. If alien life does exist then we will probably know about it fairly soon – something which should excite us and concern us in roughly equal proportion.

10 The new Creator

I saw the pale student of unhallowed arts kneeling beside the thing he had put together.
Mary Shelley

I was not around in 1953 when Stanley Miller announced that he had obtained amino acids from a simulation of the chemistry of the primeval earth – my own creation still lay a year or so in the future. So I have no first-hand knowledge of the reaction his announcement prompted in the laboratories and coffee rooms of the scientific world. There must have been some excited chatter about how quickly we might become capable of re-creating the origin of life itself; and I suspect there may have been a few optimistic souls who thought that life would soon be 'crawling at us out of a test-tube'. This book has examined the subsequent attempts to re-create the origin of life, attempts which have failed so far, but which may eventually yield success. In addition to our future efforts to re-create the origin of life, we now stand ready to create life from scratch, using the technology of genetic engineering and perhaps in other ways as well. This chapter turns its back on past failures and looks to the future, and mankind's likely role in that future as the new Creator.

First of all, what of the future of our attempts to re-create key steps in the origin of life on earth, and perhaps to re-create the origin of life itself – where do these efforts go from here? Many scientists throughout the world are busy trying to get nucleic acids, or very similar chemicals, to form and replicate under the likely conditions of the primordial earth. The fact that they have not succeeded in generating replicating 'life' so far, obviously does not rule out dramatic successes in the future, but perhaps they should return to the sort of logic which initially prompted the celebrated experiment of Miller.

Back to basics

Miller mixed together the chemicals thought at the time to have been the most likely major components of the primitive atmosphere. He then subjected the mixture to conditions of heat and electric discharge believed to have been a reasonable simulation of conditions on the early earth. After a while, he looked to see what had been produced, and was pleased to find significant amounts of amino acids. His experiment was not initially designed to yield amino acids, or bases, or sugars, or whatever – it was designed simply to mimic events on the early earth, to find out what might have happened on it. A roughly similar approach has yielded some bases and sugars, providing all of the simplest building-blocks of life.

Most efforts to take things further have been based on a different sort of approach. Instead of simply re-creating various primordial conditions, and looking to see what might have happened in them, scientists have tended to purposely try to find conditions under which bases and sugars and amino acids could have formed nucleotides, nucleic acids, peptides and proteins. They know that somehow these products were eventually formed, so they have tried to find ways of making them rather directly. Thus, many successes have been achieved in making nucleotides and nucleic acids under conditions which *partially* simulate the likely conditions of the early earth; but so far the reactions have always needed some sort of 'help' from chemicals or conditions that were unlikely to have been around on the prebiotic world. Having achieved such partial successes, scientists then try to find ways round the unacceptable help, attempting to steadily make their simulations more realistic in the hope that eventually they will be able to manage without any unacceptable help at all.

This approach might eventually lead us to acceptable answers about the origin of life on earth, but it may be fatally flawed by the handicap of knowing where that origin was ultimately heading. Since we know that eventually creatures based on nucleic acids encoding proteins had to arise, the temptation to try to head directly towards such creatures has been hard to resist. Far from helping us to unearth the secrets of life's origin, our knowledge of present-day life might actually be hindering us, by encouraging us to search for instant origins for nucleic acid and protein-based systems which may actually have originated a long way up the 'evolutionary tree', and which could never have originated without the help of simpler, lower forms of life.

So instead of obsessively looking for the direct creation of replicating nucleic acids that encode proteins, we should perhaps be returning to Miller's approach of simply re-creating the conditions of the early earth, in ever-increasing complexity, and looking to see what happens. This approach of simply thinking about (and doing experiments to see) what would have happened most easily, is of course the method which led Graham Cairns-Smith to propose a long phase of 'low-tech' crystal life which paved the way for nucleic acid and protein-based life to take over. But there may be possible forms of low-tech life other than replicating crystals, and other possible takeovers. There may be other types of molecules which could have replicated and evolved on the earth long before nucleic acids began to.

Scientists interested in life's origins are well aware of this possibility, and they do make some attempts to take it into account. They experiment, for example, with much simpler analogues of nucleic acids containing simpler smaller sugars and simpler chemical groups in place of bases, but in such attempts they are still 'hooked' on the supposed need to get to replicating nucleic acids as soon as possible. After over 30 years of aiming for nucleic acid and protein-based life directly, and failing to get very far, it might be time to start looking more closely at the broader chemical possibilities of the primordial earth. If scientists search earnestly for the most likely chemical events at that time, trying to forget that they probably gave rise to life, and without restricting the search to reactions they think might have helped give rise to life, then they might stumble on the simpler forms of replicating life which laid the foundations for our own type of life to arise.

I am not suggesting that nobody has ever tried this approach. Some have and some continue to do so, but the emphasis has certainly been on attempts to generate nucleic acid and protein-based life directly from primordial soups. Perhaps it is time to educate that group of chemists while keeping them ignorant of the nature of life on earth, and then leave them to find out what sort of replicating life the early earth might have first produced!

Prebiotic reactors

Regardless of the nature of the first replicators, there must have come a time when nucleic acids became the dominant replicators of the earth, as they have remained to this day. The literature on the origins of life bulges with speculation about what the first simple nucleic acids might have done and how they might have evolved, but we may be about to move on from speculation into the realm of hard evidence.

Scientists now have the chemical know-how to manufacture nucleic acids of specified sequence at will. These techniques were developed to assist in the genetic engineering revolution, which now allows scientists to tinker with the genetic material of all sorts of organisms from bacteria to humans. They have reached such a state of sophistication that fully automated 'synthesizers' are on the market, able to manufacture many copies of a nucleic acid of a sequence chosen by the operator (see plate 12). So scientists are now in a position to conduct a detailed investigation into the full potential of nucleic acids such as DNA and RNA. They could generate nucleic acids of widely varying sequences, in search of ones able to replicate themselves, or encourage amino acids to link up into proteins, or act as catalysts in many other ways.

In chapter 5 I suggested that the discovery that RNA molecules could act as efficient catalysts might turn out to be a major breakthrough in the attempts to understand and re-create the origins of life. The implication was that populations of RNA molecules might be capable of evolving into self-replicating RNAs and eventually into simple cellular forms of life composed of various RNAs cooperating and possibly making proteins. We are now in a position to find out.

Imagine a 'prebiotic reactor' which automatically churned out small RNA molecules of random nucleotide sequence. These RNAs could be fed into various chambers in which they would be subjected to a wide range of varying conditions mimicking different parts of the early earth. They could be exposed to hydrated electrons, to see if some types survived better than others; they could be mixed with nucleotides and subjected to cycles of heating and cooling to see if any were capable of self-replication; and so on. Many single experiments could be performed, each designed to test the abilities of one particular RNA species; or more ambitious experiments in which RNAs were created and destroyed at equal rates could be left to run for weeks, or months, or years, to see if anything interesting or even 'alive' came to dominate the population.

It has already been shown that RNA molecules can 'evolve in the test-tube', with an initial population of RNA molecules giving rise to new 'species' of variant molecules over several generations. But in order to get this 'molecular evolution' to work you must add a modern enzyme to replicate the RNAs. The presence of this modern enzyme makes these experiments completely invalid as simulations of likely events during the origins of life (a fact often ignored by teachers and textbooks). But suppose our 'random RNA generator' produced a species of RNA capable of inefficient self-replication. That species could then be expected to multiply and evolve into other species; and some of these other species might just be able to link up amino acids into proteins and mimic the steps that got the evolution of life towards us truly on its way.

So the discovery of catalytic RNA suggests many obvious experiments to explore the potential of RNA, and other nucleic acids, to initiate the evolution of life. Catalytic RNAs might well turn out to be able to both replicate and evolve into simple protein-making systems – something which would at a stroke resolve the two major difficulties facing us as we try to explain the origins of life. The only major remaining problem would then be to explain how RNAs of random sequence were generated frequently enough to eventually create the 'clever' ones that evolved into us. I await the results of the exploration of the potential of catalytic nucleic acids with interest and excitement, an excitement which will hopefully prove more justified than that which followed the Miller experiment in 1953.

Nucleic acids are not the only chemicals suited for the 'prebiotic reactor' approach. Scientists also have the chemical know-how to generate peptides and proteins of specified, or random, sequence, to discover more of the things that proteins can do. For years scientists investigating the activities of both nucleic acids and proteins have had to rely on examining *naturally occurring* examples to find out what they could do. Now, they are in position to create nucleic acids and proteins at will, to uncover the full range of their abilities, rather than being limited to the things these polymers do in the life that lives on earth now.

The exploration of the potential of peptides and small proteins might reveal species capable of catalysing important stages in the origins of life. It might even reveal proteins capable of self-replication, or at least of encouraging reactions that yield proteins of broadly similar sequence. And of course the most successful prebiotic reactors might generate both nucleic acids and proteins, mixing them together while we watch and wait until some cooperating species turn up that look likely contenders as the first components of life.

A detailed exploration of the virtually infinite potential of proteins and nucleic acids would not only be of interest to scientists searching for clues to the origins of life. It might also uncover molecules with useful industrial or medical properties which have not yet been 'discovered' by nature, or whose times of usefulness have passed.

Evolution is essentially a slow relentless exploration of the chemical abilities of nucleic acids and proteins. It proceeds by the generation of chance variants of existing forms, and then their slow 'testing' by the rigours of natural selection. Mankind could now drive that slow exploration forward in the laboratory at a phenomenally accelerated pace – searching through the entire repertoire of nucleic acids and proteins of differing nucleotide and amino acid sequence, testing for useful new varieties, and perhaps even incorporating these new varieties into new breeds of organism using the technology of genetic engineering (see later). The search to uncover our origins might at the same time lead us towards our future.

Continuous crystallizers

Before leaving the possibilities of re-creation, and turning to the possibilities of totally novel living *creations*, we should return briefly to the major alternative theory of the origin of life considered in chapter 6. Graham Cairns-Smith believes that the first living things were cooperatives of crystals able to replicate and evolve and perform many complex chemical reactions which eventually yielded organic life. He also believes that we should be able to construct simple crystal forms of life, similar to the ones that may have paved the way for the evolution of organic beings such as ourselves.

Before scientists can realistically set about constructing self-replicating and evolving crystals, they will need to learn a lot more about the things crystals can do. First of all, they need to know if crystals really can pass 'genetic' information faithfully on through many crystal generations. They need to know if crystals really can act as sophisticated 'organic chemists', catalysing the manufacture of chemicals such as RNAs and proteins to help the crystals survive and multiply. They need to investigate the extent to which one 'species' of crystal can influence the formation of other species; and they should also look carefully in the places where crystals are forming on the earth today, to see if any natural examples of crystals evolving by Darwinian natural selection can be found.

One thing that could be done in the laboratory, however, without waiting any for dramatic advances in our knowledge of crystal chemistry, would be to set up 'continuous crystallizers', in which various types of crystals could be formed and given the opportunity to evolve. Imagine a crystal reactor, with solutions of the raw materials for crystal growth flowing in at the top and eventually out at the bottom, having passed through various regions where crystal growth could begin in environments under our strict control. If we found the right conditions and set the right 'challenges', would populations of different types of crystal begin to compete for nutrients and evolve? Would the crystal population become dominated by successive waves of self-replicating crystals each better at surviving and multiplying than their successors? Under suitable conditions would some crystals begin to perform organic chemistry in ways that enhanced their chances of survival? Would the crystal population react to new challenges (such as changes in temperature, salinity, the porosity and chemistry of their living quarters and so on) by giving rise to new variant species? The experiments have not been done, so nobody knows the answers.

Various research groups throughout the world are becoming increasingly interested in finding out more about the abilities of crystals to act as catalysts and perhaps as living things. They are beginning to explore the full potential of crystal chemistry in the same way as biologists are beginning to explore the full potential of nucleic acids and proteins. The main motivation behind the future expansion of all three explorations may have little to do with the origins of life, being more concerned with the needs of industry (to find new crystalline catalysts, solar cells, semiconductors etc.), or of biotechnology (new molecular tools for genetic engineers) and medicine (new drugs and vaccines); but clues to our ancient origins may well be uncovered in the process.

So much for our attempts to re-create life's origin. The message of this book so far has been that most of the key mysteries of that origin remain stubbornly unsolved. The future may see many new breakthroughs in experiment and theory which may give us a much fuller understanding of how we might have come to be here, and perhaps even the ability to re-enact some of the first steps up the 'ladder of life'. But the problem of the origins of life on earth will always be a problem of the past – fascinating, but essentially neither soluble nor very important. No matter how plausible our theories and re-creations become, we will never really know what happened to bring us into being, and many people may ask why we should care.

The question of life's future is much more important and accessible. We are all going to know directly at least a little about that future – it arrives inevitably all the time. Life on earth and elsewhere can never be static and unchanging, since change and evolution is the very stuff of life itself. Rather than being mere observers and victims of that change, we are increasingly attempting to steer it towards our own ends.

What sort of life should there be?

Mankind is undoubtedly the pinnacle of evolution's achievements so far, in terms of intelligence and the ability to purposefully change the natural world which brought us into being. Of course, since these are the traits we are dominant in, we tend to regard them as the most fitting criteria to determine evolutionary ascendancy. We are certainly not evolution's pinnacle in terms of numbers – many different species ranging from beetles to bacteria must populate the world in far greater numbers than ourselves. In terms of biochemical abilities we are pathetic, helpless creatures compared with plants, whose photo-synthetic 'cleverness' we depend on, and a multitude of organisms from bacteria to various other vertebrates which can manufacture many more of the molecules they need to survive and grow than our vitamin-dependent selves. Our ability to rearrange or destroy the natural world, to make vast prairies of wheat, new breeds of horses and dogs, cattle and crops, to demolish rainforests and eradicate dangerous pathogens such as the virus that used to cause smallpox, has been purchased in return for a hopeless dependency on the very creatures we can manipulate or destroy.

For many years mankind has been able to act as the 'shaper of life' in various indirect ways, such as selective breeding or extermination, shepherding, cultivation and chemical control. Throughout the 1970s we became steadily able to shape new life directly, thanks to emergence of the new 'biotechnology' known as genetic engineering.

Genetic engineering is a blanket term for a host of different biochemical techniques which promise to ultimately give us complete mastery over the nature of life on the planet, and on any other planets we choose to colonize as well. All of the living things on earth today are at heart composed of genes that encode proteins. Genetic engineering allows us to tinker directly with the chemical that genes are made of – DNA. It allows us to take genes out from living things and study them. It allows us to put new genes into living things that would never have acquired such genes by more 'natural' means. It allows us to chop up genes and to change them, to swap genes around between living things, to manufacture entirely novel genes not yet discovered by evolution, and to generally explore the full potential of DNA as a carrier of genetic information at an unbeliev-ably faster rate than the slow remorseless march of conventional evolution.

Chapter 8 summarized the main mechanisms of genetic change, the change which provides the raw material for evolution. Mankind, by learning the skills of genetic engineering, has become a radical new and dramatically faster and more powerful mechanism to add to the list. Unlike the conventional mechanisms of genetic change, mankind can purposely *direct* evolution towards specific goals. We can identify a need, and set about engineering its solution directly. Thanks to the advent of genetic engineering, evolution may eventually burst forward at an incredibly accelerated pace.

You may be tempted to dismiss the changes we will bring about in the genetic structure of organisms as not 'true' evolution, but 'unnatural' man-made change; but remember, we ourselves are a part of nature. We are 'natural', and so everything we do is a natural consequence of the evolution that brought us into being. When the first photosynthetic cells began to trap the energy of sunlight directly and use it to manufacture chemical raw materials, that would have looked like an 'unnatural' new trick to any conventional cells able to comment upon it. Without this 'unnatural trick' we would not be around to create our own 'tricks' of genetic engineering. I wonder what creatures might look back at the evolutionary record from millions of years in the future and say, 'If mankind had not learned the tricks of genetic engineering, we would never have come to be?'

What is mankind likely to do, what is it already doing, with its increasing ability to determine what sort of life there should be? The first tentative steps have been very cautious (commendably cautious) and minor, but already very useful. Various bacteria and yeasts have been given the genes needed to manufacture medically useful proteins such as insulin, growth hormone and interferon. The 'engineered' microorganisms can then be grown in large numbers and induced to manufacture plentiful supplies of these valuable proteins. In this way genetic engineering is already yielding much cheaper, purer and more abundant supplies of proteins needed to treat diabetes, dwarfism, viral infections and possibly cancer. Other, less well known, proteins are also being produced by genetic engineering, which is going to increasingly supply an abundance of cheap proteins for use in medicine, industry and further research.

Genetic engineering is already being used to unravel the mysteries of how complex living things grow and develop from single fertilized egg cells; and generally to discover much more about how life based on genes that encode proteins actually works. The desire to learn more about the 'molecular biology' of life was the real motivation behind the creation of genetic engineering techniques in the first place. Scientists wanted to learn how to fiddle about with the genetic make-up of living things, simply because by fiddling about with things you can often find out how they work. And of course by learning more about how living things work, we will hopefully be much better placed to intervene when things go wrong, to prevent or cure disease.

The ways in which genetic engineering *could* be used to change life are virtually limitless, since it allows us to engineer the DNA molecules that make living things what they are. Some of the most radical current proposals involve changing the genetic make-up of plants, partly because there are fewer ethical objections to such projects than there are to attempts to meddle with the genetics of animals or humans. It might well be possible, for example, to greatly improve the nutritional value and the yields of many crop plants by fairly straightforward genetic tinkering. A few simple changes to a gene encoding a major plant protein, for example, might make the protein contain more of the 'essential' amino acids most needed in the human diet. A few changes to the genes encoding proteins involved in photosynthesis, might improve the efficiency of that process to give us greater yields.

A more ambitious idea is to free many of our staple crops from their dependency on nitrogen-containing fertilisers by giving them the genes needed to trap (or 'fix') the atmospheric nitrogen freely available in the air. At the moment only 'leguminous' plants (such as beans) can fix their own nitrogen in this way, but soon we might have created strains of rice and wheat that can do it as well.

As I write, scientists in America are about to try to protect crop plants against frost damage by using genetic engineering in a rather indirect way. They have 'engineered' a bacterium to make it less likely to assist the formation of ice-crystals than the natural bacteria found on plants. They intend to spray crops with these new 'ice-minus' bacteria, in the hope that they will displace the natural bacterial population to leave the plants much less vulnerable to the ravages of frost. Bacteria are also being genetically engineered to consume harmful pollutants and convert them into harmless wastes, and they may also be used to protect our crop plants against various insects and other pests.

Although they involve the engineering of mere plants and bacteria, the proposals considered so far have fuelled a fierce environmental debate. Many people worry about the possibilities of us 'upsetting the balance of nature' in various unpredictable and perhaps catastrophic ways by the release of our new creations. Could 'ice-minus' bacteria, for example, be carried up into the clouds to interfere with the formation of ice crystals, which initiates rainfall? By engineering our crops to be resistant to some pests, whose numbers would therefore decline, could we bring about the extinction of other important insects that feed upon these pests? The debates continue endlessly and unresolved, and they are increasingly becoming accompanied by even fiercer debates about the things we might do with genetic engineering to animals and humans.

We could well create new breeds of livestock which would give larger yields and perhaps be resistant to various diseases. Eventually we could probably create new breeds of people, if we wished. The ultimate possibilities of genetic engineering are virtually limitless, since DNA is what makes living things what they are. Obviously these limitless possibilities can be a source of great concern as well as great hope. The lessons of Nazi Germany teach us the terrible things that some people will do in the name of science and the 'improvement' of the species. It is surely ludicrous to suggest that there are no potential successors to Dr Mengele around today, or never will be in the future.

Most geneticists are keen to discount the wildest ideas (of 'super-races', mindless slaves, fearless warriors, intelligent apes, human–ape hybrids and so on) by claiming that nobody would ever be crazy enough to try them out; or simply by dismissing the required techniques as 'very far in the future'. But human history surely catalogues the exploits of a species abundantly supplied with craziness; and the future always eventually arrives, often much sooner than we expect it to.

In thinking about the potential for genetic engineering to change our world, we should not suppose that our descendants will forever live in societies similar to our own or see things in the same way as we do. Nor should the brevity of our own life-span blind us to the likely long-term consequences of our acts. In inventing genetic engineering we are giving humanity (and whatever creatures humanity evolves into) the ability to overthrow conventional evolution and determine what sort of life the earth will hold in the future. It may be a long time before that ability is put to full use, it may never be put to full use; but within a hundred years or so the complete reshaping of the nature of life on earth *could* be under way.

It is easy to laughingly dismiss the idea that the relatively trivial tinkering of today's genetic engineers could eventually lead on to the creation of such 'wonders' as photosynthetic disease-free humanoids, with regenerating brains and a life-span of many thousands of years; but genetic engineering, with its potential to take over the 'reins' of evolution from Darwinian natural selection, can make the laughable likely. If the slow march of evolution by natural selection has allowed single cells to give rise to humans, what might humans be changed into by the much faster process of purposeful genetic engineering?

Starting afresh

So far, in considering mankind's potential role as 'the new Creator', I have looked only at the possibilities of re-creating the origin of life or of reshaping the living things already in existence. It is also possible that we may soon begin to *create* completely novel forms of life unlike any ever seen before.

The new forms of life we might create could be constructed along several different lines. The most conservative possibility is the creation of novel creatures based on genes that encode proteins just as we are. The ability to manufacture DNA molecules of any sequence we desire means that we may eventually begin to manufacture entirely new genomes from scratch. Already we could probably make new types of virus, if we wished, since viruses are little more than short pieces of infectious DNA (or RNA) wrapped up in a simple protective coat. We could soon be able to manufacture entirely novel genomes as big as those inside bacteria; and ultimately manufacturing even genomes as big as our own may present no insurmountable obstacles to the fast-developing genetic technology. Making a genome, however, is only a part of the problem of making a bacterium, or a new animal as complex as a human. You must also put that genome into a suitable surrounding cell containing the enzymes and other molecules and sub-cellular components needed to allow the genome to be properly expressed, to manufacture the proteins, and ultimately the organism of your designs.

This too, might be a readily surmountable problem in the long term. At first, we could try inserting a novel genome into some pre-existing cell whose own genome had been removed. Eventually, it might be *feasible* (always assuming anyone wanted to do it) to insert completely synthetic genomes into fertilized human egg cells, having removed the native genomes, to allow complex creatures of our own designing to emerge.

You might suggest that I am taking things too far, but I am only taking the growth in our emerging genetic technologies to their ultimate conclusion. That conclusion might arrive in 50 years, or 500, or 5000; but provided our civilization does not collapse it will eventually arrive. Using the technology available today, I think scientists could manufacture a completely novel virus, if they set their minds to it. *Ultimately*, genetic engineers will surely gain the technical know-how to manufacture completely novel organisms as complex as human beings, and perhaps much more so. There are a great many *technical* problems of detail, complexity and sophistication to be solved before that day arrives, and we would need to find out a lot more about the precise way in which the genome inside a fertilized egg cell gives rise to an adult organism; but no fundamental conceptual breakthroughs would seem to be required before mankind could begin creating novel life based on genes encoding proteins.

When we learned about DNA and RNA and how they contain the information needed to make proteins, we probably learned all the really fundamental principles of how to make new life.

Computers, robots and life

Some people think that their computers are alive, some even think they might be conscious. Some people have put forward a case for considering cars to be alive, and have suggested that aliens surveying the complexities of our world might at first conclude that cars were the dominant form of life. Both computers and cars, and many other industrial artefacts, certainly multiply, although they do not really 'replicate' in the sense used in this book so far. They might also be said to evolve, although not by Darwinian natural selection. They evolve from 'generation to generation' because their creators – us – keep thinking up ways to improve them.

I have already abandoned debates about the precise meaning of the perhaps inherently imprecise term 'life', as probably unresolvable and often unhelpful, so I am not about to launch into a deep discussion on 'living computers'. But as technology advances it seems certain that our computers, robots and other artefacts are going to become increasingly competent in many of the activities that we have previously recognized as 'signs of life'. They may even begin to replicate themselves directly, without our help, and perhaps survive us or displace us to inherit the resources of the earth. Regardless of whether they involve 'living' things or not, such potential activities of our creations are surely worth a mention.

Humans have long been fascinated with the idea of creating beings of their own making, certainly long before the first simple auto-matons moved their jerky limbs and waggled their empty heads. The literature of science fiction is full of 'androids' and robots which are either close mimics of life or are considered to be living things in their own right. Now that robots have begun to assemble motor cars, and scientists are increasingly considering how computers might be made to 'think' and even become as conscious as (or much more conscious than) ourselves, the possibilities of the science fiction fantasies need to be taken seriously and properly thought through.

The problem in thinking them through is that we have to use words whose meanings we do not really know. 'Life', 'thought', 'intelli-gence', 'consciousness' – when we apply these words to humans we intuitively know what we mean, or think we do, but do they signify real clear-cut notions which can be applied to anything else? The more deeply we think about them, the more intangible and meaningless they become. We cannot really discuss whether computers or robots could become alive, or intelligent or conscious until we know what it is that makes us alive, intelligent and conscious. We know what it is that enables us to carry oxygen around our blood – it is a protein called 'haemoglobin' which can be purified and crystallized. We do not know what a 'thought' is, let alone an intelligent thought, although we assume it has something to do with electro-chemical activity in the brain. Until we have more precise answers it would be stupid to be dogmatic about the entitlement of computers and robots (now or in the future) to the status of living thinking conscious things.

Regardless of what status we should grant them, how might computers and robots become increasingly similar to forms of life? First, their multiplication would need to become increasingly automatic and independent. In other words, they would need to become increasingly capable of self-replication.

In the 1940s the mathematician John von Neumann speculated about the possibility of producing self-replicating machines, and produced a plan of the minimum requirements for such machines. He envisaged a machine able to roam about a 'stockroom' containing only very simple basic components (nuts and bolts, wire, pieces of metal, fuel etc.) supplied by us. The machine would contain a program and the necessary machinery to allow it to assemble the components into new versions of itself. It would also contain the machinery needed to copy the program (onto a new magnetic tape or disc, for example) and insert a new copy into each new version of the machine. It seems quite possible that we could construct such a machine today, leaving it to multiply out of control until the supplies in the stockroom ran dry or the growing number of machines began to bump into one another and otherwise get in each other's way.

It is easy to see why we might want to make such machines, assuming that they were also designed to do something that was useful to ourselves. Self-replicating cars and washing machines and computers appear to be technically feasible, and might well be commercially viable as well. Of course they would be totally dependent on us to keep the 'stockrooms' supplied, and they would only 'evolve' when we came up with new modifications for their programs. They would be as dependent on us as we are on plants, so they would hardly be likely to 'take over' the world in the manner envisioned in some science fiction fantasies; but other machines might not be so helpless.

Already, computer scientists are working on self-programming computers, aiming to provide computers with basic programs that will allow them to devise new programs to improve the original programs or meet future demands. Imagine a von Neuman machine containing a program designed to allow it to create new programs and try them out. A sophisticated machine built along these lines might well become capable of true 'evolution', if the original program deemed that any new programs capable of 'improving' the machine in some way, were to be used as replacements for the original program. As soon as the machine came up with a program that would allow it to replicate faster, or more efficiently, for example, that program would become the new 'base' program until further exploration of the programming possibilities came up with an even better version.

Again, there are sound commercial reasons why we might want to create and exploit such machines. We could leave them to get on with the business of inventing new and better programs and designing new and better machines for us while the human programmers and designers went off on holiday, or to the golf course, or to the unemployment bureau. They might still be dependent on humans to keep the stockrooms supplied, but perhaps our lazy descendants might wish to make them able to roam the earth searching for supplies themselves, digging up iron ore and coal and crafting it into steel and nuts and bolts and whatever else they required. And then, if humanity expired, perhaps a few of our versatile (and perhaps 'intelligent' and 'conscious') self-programming machines could survive and continue to evolve by inventing new programs to cope with life's changing demands. Would anyone discovering an earth inhabited by such creations realize that they were the results of a takeover, of organic life by its machines; or perhaps of two takeovers, of crystals, by organic life, by machines? Or would they come up with implausible ways for the ancestors of the first von Neumann machines to have originated spontaneously without assistance?

More 'natural' paths

With civilization and technology at their present stage, it is hard to take fantasies about self-replicating, self-programming, conscious robots inheriting the earth too seriously. Robots and computers constructed out of silicon chips and nuts and bolts and plates of polished steel seem too unnatural to ever survive and reproduce without our help. If that is the case, there may well be more 'natural' paths along which living things of our own making could develop, and there are good commercial reasons why we might wish to bring them into being.

Life based on genes that encode proteins can clearly survive and reproduce on planet earth – it is virtually impossible to stop it from doing so. So could we build computers and robots based on similar biological principles, and then leave them to multiply and evolve into ever more useful servants for ourselves. Work aimed at producing 'biochips', 'biocomputers' and ultimately self-reproducing and self-assembling biocomputers is already under way.

The first step towards living biocomputers is to manufacture microchips whose logical circuitry is constructed out of biological molecules such as proteins and RNAs. Many research groups throughout the world are already busy working towards that goal. They are spurred on by the great advantages of scale offered by biochips (the working parts of silicon microchips are usually massive compared to the tiny molecular working parts of the cell); and by the prospect of constructing *three-dimensional* logic circuits rather than the two-dimensional arrays of conventional technology.

If it turns out that microchips and computers can be constructed out of proteins and RNAs, the next logical step will be to construct the genomes that will encode these components automatically, and allow them to be self-assembled as parts of living cells and organisms. Dr Kevin Ulmer of the genetic engineering company Genex has already spoken of his hope 'to develop a complete genetic code for the computer that would function as a virus does, but instead of producing more virus, it would assemble a fully operational computer inside a cell'. Once we have constructed cells that are living computers, natural and artificial selection might then give rise to ever more efficient and versatile cellular and multicellular forms of computer life. Any such life-forms might be well capable of surviving on their own without our help, a few might even escape to evolve into the bugs or predators or vastly more intelligent masters that will ultimately drive us to extinction.

This book is being written on an Amstrad PCW 8256 personal computer, which is so far doing a great job, but I will presumably be forced to invest in a replacement when it eventually wears out. Writers of the twenty-first, or thirty-first, century might have no such worries. Having completed a book, they might go off on a well-deserved holiday while leaving their tired old Amstrad in a warm place surrounded by a broth of suitable nutrients. On returning from their break they might find a new generation of personal computers fresh and ready to help them on their next literary endeavour!

Such fantasies aside, is it really feasible to construct computers out of proteins and RNAs? One argument suggests not, because proteins and RNAs do not seem to be really suitable materials from which to construct logical electronic circuitry similar to the circuitry within microchips. The movement of electrons is generally highly restricted within biological materials, and many scientists feel that attempts to turn proteins and RNAs into logical electronic devices are doomed to failure. The counter-argument points out that proteins and RNAs are able to form the brains which invented microchips in the first place, although the problem with brains is that they work much more slowly than today's computers; and today's computers are presumably going to be replaced by new 'generations' of ever-faster and more versatile ones.

It may be that the advantages of self-reproducing and self-assembling computers will be purchased at the expense of speed and efficiency; but perhaps not, because it might be possible to construct biocomputers whose logic circuits do not depend on the movement of electrons, but on the transition of organic molecules between different structural states, or other forms of more 'biological' change. The predigious logical powers of modern computers are essentially based on a multitude of electronic 'switches' which can either be 'on' or 'off'. Anything that can change between two (or more) reasonably stable states in a controlled manner might be used to construct alternative logic circuits. Biocomputers need not be constructed out of protein-based transistors and diodes and so on, they might be constructed out of whatever organic chemicals seem best, perhaps employing 'switches' that do not involve the movement of electrons at all, and all assembled and controlled by the activities of proteins encoded by genes.

But even if nucleic acid genes encoding proteins cannot be used to construct biocomputers, alternative avenues towards computer life might still remain. It might be feasible to construct novel genes based on genetic polymers that bear no resemblance at all to nucleic acids, other than their ability to hold coded information. These new synthetic genes might encode versatile catalytic polymers of our own choosing, which are not proteins, but which have the electronic properties we require. Genes based on nucleic acids encoding proteins might have been the only feasible type of genes to arise on the early earth, but that does not mean they are the only possible type of genetic material, or that proteins are the only possible catalysts of life. The science of molecular biology has taught us how genes made of DNA can make complex living things based on proteins. That knowledge leaves us ready to explore the perhaps infinite possibilities of genes made of other chemicals which may make complex living things based on catalysts and structural polymers other than the proteins.

Compared to the previous chapters of this book, this one has obviously been a highly speculative 'flight of fancy' which should neither be taken too seriously nor too lightly. Many past generations of humans would undoubtedly have been astounded to learn of the life their descendants would be leading ten or twenty generations on. Why should we be any different? As molecular biology unlocks the secrets of how life manages to live, it seems our interest in our own origins may be increasingly swamped by a desire to be the originators of other forms of life. We may create these new living things out of commercial, medical and military interest, or simply out of curiosity and fascination. They may free us from drudgery and starvation, enslave us, or completely displace us. Whatever happens, this present 'twentieth' century, which is actually about the forty-millionth century of life on earth, could well be remembered as the one in which life on earth began to be completely transformed by the effects of mankind – the new Creator.

Epilogue

I know not whence I came, nor whither I go, nor who I am.
Erwin Schrödinger

Nobody knows how life originated, either on earth or anywhere else. Nobody knows if there is life elsewhere in the universe, although we might know soon. Nobody knows what will happen to life in the future. It may continue to blossom by conventional Darwinian evolution into new and ever more versatile forms – mobile photosynthetic 'animals', thinking plants, intelligent space-faring insects . . .; and perhaps all based on genes that encode proteins containing a larger variety of amino acids than the proteins of here and now, or based on genes which are not nucleic acids and which do not encode proteins. It may race off in entirely new directions determined by our tinkering selves. It may shortly be destroyed for ever.

The past and future of life, and even much of its present, remains mysterious, although we know it to be based on chemicals we call genes which encode others we call proteins. We certainly do not know what the consciousness which allows us to ponder it all really is. To pretend to know the events which first yielded life many thousands of millions of years ago is, at the moment, a preposterous conceit.

It is no disgrace that modern science cannot say with certainty how life began, and the 'generally accepted' ideas about its origin might be very close to the truth. The fact that attempts to simulate that origin have yet to record any dramatic successes does not mean that they must be based on flawed ideas. It might simply be ridiculous to expect to re-create in the laboratory significant portions of an origin which may have taken many millions of years. Scientists might, however, be searching for the origins of life along completely the wrong lines, and in completely the wrong places.

In conclusion, the efforts of scientists to explain our origins have so far yielded a few vague and very general notions which may hold part of the truth; but unless we become able to convincingly re-create all or significant parts of the spontaneous origin of life ourselves, that origin will remain a deep mystery. It will always be somewhat a mystery, even if our ideas become much more secure than they are now, unless our descendants learn to see backwards into time.

Further reading

This is a short and selective list of some books and papers (in the more accessible scientific journals), from which readers will be able to find out more about the subjects covered in this book. The references contained within the works referenced here will lead you ever deeper into a fascinating puzzle. Any readers wishing to investigate the subject in detail should also look up the scientists mentioned in the book in the *Science Citation Index*; and the subject headings 'Life – origin of' in *Chemical Abstracts*, and 'Biogenesis' in *Index Medicus*. They might also wish to consult recent issues of the specialist journals – *Origins of Life*, *Journal of Molecular Evolution* and *Molecular Biology and Evolution*.

Chapter 2   Sparse fabric

The Forces of Nature, by Paul Davies, Cambridge University Press, 1979.
Superforce, by Paul Davies, Unwin, 1984.
The Second Law, by Peter W. Atkins, W. H. Freeman, 1984.
The Cosmic Onion, by Frank Close, Heinemann, 1983.
The Cosmic Code, by Heinz R. Pagels, Penguin, 1982.
Time, Space and Things, by B. K. Ridley, Cambridge University Press, 1984.
Introducing Chemistry, by Hazel Rossotti, Penguin, 1975.

Chapter 3   Life on earth

The Chemistry of Life, by Steven Rose, Penguin, 1979.
Molecular Biology of the Cell, by Bruce Alberts, Dennis Bray, Julian Lewis, Martin Raff, Keith Roberts and James D. Watson, Garland Publishing, 1983.
The Cartoon Guide to Genetics, by Larry Gonick and Mark Wheelis, Barnes & Noble, 1983.
In Search of the Double Helix, by John Gribbin, Corgi, 1985.

Chapter 4   Stardust in a pond

The First Three Minutes, by Steven Weinberg, Fontana, 1983.
Genesis on the Planet Earth, by William Day, Yale University Press, 1984.
The Origins of Life on the Earth, by Stanley Miller and Leslie Orgel, Prentice-Hall, 1974.
Genesis, by John Gribbin, Delta, 1982.
The Selfish Gene, by Richard Dawkins, Paladin, 1976.
The Structure of the Early Universe, by John D. Barrow and Joseph Silk, *Scientific American*, April 1980, pp. 98–108.

Chapter 5   A gulf unbridged

Molecular Approaches to Evolution, by Jacques Ninio, Pitman, 1982.
Selection in the Soup, by John Scott, *The Sciences*, **23**, 38–42, 1983.
See also, *Genesis on the Planet Earth* and *The Origins of Life on the Earth*, under chapter 4.

Chapter 6   Crystalline life

The Life Puzzle, by A. G. Cairns-Smith, Oliver & Boyd, 1971.
Genetic Takeover, by A. G. Cairns-Smith, Cambridge University Press, 1982.
Seven Clues to the Origin of Life, by A. G. Cairns-Smith, Cambridge University Press, 1985.
The First Organisms, by A. G. Cairns-Smith, *Scientific American*, June 1985, pp. 90–100.

Chapter 7   An infected world

Life Itself, by Francis Crick, Touchstone, 1982.
Evolution from Space, by Fred Hoyle and Chandra Wickramasinghe, J. M. Dent & Sons, 1981.
The Quest for Extraterrestrial Life – a book of readings, edited by Donald Goldsmith, University Science Books, 1980.
Can Spores Survive in Interstellar Space?, by Peter Weber and J. Mayo Greenberg, *Nature*, **316**, 403-407, 1985.

Chapter 8   From proteins to palaeobiologists

The Theory of Evolution, by John Maynard Smith, Penguin, 1975.
Science on Trial – the case for evolution, by Douglas J. Futuyma, Pantheon, 1983.
Evolution Now, edited by John Maynard Smith, Macmillan Press, 1982.
Darwin for Beginners, by Jonathan Miller, Unwin, 1982.

The Mechanisms of Evolution, by Francisco J. Ayala, *Scientific American*, September 1978, pp. 48–61.
The Evolution of the Earliest Cells, by J. William Schopf, *Scientific American*, September 1978, pp. 85–102.
The Evolution of Multicellular Plants and Animals, by James W. Valentine, *Scientific American*, September 1978, pp. 105–117.
The Oldest Eukaryotic Cells, by Gonzalo Vidal, *Scientific American*, February 1984, pp. 32–41.

Chapter 9   Worlds such as this one

The Quest for Extraterrestrial Life – a book of readings, edited by Donald Goldsmith, University Science Books, 1980.
Recent Progress and Future Plans on the Search for Extraterrestrial Intelligence, by Michael D. Papagiannis, *Nature*, **318**, 135–140, 1985.
Titan, by Tobias Owen, *Scientific American*, February 1982, pp. 76–85.
Habitability of Europa, by Ray T. Reynolds, Steven W. Squyres, David S. Colburn and Christopher P. Mckay, *Icarus*, **56**, 246–254, 1983.

Chapter 10   The new Creator

Man Made Life, by Jeremy Cherfas, Basil Blackwell, 1982.
The Eighth Day of Creation, by Horace Freeland Judson, Simon & Schuster, 1979.
Setting Genes to Work, by Stephanie Yanchinski, Penguin, 1985.
What Sort of People Should There Be?, by Jonathan Glover, Penguin, 1984.
Reinventing Man, by Igor Aleksander and Piers Burnett, Penguin, 1983.
Computer Power and Human Reason, by Joseph Weizenbaum, Penguin, 1976.
The Molecular Electronic Device and the Biochip Computer: Present Status, by R. C. Haddon and A. A. Lamola, *Proceedings of the National Academy of Sciences of the USA*, **82**, 1874–1878, 1985.

Index